Santa Barbara & Ventura Counties

Automobile Club of Southern California

Cover Photo
Mission Santa Barbara by John Austerman

Writer................Norma E. Palmer
Artist................Virginia Matijevac
Cartographer .....Michael Stewart

Editor...........Judy van Wingerden

ISBN: **1-56413-186-6**
Printed in the United States of America

GET EVERYTHING FOR YOUR TRIP. FREE.

Maps, TourBooks®
& Area Guides

Fee-Free American Express®
Travelers Cheques

Car Rental Reservations & Discounts

AIRLINE
TICKETS

Complete Airline &
Travel Reservations

Hotel/Motel Reservations & Discounts

Dependable Emergency Road Service

Join the Auto Club of Southern California today and we'll give you everything you need for your trip. ✦ Free maps ✦ Free TourBooks®, CampBooks® and area guides ✦ Fee-free American Express® Travelers Cheques and ✦ Free Triptiks®, a personalized, mile-by-mile routing of your entire trip. And you'll love saving money with Member-only discounts on ✦ Tours and cruises ✦ Hotel/motel reservations ✦ Rental cars and ✦ Popular attractions across the country. All of these great travel benefits can be yours for $38 a year plus a $20 enrollment fee -- a total of just $58. So why wait? Join AAA today and get everything for your trip. Free!

Call 1-800-882-5550, Ext. 152
(Outside So. CA: 1-800-AAA-HELP)

Associate memberships for your spouse and children are available for a nominal fee. Membership dues are subject to change without notice.

Contents

Santa Barbara and Ventura Counties

Santa Barbara and Ventura are contiguous counties that lie along the Pacific Ocean's Santa Barbara Channel, a waterway named by a 17th-century Spaniard seafarer. Strong ties to a Spanish and, later, an American pioneering heritage are evident through architecture, place names and historically oriented annual events. At the same time, the region sustains a contemporary vitality represented by numerous cultural activities, points of interest, recreational areas and well-developed tourist services. Those things to see and do, as well as where to stay in Santa Barbara and Ventura counties, are detailed in this travel guide, which includes maps of popular destinations.

The history of Santa Barbara and Ventura counties is not unlike that of Southern California in general. Chumash Indians were the Central Coast's native inhabitants when Portuguese and Spanish explorers arrived in the 16th and early 17th centuries. In the 18th century, four missions established by Spain flourished until Mexico gained control of California, at which time the vast mission holdings were divided into ranches. The arrival of the stagecoach, and a little later the railroad, signaled the beginning of land subdivision and the coming of settlers from around the world.

Lying northwest of Ventura and south of San Luis Obispo counties, Santa Barbara County is made up of a series of coastal plains and interior valleys separated by gently rolling hills and rugged mountain ranges. Southeast of Santa Barbara County, Ventura County is bordered by Los Angeles County to the south and east, and most of the northern edge of its backcountry meets Kern County. Ventura County's look is much the same as that of Santa Barbara in that geographical features in the two counties range from sky-high mountain peaks to dramatically eroded canyons to flat grasslands to rocky and sandy seashores.

Geography, climate and geology within the counties' various regions naturally contribute to the economic base of each. The climate of the Santa Barbara and Ventura coasts and their coastal valleys are strongly influenced by ocean breezes. These winds, along with occasional fog, combine with rich soil to create an abundance of agricultural and horticultural products. Because of their south-facing position in relation to the sea, the Santa Barbara and Ventura coasts are less susceptible to fog, and daytime temperatures are usually several degrees warmer along the coast than in the valleys. These climatic conditions, ideal for growing avocados, citrus fruit and flowers, also support a banana plantation.

In Santa Barbara County the Santa Ynez and interior Santa Maria valleys garner some ocean winds, but more importantly, the warm afternoon sunshine and cool evening breezes account for the growth of grapes and the subsequent emergence of these regions as major California wine producers.

Citrus fruit occupies much of Ventura County's interior valleys, particularly in the Ojai and Santa Paula areas. Lemons are the most important crop, with almost half the lemons grown in the United States coming from Ventura County. Nearer the coast, vast fields of vegetables and citrus and avocado groves cover the landscape. Beneath the surface of both counties, particularly Ventura, lie great pools of "black gold," and oil pumpers have risen in the valleys, along the coast and offshore.

In addition to farms, orchards, vineyards and oil wells, many of the grass-covered hills throughout the counties support horse ranches or herds of cattle. Other economic endeavors in the region include tourism, light industry, mining and space exploration.

The Santa Barbara coast, extending from Carpinteria to Gaviota State Park, is an east-west coastal plain encompassing the communities of Carpinteria, Santa Barbara, Goleta and several beaches along US 101. North from the coast over the Santa Ynez Mountains is the Santa Ynez Valley, with its popular tourist destinations of Buellton and Solvang, along with several small agricultural and farming hamlets known for their country charm and hospitality.

Immediately west of the Santa Ynez Valley lies the Lompoc Valley, with its diverse economy ranging from oil and space exploration to flower-seed production. The valley's sprawling Vandenberg Air Force Base, the second largest military air base in California, is the launch site for NASA and Defense Department satellites placed in polar orbits around the earth, and it is also an important test range for ballistic missiles.

Occupying the northwest corner of the county is the Santa Maria Valley, a flat, 20-mile-wide, coastal-inland plain noted for its agricultural produce and horticulture.

The Santa Ynez Valley in Santa Barbara County is considered an established wine region and produces award-winning vintages. Many wineries in this valley, as well as in the Santa Maria Valley, offer public tours of the premises and tasting of their products. A free brochure, published by the Santa Barbara County Vintners' Association, contains a listing of area wineries with daily hours and handy maps pinpointing locations. The brochure can be obtained at all county chamber of commerce offices (see *Santa Barbara*

Area Chambers of Commerce/Tourism Offices).

Ventura County has a considerably more limited viniculture. Among its less than a half dozen wineries one is near the coast about five miles east of the center of Ventura and the other inland, just south of Oak View. For more information about wineries in both counties and throughout California, the Auto Club's *California Winery Tours* book is available to members at local district offices and to nonmembers at selected bookstores in California.

The Ventura coast begins at the northern border of Leo Carrillo State Beach, skirts the seaward edge of the Santa Monica Mountains, including Point Mugu State Park, continues as a coastal plain until the city of Ventura, then provides dramatic vistas as it becomes a narrow strip between steep hills and the sea. In addition to Ventura, coastal area communities include Port Hueneme, with its Seabee base; Oxnard, combining agricultural and maritime pursuits; and Camarillo, an important residential and business center.

In the area between US 101 and SR 118, Simi Valley and Thousand Oaks are among attractive and burgeoning towns that serve largely as bedroom communities for Ventura and Los Angeles counties. From US 101 south of the city of Ventura, SR 126 leads east past citrus groves and oil fields to the small, but historically and agriculturally important, towns of Santa Paula and Fillmore.

North of Ventura, SR 33 goes north off US 101 through a wonderfully scenic inland area. Along the way are Lake Casitas and the town of Ojai, with varied activities, sights and accommodations for the traveler. Then SR 33 winds through a portion of Los Padres National Forest, where mountain ranges look down on deep valleys cut by creek beds.

Los Padres National Forest covers nearly one-third of Santa Barbara County and half of Ventura County and offers such recreational activities as camping, hiking, fishing and horseback riding. Besides the extensive recreational opportunities in Los Padres National Forest, the counties' 150-mile-long coastline contains many beach parks offering all types of water sports. Public swimming pools, golf courses and tennis courts can be found in many communities.

Shopping opportunities can be found throughout both counties, from large shopping malls to small antique shops. Seven major shopping complexes feature large department stores and numerous retail outlets: Town Center in Santa Maria and, in Santa Barbara, La Cumbre Plaza and Paseo Nuevo; The Oaks Mall in Thousand Oaks; Buenaventura Mall and Telephone Plaza in the city of Ventura; Centerpoint and the Esplanade in Oxnard.

Shops in the town of Los Alamos and along Brinkerhoff Avenue in Santa Barbara are noted for antiques, while the Danish-American city of Solvang offers a wide assortment of merchandise with an emphasis on imported Danish handicrafts. A number of stores are situated in historic buildings, such as those housed in the Casa de la Guerra, built in 1826, and now part of the picturesque El Paseo shopping arcade in downtown Santa Barbara.

In the city of Ventura, antique collectors can spend hours going in and out of all the shops along Main Street, west of Seaward Avenue. Ojai and Santa Paula are among the small towns that offer charming shops filled with antiques and collectibles. Every museum in both counties—historic, art or special interest—has a shop with attractive, unusual merchandise just right for souvenirs or gift-giving.

The harbor and marina areas of Ventura and Oxnard offer tourist-oriented shopping with a nautical theme: Ventura Harbor Village in Ventura includes 40 shops, restaurants and a carousel, as well as live community theatrical presentations. Fisherman's Wharf in Oxnard offers specialty shops and restaurants, and is the site of the Ventura County Maritime Museum. Harbor Landing near Port Hueneme has a good selection of eating places, some of which are housed in a round building reminiscent of a merry-go-round.

Art fanciers rejoice in the large selection of locally produced works sold at several galleries in Santa Barbara and in Ojai. The city of Santa Barbara hosts an arts and crafts show every Sunday, weather permitting, along Cabrillo Boulevard east from State Street. The small town of Los Olivos is a haven for western-style artists, and several art galleries in the community sell their works.

In Ojai the shops along The Arcade are known for their one-of-a-kind jewelry and other works of art, much of which is locally handcrafted. It's often possible to visit the studios of some of the Ojai area artists, watch them work and purchase original paintings, sketches or sculpture. On Sundays an outdoor art exhibit is held in downtown Ojai.

Cultural activities and the arts flourish throughout Santa Barbara and Ventura counties. Museums contain art and photography exhibits, history and natural history collections, and maritime and land-transportation artifacts. Many historically significant structures have been preserved, including some adobes and four Spanish California missions. Several buildings designated as state historic landmarks are open to the public as shops, bed and breakfast inns, hotels and dining establishments.

The Santa Barbara Symphony Orchestra, along with visiting orchestras, opera and ballet companies, regularly perform at the Arlington Center for the Performing Arts in Santa Barbara, and the nearby Lobero Theatre hosts a year-round program of drama, music and dance. The Pacific Conservatory of the Performing Arts troupe presents a series of plays and musicals year round in Santa Maria and during the summer months in Solvang.

The Ventura County Symphony offers an annual season of classical music in Oxnard. Ojai offers drama and music with a Shakespeare festival and a contemporary classical music series.

Most colleges and universities present high-caliber music and drama programs on their campuses, and dinner theater is alive and well in both counties. Many towns have thriving community theaters that present dramas, comedies, musicals and children's fare.

Visitors' services are plentiful in most communities in both counties and along the major highways, with the most notable exception being the mountain roads within Los Padres National Forest. Chambers of commerce can provide additional specific information about events; their addresses and phone numbers appear on page 232. Information about campgrounds and AAA-approved lodgings and restaurants appears in this book under *Recreation* and *Lodging & Restaurants*.

Following the *Annual Events* listings in this book, a section on Santa Barbara County covers its attractions, recreation and accommodations. This is followed by the same type of information for Ventura County. Each county has been divided into sections that reflect the geographical makeup of the counties. (Maps on pages 36 and 156 indicate the boundaries for these areas.)

AUTO CLUB DISTRICT OFFICES

Automobile Club of Southern California district offices can help members in preparing a trip to Santa Barbara and Ventura counties by making reservations for lodging and transportation and by providing weather, routing and emergency road service information. Auto Club maps of the area are available: *Santa Barbara County, Ventura County*

(covering Oxnard, Port Hueneme and Ventura), *Cities of Santa Barbara County* (covering Santa Barbara and vicinity, Carpinteria, Santa Ynez Valley, Lompoc and Santa Maria), *Simi and Conejo Valleys* (covering, among several others, Camarillo, Moorpark, Simi Valley and Thousand Oaks) and *Ojai Valley Area* (including Fillmore, Ojai and Santa Paula).

Following are the Auto Club's district offices within the two counties. Hours at these district offices are 9 a.m. to 5 p.m. Monday through Friday.

Lompoc District Office
816 East Ocean Avenue
Lompoc
(805) 735-2731

Santa Barbara District Office
3712 State Street
Santa Barbara
(805) 682-5811

Santa Maria District Office
2033-B South Broadway
Santa Maria
(805) 922-5731

Simi Valley District Office
2837 Cochran Street
Simi Valley
(805) 522-7330

Thousand Oaks District Office
100 East Wilbur Road
Thousand Oaks
(805) 497-0911

Ventura County District Office
1501 South Victoria Avenue
Ventura
(805) 644-7171

History

Santa Barbara and Ventura counties' history could be said to consist of four overlapping periods: Native American, Mission, Rancho and American. Historians and anthropologists believe that Native Americans occupied the coastal and inland areas along the Santa Barbara Channel for thousands of years before European exploration began. During the heyday of Spain's territorial expansion in the 18th century, Native Americans became both religious converts and servants as Spain established missions, constructed forts and began settlements from Mexico to Northern California. With Mexico's independence from Spain in 1821 came the break-up of mission lands and the beginning of the great ranchos. These in turn gave way to smaller holdings bought up by American farmers and ranchers. Add astute businessmen, and the nucleus of a settlement was born. As the 20th century progressed, settlements grew into towns and cities, railroads took produce out and brought settlers in, oil was discovered in great pools beneath the ground, and America's military found the area ideal for naval and air stations.

NATIVE AMERICAN PERIOD

While little is known of the earliest people to inhabit California's central coast area some 10,000 to 12,000 years ago, there are many clues to the culture of the Chumash people that began about 1000 years ago. Archaeologists have discovered that as the final stages of prehistory evolved, numerous Chumash villages appeared along the coast, in the inland valleys and on the Santa Barbara Channel Islands. (*Chumash* is apparently an English term based on the Indian name *Mi-tcu-mac*.) Among the memorable accomplishments of the Chumash were the canoes which they fashioned of planks. These craft were worked with tools of shell and flint and caulked with the tar (asphaltum) that came from seashore and inland deposits. For their time, the canoes were swift and constructed to withstand the rough waters of the open sea.

Chumash houses, often measuring from 12 to 20 feet in diameter, were made of willow poles lashed together at the center to form a dome shape. Tule (bulrush-type reeds growing wild in marshy areas) covered the willow structures, with a hole left at the top for escaping smoke from a circular fire pit. The village sites, established near the ocean, provided a livelihood based on fishing and using shells for ornamental and trading purposes. Food sources from the nearby hills and valleys were provided by acorns and grasses and small mammals, such as rabbits.

Among the relics of early Chumash culture are baskets, wooden tools and stone vessels that demonstrate careful attention to design and workmanship. Some of these relics are on display in the Ventura County Museum of History and Art, Santa Barbara Museum of Natural History and the Carpinteria Valley Museum of History. Paintings on the rock walls of caves hidden in the Santa Ynez and San Rafael mountains reflect Chumash culture.

With the coming of Europeans, time and lack of immunity to the white man's diseases took their toll, drastically diminishing the Chumash population. Since the beginning of the 20th century, the Chumash population—albeit of mixed blood—has rebounded, and there are now approximately 3000 people of Chumash ancestry living throughout the United States; the 126-acre Santa Ynez Chumash Indian Reservation, 33 miles northwest of Santa Barbara, supports a population of about 320.

In the 16th century, Spain, already a power in Mexico, was looking northward with the intention of increasing her empire. The Portuguese explorer Juan Rodríguez Cabrillo was commissioned by Spain to find the fabled waterway connecting the Atlantic and Pacific oceans. In 1542 he sailed up the California coast, mapping the shoreline and claiming the land for Spain. In the autumn of that year Cabrillo passed through the channel that would be called Santa Barbara. It is possible that he may have come ashore near what is now the city of Ventura. In any case, he made note of the friendly natives in their well-crafted canoes caulked with tar.

Sixty years later, on December 4, 1602, a Spanish seafaring merchant, Sebastián Vizcaíno, entered the channel. Because that date was the feast day of the legendary third-century martyr Saint Barbara, Vizcaíno named the channel in her honor.

MISSION PERIOD

After more than 150 years of neglect, Spain returned her attention to Alta (Upper) California in 1768, when Charles III ordered the Viceroy of Mexico to establish presidios (garrisons) and missions in California. An expedition led by Captain Gaspar de Portolá set out in 1769 and included Father Junípero Serra, whose job it was to lay the groundwork for the missions; Father Juan Crespí served as historian.

In August 1769 Portolá and his men reached what is now Ventura County. For three successive nights they camped close to Indian villages that lay near present-day Fillmore, Santa Paula and Saticoy. On August 14 the party stopped near the site of what became the city of Ventura; Crespí named the village *La Asunsión de Nuestra Señora* (The Ascension of our Lady), expressing the hope that it would become the site of a good mission. Unfortunately, supply problems, then political and military considerations, delayed for years the founding of a mission.

It was not until March 31, 1782, under Governor Felipe de Neve, that Father Serra founded Mission San Buenaventura, a few hundred yards south of its present site. (*San Buenaventura*, St. Good Fortune, was named for a 13th-century Italian saint.) This, the last mission that Father Serra would found, began with a chapel, living quarters for the priests and guards, and a surrounding stockade. Immediately back of the mission, on *La Loma de la Cruz* (the Hill of the Cross), a cross was erected, as was the custom—not only as a religious symbol but as a beacon for travelers in search of the mission. The cross that stands today replicates the original.

While Spain planned to maintain only a mission in San Buenaventura, it was felt that Santa Barbara should have both a mission and presidio, so three weeks later Father Serra and a contingent of soldiers under the command of Lieutenant José Francisco de Ortega set out northward. In mid-April they made camp on what was then the shore of a large lagoon. On April 21, a shelter with an altar and cross was erected; Father Serra celebrated mass, and the land was formally claimed for Spain. Thus was the Royal Presidio of Santa Barbara founded, its site cutting at an angle through the present intersection of Santa Barbara and Canon Perdido streets.

Father Serra had expected that the founding of the mission would soon follow; however, at Governor Neve's insistence, work on the presidio began first. A wall, approximately eight feet high and more than three feet thick, was built to enclose barracks, a chapel, officers' quarters and storerooms bordering a large open area. It is believed that work was completed in the 1790s; the presidio chapel was dedicated on December 12, 1797. The town of Santa Barbara had its start as active and retired soldiers and their families began building homes just outside the presidio.

The Santa Barbara Mission was founded two years after the deaths of Father Serra and Governor Neve. An elevated site was chosen, with views of the valley, presidio and ocean; nearby ran a stream of clear water. On December 16, 1786, Padre Fermín Francisco de Lasuén conducted the official dedication of the site, and work on the first mission buildings began the following spring.

During the years that followed, the mission's growth exceeded that of the presidio. As large numbers of Chumash came into the mission community, it was necessary to increase the size of the church. By 1812 three churches had been built, each one larger than the one before. An earthquake in 1812 virtually destroyed the existing church and a new one was built, with the dedication taking place in 1820. In addition to the church, mission structures included living quarters, a granary, gristmill and rooms for tanning hides and weaving. Another temblor in 1925 necessitated extensive restorative work on the church's towers and facade, but the 1820 appearance of the mission was largely unchanged.

Norma E. Palmer

Mission Santa Barbara, known as "Queen of the Missions," features classic Roman and Spanish architecture.

The mission's water system also contributed to its growth. The water of the stream behind the mission was dammed, held in small ponds and carried in a stone aqueduct to reservoirs on the mission grounds. The water was also used to power a gristmill at the mission. This system was so well built that parts of it are still in good condition. The dam can be seen on the grounds of the Santa Barbara Botanic Garden.

Meanwhile, from 1782 to 1816, Mission San Buenaventura grew into a thriving community with land holdings that ultimately extended to the Sulphur Mountain foothills and along the Santa Clara and Ventura river valleys. The mission's structures closely followed, in form and function, those of Mission Santa Barbara—a plan which Spain had established in Mexico. Most of San Buenaventura's buildings were built between 1790 and 1810, with construction beginning on the main church in 1792 and completion celebrated in 1809. The 1812 earthquake which had nearly destroyed Mission Santa Barbara's church caused heavy damage at San Buenaventura. A new bell tower and reinforcement of the church with an immense buttress was accomplished within less than two years.

In order to provide water for the mission's people, crops, orchards and gardens, an aqueduct was built that probably began near the juncture of San Antonio Creek with the Ventura

River. From there, water was carried about seven miles through an aqueduct of adobe bricks and cobblestones to a primitive but effective charcoal filtering plant where it was treated for cooking and drinking. Turning a gate allowed a portion of the water to be diverted into an irrigation channel before it reached the filtration plant.

In addition to acreage owned by the church, occasional grants from the governor enabled favored individuals to hold large amounts of California land. The land was used primarily for cattle raising, and the resulting hides were used for everything from jackets to beds (a rawhide stretched between four posts). Additionally, many of these land grants ultimately formed the nucleus of settlements which became the towns of today's Santa Barbara and Ventura counties.

Although trade with any country other than Spain was officially forbidden, illicit dealings were often conducted with foreign vessels in sheltered coves along the coast. These transactions furnished the residents of Santa Barbara and Ventura with luxuries as exotic as Chinese silks or as prosaic as American shoes. Rawhides used in trading soon came to be known as "California currency."

RANCHO PERIOD

When Mexico gained its independence from Spain in 1821, the regions that are now Santa Barbara and Ventura counties were placed under Mexican rule. In 1834 Mexico's government decreed that vast tracts of land be removed from control of the Catholic church and divided into ranchos, and that the missions were to be secularized. The new owners of the ranchos, usually former military officers, expanded the economic base from primarily cattle raising to include other livestock, grain, and citrus and nut trees.

Ranchos were much like self-sufficient small towns, with a work force of Chumash, who received shelter, food and clothing for their labor. The ranch owners were *Californios*, (Mexican and Spanish residents of California), famous for a hospitality that included rodeos, feasting and fiestas. Among ranchos whose names continue as place names on today's maps is Camulos. Rancho Camulos, about 10 miles east of present-day Fillmore, is believed to have been instrumental in providing the title character for Helen Hunt Jackson's romantic novel, *Ramona*. About 30 miles to the west stands the Olivas adobe, which once presided over 4692 acres. It is now open to the public as Olivas Adobe Historical Park, south of downtown Ventura.

As the ranchos prospered, settlements in the area were beginning to grow, with Santa Barbara changing from a fort to a town as the port attracted commerce, and seafarers made it their home. Early settlers in Ventura were soldiers or civil servants living near the mission, and by 1866 several dozen adobe homes formed the nucleus for what was to be the city of San Buenaventura.

Santa Barbara County, including the land which later became Ventura County, was incorporated in February 1850. (California was admitted to the Union seven months later.) Only after many years of planning, petitioning and politics, did Buenaventura officially become a separate county in 1873. It is not known precisely when or why *Buenaventura* was shortened to *Ventura*; it legally became Ventura in the 1880s and has remained so ever since. Throughout the 1850s and 1860s Santa Barbara and Ventura counties continued to grow and prosper as more Americans acquired title to land, and towns began to rise along the coast and in the inland valleys.

AMERICAN PERIOD

In the area which was to become Ventura County, interest began to center around that heavy, black substance seeping up from under the ground. Early prospectors in the Ojai/Santa Paula area managed, after painstaking drilling through rock and shale, to reach oil. In 1861 one pioneering entrepreneur shipped a few thousand gallons of "lamp oil" (kerosene) to San Francisco from a small refinery near the Ventura River. Within only a few months, however, a fire destroyed the operation.

Wealthier and more ambitious oil speculators followed, and during the early 1860s oil rights were obtained to the enormous land holdings of some of the area's great ranchos. As time went on, and a severe drought in 1864 made ranchlands cheap, more land for oil speculation was obtained between Ojai and Ventura, the Simi Valley and portions of the plain between Camarillo and Oxnard.

In spite of the excitement and endless speculation, the oil industry began to dwindle in the late 1860s. In the first place, drilling for oil was a difficult proposition since the earth held problematic tilted and folded strata. Then there was the competition from cheaper kerosene imported from the eastern states. Lastly, as more settlers began arriving in the county, land speculation became more profitable than oil speculation. Thanks to perseverance and improved equipment, however, the oil industry made a spectacular comeback in the 1880s and remains an important factor in the counties' economic base.

Following passage of the Homestead Act in 1868, Civil War veterans came to Santa Barbara County to take advantage of the free arable land offered there. A year before that, 17,000 acres of fertile land—part of a rancho—were offered for $10 an acre, payable over 10 years. Such bargains as these were irresistible to venturesome farmers both in California and those arriving by steamship and stagecoach. Among the major cash crops were grain, citrus fruit, nuts and olives. When the Southern Pacific Railroad reached Ventura and Santa Barbara in 1887, it became a simple matter to move the produce to markets outside the valley.

The coming of the railroad also signaled the growth and prosperity of towns in the counties. In addition to moving freight, the railroad brought settlers and tourists. Today highways US 101 and, to a lesser extent, Interstate 5 carry the cars and trucks that serve the area.

Transportation

Towns and recreational areas within Santa Barbara and Ventura counties are served by modes of transportation that run the gamut from jet planes to small buses. Additionally, modern multi-lane freeways serve the heavily populated areas, and well-maintained highways lead into the backcountry.

Traveling to Santa Barbara and Ventura Counties

AIR

Santa Barbara

Currently six carriers operate daily at Santa Barbara Municipal Airport: two long-distance jet services and four commuters with frequent flights to and from Northern and Southern California cities, as well as Denver. All flights land at the Municipal Airport in Goleta, which is about a 15-minute drive from downtown Santa Barbara.

Santa Maria Valley

Visitors to the Santa Maria and Lompoc valleys are served by three commuter airlines at the Santa Maria Public Airport. Nonstop flights to Santa Maria originate in San Francisco, Las Vegas and Los Angeles. The airport is about a 10-minute drive from downtown Santa Maria and approximately 30 minutes from Lompoc. For complete schedule information, reservations and help in arranging connecting flights, contact any Travel Agency office of the Automobile Club of Southern California.

Ventura County

Air commuters to Ventura County are served by Oxnard Airport, located on West Fifth Street, between Ventura Road and Victoria Avenue. American Eagle and United Express each have daily flights to Oxnard from Los Angeles.

General aviation airports for private and charter planes are located in Camarillo off Pleasant Valley Road at Freedom Park Drive and in Santa Paula, off Santa Maria Street, just east of Eighth Street.

AUTOMOBILE

The majority of travelers who choose Santa Barbara and Ventura counties as their destination arrive by automobile. US 101 is usually the route of choice through the counties since it is a multi-lane, divided highway with limited access. The city of Santa Barbara is situated on US 101, 95 miles northwest of Los Angeles and 339 miles southeast of San Francisco. West of Santa Barbara, US 101 provides access to Goleta, the Santa Barbara Municipal Airport, El Capitan and Refugio state beaches, Gaviota State Park and Santa Maria. East of Santa Barbara, US 101 travels through Montecito, Summerland and Carpinteria.

At the north end of Gaviota State Park, SR 1 heads northwest from US 101 to the city of Lompoc, then goes to Vandenberg Air Force Base. Just north of Santa Maria, SR 166 goes east off US 101 through the Los Padres National Forest and connects northern Santa Barbara County with the San Joaquin Valley. At the western edge of downtown Santa Barbara, SR 154 (San Marcos Pass Road), goes north through the Santa Ynez Mountains and provides access to Lake Cachuma and communities in the Santa Ynez Valley, including Solvang, Buellton and Los Olivos.

The city of Ventura lies about 30 miles southeast of Santa Barbara on US 101. The highway runs along the coast between Carpinteria and Ventura and makes a turn away from the coast southeast of Ventura, passes through Camarillo and, east of Thousand Oaks, enters Los Angeles County. At Thousand Oaks, SR 23 goes north to the Simi and Conejo valleys and connects with SR 118, which in turn connects with I-5 in Los Angeles County's San Fernando Valley. South of Ventura at Oxnard, US 101 connects with SR 1, the coast route to Los Angeles County.

Off US 101, north of Ventura, SR 33 leads to SR 150 which in turn goes west to Lake Casitas, and east and south to Ojai, Santa Paula and Fillmore, connecting with SR 126. Eastward, SR 126 reaches I-5 along the edge of Angeles National Forest. Northwest of Ojai, SR 33 becomes a scenic route through Los Padres National Forest.

BUS

Greyhound Bus Lines offers service to the following Santa Barbara and Ventura county communities from almost every town in California. One-way tickets can be purchased up to two months prior to departure and up to 12 months for round-trip tickets. For information, contact the ticket office of the nearest bus terminal.

Oxnard
201 East 4th Street
(805) 487-2706

Santa Barbara
Carrillo and Chapala streets
(805) 965-3971

Santa Maria
313-A North Broadway
(805) 925-8841

Ventura
291 East Thompson Boulevard
(805) 653-0164

For nationwide schedule and rate information call (800) 231-2222.

Santa Barbara Airbus offers daily service to Los Angeles International Airport from Carpinteria, Goleta, Isla Vista and Santa Barbara; phone (800) 423-1618. **The Great American Stage Line** goes to Los Angeles International Airport from Camarillo, Oxnard, Thousand Oaks, Ventura, Westlake Village and Woodland Hills; phone (805) 499-4316.

TRAIN

The city of Santa Barbara is served daily by Amtrak's "Coast Starlight" and "San Diegan" trains. The "Coast Starlight" runs between Los Angeles and Seattle, with stops in Glendale, Simi Valley, Oxnard and Santa Barbara before proceeding north along the Central California coast. The "San Diegan" starts at the Amtrak Depot in San Diego, and makes stops in Del Mar, Oceanside, San Juan Capistrano, Santa Ana, Anaheim, Fullerton, Los Angeles, Glendale, Van Nuys, Chatsworth, Simi Valley, Moorpark, Oxnard, Ventura and Santa Barbara. The Amtrak station in Santa Barbara is located between State and Chapala streets, just south of US 101; the telephone number is (800) 872-7245. In Oxnard the Amtrak station is located at 201 East 4th Street, near the corner of 5th Street and Oxnard Avenue; the telephone number is (805) 487-8787.

For complete schedule information, reservations and help in arranging connecting trains from cities without direct service, contact any Travel Agency office of the Automobile Club of Southern California.

John Austerman

Passengers prepare to board a northbound Amtrak train at Santa Barbara station.

Transportation Within the Counties

AUTOMOBILE

Getting around Santa Barbara County by automobile is an easy matter. The motorist should be aware, however, that a few of the north-south downtown streets in the city of Santa Barbara are one way.

Traffic delays in Solvang can be expected, especially on weekends and during the summer months. Parking is free along the downtown streets and in a few public parking lots.

Ventura County likewise presents few problems for the motorist. Within the larger Ventura County cities, such as Camarillo, Oxnard, Simi Valley, Thousand Oaks and Ventura, commuter traffic may be heavy on freeways and major surface streets from about 7 to 9 a.m. and 4 to 7 p.m.

The highways and roads leading to Lake Casitas and Ojai are usually heavily traveled during the summer and during special events.

BUS

Santa Barbara

Santa Barbara Metropolitan Transit District (MTD) operates 25 lines serving an area that extends from approximately five miles west of Goleta to Carpinteria on the east; most buses run daily except on major holidays. The base fare is 75¢, with a reduced fare of 30¢ for senior citizens and people with disabilities; children under five ride free (limit three children per adult).

Information, schedules, change and tokens are available at the MTD Transit Center at 1020 Chapala Street (near Carrillo Street), Santa Barbara; (805) 683-3702.

An electric-powered shuttle bus ferries passengers daily all year along State Street between Stearns Wharf and downtown Santa Barbara, and also along the waterfront on Cabrillo Boulevard between the Santa Barbara Zoo and the municipal harbor. The free shuttle operates every 10 to 15 minutes on State Street and every 30 minutes along the waterfront from 10 a.m. to 5 p.m. Sunday through Thursday and until 8 p.m. Friday and Saturday.

Santa Maria Valley

Santa Maria Area Transit (SMAT) has five routes servicing the Santa Maria and Orcutt areas Monday through Saturday. Base fare is 90¢, students 65¢, seniors and handicapped persons 45¢, children five and under free. On Tuesday and Thursday, SMAT operates between Santa Maria and Guadalupe, and between Santa Maria and Santa Barbara. Information, schedules and tickets are available at the SMAT office at 615-A South McClelland Street, Santa Maria; (805) 928-5624.

Demand Response Service

Service is available Monday through Saturday in Lompoc, Vandenberg Village and Mission Hills from **Lompoc Transit,** 1300 West Laurel Avenue, Lompoc; (805) 736-4722,

736-7666 or 735-7342. Base fare is 50¢ for service in Lompoc and $1 for Mission Hills and Vandenberg Village.

Ventura, Ojai and Santa Paula Areas

South Coast Area Transit (SCAT) operates throughout Ventura County; the service areas include Ojai, Oxnard, Port Hueneme, the city of Ventura, Santa Paula and the county area between these cities. Most routes run daily except on major holidays. Base fare is $1, students 75¢, seniors and handicapped persons 50¢, children five and under free. SCAT also offers multiple ride tickets for 10, 20 and 30 rides at reduced rates, as well as monthly passes with unlimited rides during any given month. For information on schedules and routes call (805) 487-4222, 643-3158 or 647-4241.

Camarillo Area Transit (CAT) serves Camarillo Monday through Saturday, with a base fare of $1; reduced fare for seniors, disabled persons and students. For schedules and routes call (800) 438-1112.

Simi and Conejo Valleys

Simi Valley is served by **Simi Valley Transit**, with a base fare of 75¢; seniors 25¢. For information call (805) 584-6287. Moorpark is served by **Moorpark City Bus**, with a base fare of 75¢, seniors 25¢. For information call (805) 529-6864. **Thousand Oaks Transit** provides service throughout Thousand Oaks Monday through Friday, except major holidays, with a base fare of 75¢; reduced fare for seniors, children and handi-

capped; call (800) 438-1112 for schedules and routes. **Interconnect** runs buses from Thousand Oaks to Camarillo, Oxnard and Ventura Monday through Friday, except major holidays, with a base fare of $1.25 to Oxnard or Ventura; call (800) 438-1112 for schedules and routes.

TRAIN

Simi and Conejo Valleys

Metrolink, the regional commuter rail system in Southern California, serves Simi Valley and Moorpark in Ventura County. The Ventura County Line offers five trains in each direction between Union Station in Los Angeles, and Simi Valley and Moorpark via stations at Chatsworth, Van Nuys, Burbank and Glendale. The Metrolink system also reaches San Bernardino, Riverside and Santa Clarita. In May, service will begin to Oceanside in San Diego County via Orange County. Metrolink operates Monday through Friday. For exact schedule and fare information call (800) 371-5465.

The Moorpark Metrolink Station is at 300 High Street east of Moorpark Road (SR 23), and the Simi Valley station is at 5050 Los Angeles Avenue, west of Stearns Street. Amtrak trains also stop at these stations.

RENTAL CARS

Visitors who come to Santa Barbara and Ventura counties via public transportation and wish to sightsee may choose to rent a car. A number of car rental agencies are located in the county—nationwide companies, as well as smaller, independent agencies; many companies have offices at Santa Barbara, Santa Maria and Oxnard airports. The various city telephone directory yellow pages are the best source of names and telephone numbers for car rental agencies (see Automobile Renting and Leasing).

Cards entitling AAA members to discounts from Hertz agencies may be obtained from any Auto Club district office. Hertz offers information and reservations for AAA members at (800) 654-3080. Callers to Hertz should be sure to identify themselves as Auto Club members. Auto Club Travel Agency offices will also quote rental rates and make reservations.

TAXI

Yellow Cab offers service in various cities throughout Santa Barbara and Ventura counties. Base fare runs about $1.80, to which approximately $1.80 per mile is added. Yellow Cab and other taxi companies are listed in the Santa Barbara and Ventura yellow pages.

Entertainment

Diverse types of entertainment can be found throughout Santa Barbara and Ventura counties.

In addition to movie theaters, drive-in as well as walk-in, dinner theaters include the Circle Bar B at 1800 Refugio Road (805/965-9652), west of Goleta and Starlight Entertainment at Villa Santa Barbara, located in downtown Santa Barbara at 227 East Anapamu Street (805/964-3688). Ventura County's dinner theaters include Theatre by the Sea, a community playhouse located in Ventura Harbor Village, offering murder mysteries with dinner (805/655-7790).

Several hotels have lounges offering live entertainment and dancing. Among those in the Santa Barbara area are the Four Seasons Biltmore Hotel, Sheraton Santa Barbara Hotel and Maxi's in Fess Parker's Red Lion Resort. In Santa Maria the Santa Maria Inn Restaurant has entertainment.

Arlington Center for the Performing Arts, located at 1317 State Street, Santa Barbara, presents entertainment in an unusual setting. The entryway is in the style of a Spanish courtyard, the lobby ceiling has a mural depicting fiesta dancers, and the theater's interior walls are con-structed to resemble a Spanish town with a starry sky. Home of the Santa Barbara Symphony, Arlington Center also presents visiting orchestras and ballet companies, dramatic and musical programs, and motion pictures. For program information call (805) 963-4408.

The Ventura County Symphony offers an annual season of classical music from October through the first week in May at the Oxnard Civic Auditorium. For program information call (805) 643-8646.

Summertime in Ojai is drama and music time, with Libbey Park the scene of two well-attended annual events: a Shakespeare festival and a contemporary classical music series (see *Annual Events*). For those whose taste runs to rock music, the Ventura Concert Theatre in the city of Ventura offers year-round entertainment; call (805) 648-1936. Summer Concerts in the Park is an important series of outdoor concerts in Thousand Oaks, featuring popular music for all ages. Detailed information is available by calling (805) 499-4355.

A sparkling fountain welcomes visitors to Libbey Park in Ojai, site of activities as varied as tennis tournaments and symphonic concerts.

In Santa Barbara, the Lobero Theatre at 33 East Canon Perdido Street, a city- and state-designated historic landmark, is among the oldest legitimate theaters in California. In 1873 an Italian gentleman known as José Lobero brought a new cultural dimension to Santa Barbara by enlarging a school building so that he would have a place in which to present concerts and other staged entertainment. The present theater was built in 1924 and currently hosts a year-round program of drama, music and dance. For program information call (805) 963-0761.

The Pacific Conservatory of the Performing Arts (PCPA) presents a year-round series of music and drama in repertory at the Marian Performing Arts Center on the campus of Allan Hancock College in Santa Maria, 800

South College Drive, and in Solvang at the Solvang Festival Theater, 420 2nd Street. The professional productions range from musicals to classic drama. For program information phone (800) 549-7272. The Festival Theater in Solvang is an outdoor amphitheater, so patrons should dress accordingly.

The University of California at Santa Barbara, Santa Barbara City College, Westmont College, Allan Hancock College and Music Academy of the West play an important part in the cultural lives of their communities. Throughout the year they present high-caliber music and drama programs on their campuses.

Live performance venues in Ventura County include the Plaza Players, a community theatrical group at the

Major theatrical productions are presented year-round in Santa Maria and during the summer in Solvang by the Pacific Conservatory of the Performing Arts (PCPA).

Livery Arts Center in Ventura, where presentations range from children's theater to adult drama to Broadway musicals. The Conejo Players Theatre in Thousand Oaks presents good calibre community theater entertainment. During the summer Thousand Oaks also boasts free concerts that cover the field: jazz, country, salsa and more at Conejo Community Park. The Santa Paula Theatre Center offers classic drama, modern comedy and children's theater. Presentations at the Magnificent Moorpark Melodrama & Vaudeville Company combine both amateur and professional talent.

Automobile Club of Southern California district offices have current listings of most stage events in the counties. For additional information, consult Santa Barbara and Ventura counties' newspapers, *This Week in Santa Barbara* or *The Ventura County and Coast Reporter.*

Activities for Children

Points of interest and recreational activities geared to children can be found throughout both counties.

In the city of Santa Barbara, youngsters of all ages can visit the nearly 500 animals from around the world at the Santa Barbara Zoological Gardens. The zoo also has picnic grounds, a small carousel and a miniature train that gives riders glimpses of the adjacent coast and bird refuge. About a mile west, the Sea Center on Stearns Wharf displays life-size models of a California gray whale and her calf, aquariums and a hands-on exhibit that houses sea life native to the Santa Barbara Channel.

A boat trip out to Channel Islands National Park from the Ventura harbor will delight children of all ages. Also in the harbor area, the Maritime Museum in Oxnard introduces children to all types of sea-going craft. In case the kids think that bananas grow in supermarkets, let them see the trees at the Seaside Banana Garden. Gull Wings Children's Museum in Oxnard will give children plenty to do, from putting on a puppet show to playing "dress-up" to discovering fossils and minerals.

A letter postmarked from "Santa Claus," especially timely when mailed in December, can be sent when visiting the Santa Claus shopping area near Carpinteria. The complex includes a bakery and candy kitchen, along with shops featuring toys, dates and gifts.

Nishiki Koi Ponds on Montecito Street in Santa Barbara offers visitors a chance to observe, feed and even make a purchase from among the hundreds of brightly colored koi in a pleasant outdoor setting. Fish that make up in numbers what they lack in color can be observed at the Fillmore Fish Hatchery, about two miles east of Fillmore on SR 126. Over two million rainbow trout are raised here from eggs to catchable size, and a vending machine allows visitors to feed them.

The Danish-American city of Solvang in Santa Barbara County's Santa Ynez Valley offers a charming village atmosphere and some unusual activities for children. They can ride aboard a horse-drawn streetcar, sample freshly baked Danish pastries and marvel at working windmills. A parade in early December and special

Santa Barbara Zoological Gardens

shop window displays throughout that month lend a festive holiday atmosphere.

Also in Solvang is Santa Inés Mission, one of four California missions located in Santa Barbara and Ventura counties. Santa Inés, along with La Purísima Mission in Lompoc, Santa Barbara Mission and Mission San Buenaventura in Ventura, offer self-guided tours where youngsters can observe firsthand what life was probably like for California's early settlers.

The Parks-Janeway Carriage House in Santa Ynez showcases one of the West's finest collections of horse-drawn vehicles. Original covered wagons and stagecoaches provide children with an idea of what transportation was like before the automobile.

Nearly every outdoor recreational activity imaginable awaits visitors of all ages to Santa Barbara and Ventura counties. Rolling hills and wide valleys welcome bicyclists. The many city, county and state beaches are also popular destinations. Daily lifeguard service is provided at most beaches during the summer months and on weekends during the rest of the year. Beachcombing and surfing are especially good at Carpinteria State Beach, Rincon Point in Carpinteria, San Buenaventura State Beach in Ventura, Hollywood and Silver Strand County beaches in Oxnard and Port Hueneme Beach Park. For those who prefer freshwater swimming, several cities have municipal pools, while many AAA-approved hotels and motels have similar facilities for their guests.

Lake Cachuma County Park in the Santa Ynez Valley has two public swimming pools and offers camping, boating, freshwater fishing and hiking. Lake Casitas Recreation Area in Ventura County has camping, boating, fishing and hiking.

Children can test their mettle in landing a big fish at two Santa Barbara County fishing ponds. One is located at River Park in Lompoc and the other at Waller County Park in Santa Maria. The latter also offers children's pony rides. A small lake at Rancho Simi Conejo Park in Simi Valley also gives children a chance to try their fishing skills.

Annual Events

In addition to the points of interest and recreational activities offered for all-year enjoyment, these counties host a wide variety of once-a-year events. Members can obtain further information by calling the telephone numbers shown or by contacting any district office of the Automobile Club of Southern California.

JANUARY

Pro-Am Golf Tournament *Sandpiper Golf Course, Goleta (805) 962-7661, ext. 401.* Professionals and celebrities join amateurs; spectators are welcome. Proceeds benefit Saint Francis Medical Center of Santa Barbara.

FEBRUARY

International Festival *Veteran's Memorial Cultural Center, Santa Maria. (805) 925-0951, ext. 206.* This annual festival features ethnic arts, food and entertainment.

Storytelling Festival *Solvang. (805) 688-8000.* Professional and amateur storytellers share their tales during this 12-hour event.

MARCH

International Orchid Show *Earl Warren Showgrounds, Santa Barbara.*

(805) 967-6331. Spectacular displays compete for awards. A commercial sales area is included.

Orchids and Art Show *Veteran's Memorial Cultural Center, Santa Maria. (805) 925-0951, ext. 206.* The show features colorful displays of orchids, fine arts, food and entertainment.

Santa Barbara International Film Festival *Santa Barbara. (805) 963-0023.* The festival premieres U.S. and international films, and includes workshops, seminars and evenings with selected stars.

Spring Ojai Renaissance Festival *Lake Casitas. (805) 640-0400.* Music and plays, jousting and archery, food and crafts are set in a re-creation of a Renaissance village. (This event also takes place in September.)

APRIL

Ojai Tennis Tournament *Libbey Park and other tennis courts, Ojai.*

(805) 646-7241. Well over 1500 amateur tennis players compete in 34 divisions, which include the Big West Championships and the PAC 10 Championships

Santa Barbara County Vintner's Festival *Santa Ynez. (805) 688-0881.* Wine, food and entertainment highlight this two-day festival.

California Beach Party *Harbor Boulevard and California Street, Ventura (805) 648-2875.* Live music, wind-surfing, 5K and 10K runs and walks, food, and arts and crafts stands highlight this spring event.

Channel Islands Harbor Food & Wine Festival *Harbor Boulevard and Channel Islands Boulevard, Oxnard (800) 994-4852.* Local musicians provide a background for food, beverages and children's activities.

APRIL-AUGUST

Mission Life Days *La Purísima Mission State Historic Park, Lompoc. (805) 733-3713.* One day each month the public can see and participate in craft and food-preparation activities similar to those of the mission's early inhabitants.

MAY

Arabian Horse Show *Earl Warren Showgrounds, Santa Barbara. (805) 967-6331.* Beautiful animals are put through their paces.

Cajun/Creole Music Festival *Los Angeles Avenue near Tapo Canyon Road, Simi Valley (805) 520-4894.* Simi Sunrise Rotary Club sponsors

Cajun and Creole flavored food, music, arts and crafts and dancing.

Eagle Point Pow-Wow *Lake Casitas. (805) 640-0400.* A two-day celebration of Native American music and dance presents an opportunity to enjoy Indian culture, foods, arts and crafts.

Early California Days Festival *Fillmore. (805)524-0351.* A parade, carnival, barbecue, food and game booths celebrate Fillmore's heritage.

Gourmet Century Bike Ride *Santa Ynez Valley. (805) 688-6385.* Participants bicycle a 100-mile course around Santa Ynez Valley and enjoy gourmet offerings at several stations along the way.

Huck Finn Fishing Derby *Rancho Simi Community Park, Simi Valley. (805) 584-4400.* Children under age 15 compete for prizes in catching fish from the park's freshly stocked lagoon.

JUNE

Art Walk *Exxon Company USA Building, 225 West Hillcrest Drive, Thousand Oaks (805) 373-0054.* A two-day art exhibit showcases the work of local and California artists.

Elks Rodeo and Parade *Santa Maria. (805) 922-6006.* A parade, various contests, a rodeo, dances and barbecues are featured.

Flower Festival *Lompoc. (805) 735-8511.* Tours of the flower fields, a parade, carnival, arts and crafts booths, flower show and special entertainment highlight this event. **(See ad on page 33.)**

Ojai Festival *Libbey Park, Ojai. (805) 646-2094.* Contemporary classical music is presented by professional music groups under the baton of renowned conductors.

Ojai Wine Festival *Lake Casitas. (800) 648-4881.* This is a leisurely afternoon of wine tasting, sampling the cuisine of Ojai Valley restaurants, and browsing arts and crafts displays.

Old Santa Ynez Days *Santa Ynez. (805) 688-5318.* The town celebrates its birthday with cowboys, food and entertainment.

Summer Solstice Celebration *Santa Barbara. (805) 965-3396.* In celebration of the coming of summer, performers and artisans display their talents, and a lively parade winds through the city streets, followed by a festival featuring music, dance and food.

JUNE-JULY

Semana Nautica Sports Festival *various locations in Santa Barbara. (805) 564-2052.* This 10-day sports-oriented event takes place on land and sea, and includes sailing and swimming competitions, a sports medicine symposium, an art show, skin diving and a 15K race.

JUNE-AUGUST

Music Academy of the West Summer Concert Series *various Santa Barbara locations. (805) 969-4726.* Student and professional performances are set in gardens and theaters.

JULY

4th of July Celebration *Ventura Pier and Main Street in downtown Ventura. (805) 648-2875.* A 5 a.m. fireworks display at the Ventura Pier begins the day. Later on, food booths, bands, games, a children's parade, and an arts and crafts show light up the city.

Fourth of July Fireworks *Hilltop north of The Oaks Mall, 222 West Hillcrest Drive, Thousand Oaks. (805) 495-4671.* Fireworks light up the sky to celebrate Independence Day in Thousand Oaks.

July 4th Fireworks *Fillmore High School football field, 2nd Street and Central Avenue, Fillmore. (805) 524-0351.* A fireworks display celebrates the Fourth of July.

Santa Barbara County Fair *Santa Barbara County Fairgrounds, Santa Maria. (805) 925-8824.* Billed as a "real" country fair, this event includes 4-H exhibits, horse shows, animal judging, homemade food, a carnival, music and entertainment.

Santa Barbara Kennel Club Show *Stevenson Field, Buellton.* This is one of the largest one-day dog shows in the nation; free transportation from downtown Santa Barbara.

JULY-AUGUST

Ojai Shakespeare Festival *Libbey Bowl, Ojai. (805) 646-9455.* Matinee and evening performances of at least two of the Bard's plays take place on Saturdays and Sundays in an outdoor setting.

AUGUST

Mission Santa Inés Fiesta *1760 Mission Drive, Solvang. (805) 688-4815.* Food and game booths, a barbecue and folk dancing highlight this event that raises money for mission restoration.

Old Spanish Days Fiesta *various locations in Santa Barbara. (805) 962-8101.* Arts and crafts displays, two parades, two marketplaces and a rodeo are a few of the fiesta's exciting, colorful activities. This extravaganza, enjoyed every year for over half a century, celebrates the city's Spanish and Mexican heritage.

Ventura County Fair *Ventura County Fairgrounds, off US 101 at California Street (going west), Ventura Avenue (going east), Ventura. (805) 648-3376.* Included in this seaside fair are livestock auctions, a chili cookoff, free entertainment, a carnival, rodeo and fireworks over the ocean every night.

SEPTEMBER

Simi Valley Days *southeast corner of Los Angeles Avenue and Madera Road, Simi Valley (805) 520-4894.* There's something for everyone in this Rotary Club event: barn dance, chili cook-off, horse show, parade, carnival, 5K and 10K runs and a golf tournament.

Concours d'Elegance *Santa Barbara Polo & Racquet Club, 3375 Foothill Road, Carpinteria. (805) 969-2667.* A winner's parade follows the exhibiting and judging of classic and vintage cars.

Danish Days *Solvang. (805) 688-3317, 688-6144.* Parade, entertainment, dancing and special foods reflect Solvang's pride in its Danish heritage.

Day in the Country *Los Olivos. (805) 688-5083.* Held the fourth Saturday of the month, this event includes crafts, music, food and buggy rides in the country.

Fall Ojai Renaissance Festival *Lake Casitas. (805) 649-2233.* Music and plays, jousting and archery, food and crafts are set in a re-creation of a Renaissance village. (This event also takes place in March.)

Golden State Air Fair *Santa Maria Public Airport, Santa Maria. (805) 922-1726.* Performances by private and military aircraft share the spotlight with skydiving demonstrations, aircraft displays, food booths and concessions.

Mexican Fiesta *Libbey Park, Ojai (805) 646-5997.* Mariachi, ballet folklorico and authentic Mexican food are all part of a fiesta to benefit Mexican-American scholarships.

Santa Barbara Triathlon *East Beach Cabrillo Bath House & Art Center, Santa Barbara.* Participants swim one mile, bicycle 34 miles and run 10 miles, or they can opt for a shorter "sprint" course with a 500-yard swim, a six-mile bike ride and a two-mile run.

Zoo-B-Que *Santa Barbara Zoological Gardens, Santa Barbara. (805) 962-6310.* Family barbecue and entertainment help support the zoo.

OCTOBER

Artists' Studios Tour *Ojai, various locations (805) 646-8126.* Many of Ojai's finest painters, sculptors, print makers and potters open their private studios to visitors.

Autumn Arts Festival *Veteran's Memorial Cultural Center, Santa Maria. (805) 925-0951, ext. 206.* Included are a farmers market, arts and crafts show, food booths, live entertainment, a kids' world, car show, art demonstrations and a fine arts show.

Bowlful of Blues *Libbey Bowl in Libbey Park, Ojai. (805) 646-7230.* Top-flight musicians celebrate American music in blues, zydeco and gospel.

California Avocado Festival *Linden Avenue, Carpinteria. (805) 684-0038.* A food fair honoring the avocado joins live entertainment, an art fair, athletic events and exhibits.

Goleta Valley Days Festival *Goleta. (805) 967-4618.* Parade, concerts, Old-Time Fiddlers' Convention, crafts, golf tournament, chili cook-off, barbecue and food fair are included in this celebration.

Harvest Arts Festival *Lompoc. (805) 736-4567.* A 12 x 48-foot mural is painted in one day by 15 professional artists. The event also features hands-on art activities, entertainment and food booths.

Pt. Mugu Air Show *Naval Air Station, 4 miles south of Port Hueneme via Las Posas Road off SR 1. (805) 989-8786.* Military and civilian pilots perform air maneuvers in a variety of aircraft—from vintage to current experimental. The Blue Angels team performs every other year. Free admission; fee for grandstand seats.

NOVEMBER

Dixieland Jazz Festival *Solvang. (805) 688-8000.* Top Dixieland bands from around the country appear the third weekend of the month.

DECEMBER

Christmas Parade and Bazaar *Central Park, Fillmore. (805) 524-0351.* In addition to a parade featuring Santa Claus, food and craft booths delight visitors.

Holiday Street Festival *Main Street, downtown Ventura. (805) 648-2875.* Food booths, bands, choirs and plenty of arts and crafts start off the holiday season.

Parade of Lights *Channel Islands Harbor. (805) 985-4852, (800) 994-4852.* Dozens of boats parade in their finery of Christmas lights.

Santa Maria Christmas Parade *Santa Maria. (805) 925-8113.* This Christmas tradition features a parade of lights with bands, floats and Santa Claus.

Winterfest *Solvang. (805) 688-6144.* A parade, evening carriage rides, caroling, tree-lighting ceremonies and special store window displays celebrate the Christmas season.

Santa Barbara County

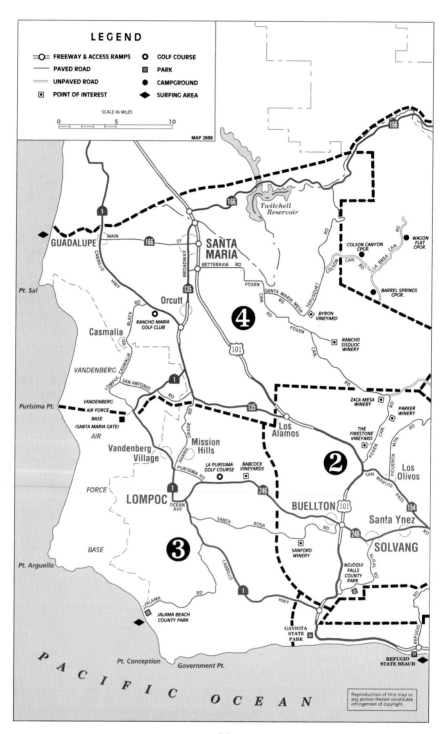

LEGEND

═◯═ FREEWAY & ACCESS RAMPS
── PAVED ROAD
═══ UNPAVED ROAD
⊡ POINT OF INTEREST
◯ GOLF COURSE
◼ PARK
● CAMPGROUND
◆ SURFING AREA

SCALE IN MILES
0 ___ 5 ___ 10

MAP 2688

Twitchell Reservoir

166

GUADALUPE
MAIN
166
ST

SANTA MARIA
BROADWAY
BETTERAVIA RD.

Pt. Sal

FOXEN
SANTA MARIA MESA RD.
SUISQUOC

COLSON CANYON CPGR.
WAGON FLAT CPGR.
CAN. RD.
LA BREA CAN.
COLSON CAN. RD.

135

Orcutt
BLACK RD.
RANCHO MARIA GOLF CLUB

BARREL SPRINGS CPGR.

4

Casmalia

BYRON VINEYARD

101

FOXEN

RANCHO SISQUOC WINERY

VANDENBERG
LOMPOC CASMALIA RD.
SAN ANTONIO

Purisima Pt.

ZACA MESA WINERY
PARKER WINERY

VANDENBERG AIR FORCE BASE (SANTA MARIA GATE)

HARRIS GRADE RD.

135

Los Alamos

THE FIRESTONE VINEYARD
FOXEN CAN. RD.
FIGUEROA MTN RD.

AIR

Vandenberg Village

Mission Hills

LA PURISIMA GOLF COURSE

BABCOCK VINEYARDS

Los Olivos

FORCE

PURISIMA RD.

246

SAN MARCOS PASS

2

154

BASE

LOMPOC
OCEAN AVE

BUELLTON
101

246

Santa Ynez

RD.

SANTA ROSA

SANFORD WINERY

SOLVANG

Pt. Arguello

3

ALISAL RD.

NOJOQUI FALLS COUNTY PARK

CABRILLO

JALAMA RD.

JALAMA BEACH COUNTY PARK

HWY

1

GAVIOTA STATE PARK

REFUGIO RD.

REFUGIO STATE BEACH

Pt. Conception   Government Pt.

P A C I F I C   O C E A N

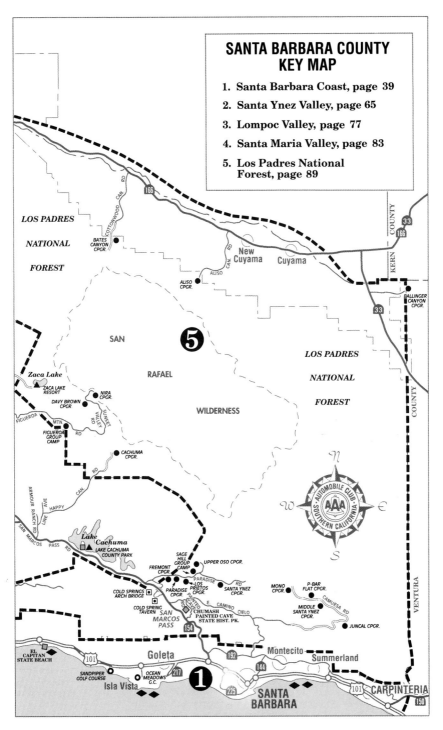

SANTA BARBARA COUNTY KEY MAP

1. **Santa Barbara Coast, page 39**
2. **Santa Ynez Valley, page 65**
3. **Lompoc Valley, page 77**
4. **Santa Maria Valley, page 83**
5. **Los Padres National Forest, page 89**

A visit to the tower of the Santa Barbara County Courthouse provides good views of the city.

Santa Barbara Coast

Extending for more than 50 miles from Rincon Point on the eastern flank to Point Conception on the west, the Santa Barbara Coast includes the communities of Carpinteria, Santa Barbara and Goleta. Nestled between the rugged Santa Ynez Mountains on the north and Pacific beaches on the south, this long, east-west plain is never more than 10 miles wide. The area's south-facing configuration and protective mountains guarantee a mild, Riviera-style climate throughout the year.

The region possesses a varied economy that reflects its ties with the past and its expectations for the future. Agricultural production (particularly lemons, avocados and vegetables) and flower cultivation continue to flourish today in the favorable climate and fertile soil. Such contemporary industries as oil exploration and research and development for electronics and space technology also contribute significantly. Lastly, tourism draws large numbers to the area, especially the city of Santa Barbara.

The principal and most populous city along this coast, Santa Barbara serves as the county seat. It is especially attractive to visitors with its many points of interest, accommodations, restaurants, entertainment complexes, shopping areas and recreational facilities. To the east lies Carpinteria, which proudly boasts of its broad state beach, while Goleta on the west serves as home to the University of California at Santa Barbara.

CARPINTERIA

Carpinteria, a city of approximately 13,750 people, is located 12 miles east of Santa Barbara in a small valley between the Santa Ynez Mountains and the coast. It reputedly acquired its name in 1769 when Spanish soldiers in Gaspar de Portolá's exploratory expedition, intrigued with the Chumash Indians' canoe building, called the area Carpinteria, meaning "carpenter shop."

The valley's agricultural production, which is still vital to the local economy, was originally slow to develop. Land division didn't begin until the mid-1800s because the entire Carpinteria Valley was considered a prized location for large Spanish and Mexican land grants to Indians and retired military personnel. In 1858 the first American rancher began acquiring orchard land and over time developed the world's largest walnut grove. Lima

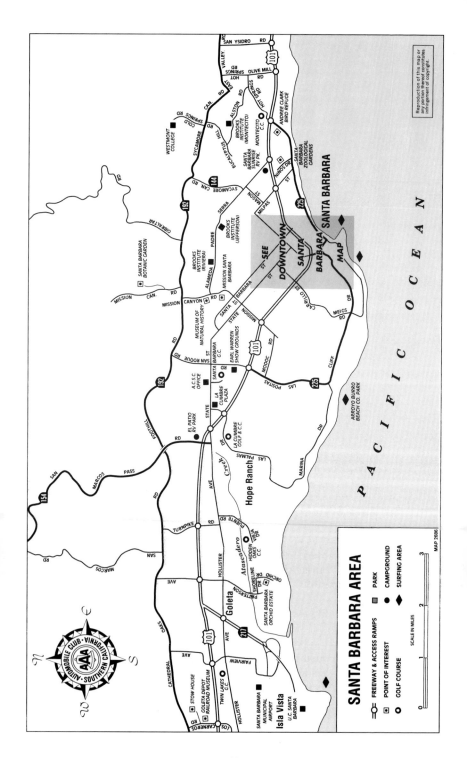

SANTA BARBARA AREA

FREEWAY & ACCESS RAMPS
POINT OF INTEREST
GOLF COURSE
PARK
CAMPGROUND
SURFING AREA

SCALE IN MILES

MAP 2686

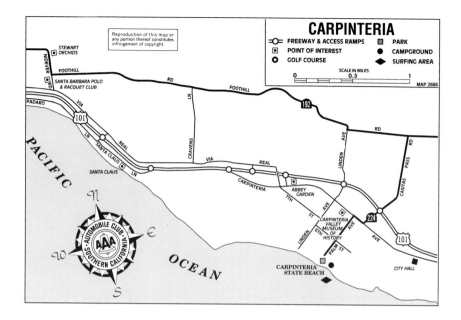

beans were first introduced as a commercial crop here about 30 years later.

In addition to farming, strip mining for tar occurred along the coast from 1875 to the early 1920s. The tar was so pure that is was not only used for paving and roofing but also for producing printers' ink and artists' colors.

Despite its early successes in farming and mining, the Carpinteria Valley was slow in drawing tourists into the area because the slopes of adjacent Rincon Mountain drop directly to the sea, severely limiting access by land. A roadbed along the shore for stagecoaches was almost impossible to maintain because of constant slides. In order to get through, stages had to wait for low tide. Finally in 1887, the Southern Pacific Railroad carved out a right-of-way and built a mile-long ledge for track out of the side of the

mountain, thus opening the Carpinteria Valley to visitors. In 1912 the Rincon Causeway, with its 6100-foot viaduct of wood planks over eucalyptus pilings spanning the water, opened to allow automobile traffic into Carpinteria. A paved highway was completed 10 years later, replacing the causeway.

Today Carpinteria's residents are proud of their shore, which has been called the "world's safest beach," because of its natural reef breakwater and absence of riptides. One of California's largest public beach camping units is at Carpinteria State Beach, and Rincon Point is considered one of the best surfing spots in Southern California. Beachcombing for shells and pebbles is another favorite activity for visitors at Carpinteria beaches.

John Austerman

Abbey Gardens Cactus and Succulent Nursery houses more than 2000 species of botanical curiosities.

The Carpinteria Valley is also a major flower-growing region because of its sunny, mild climate and fertile soil. It is recognized as one of the world's orchid capitals and the largest producer of cymbidiums in the nation. Other flowers grown here include carnations, azaleas, roses and tulips.

Carpinteria has one AAA-approved motel, and numerous eating establishments and shops are clustered along the palm-lined streets of downtown.

Unless otherwise noted, all grid coordinates refer to the Carpinteria city map on the *Cities of Santa Barbara County* street map.

ABBEY GARDEN CACTUS AND SUCCULENT NURSERY *4620 Carpinteria Avenue (B-3). (805) 684-*

5112. Visitors can view 2000 species of cacti and succulents—all under one roof. A wide variety of cactus forms makes this a place to indulge one's imagination, while cactus flowers add vivid splashes of color. The nursery and its gift shop are open Tuesday through Sunday from 9 a.m. to 5 p.m.; closed Monday. Group tours are offered by appointment only May through October. Admission is free.

CARPINTERIA VALLEY MUSEUM OF HISTORY *956 Maple Avenue (C-3). (805) 684-3112.* Many of the exhibits depict a typical turn-of-the-century lifestyle by means of household furnishings and clothing contributed by descendants of Carpinteria's pioneer families. A new wing contains agricultural and oil-boom artifacts and a turn-of-the-century schoolroom. A number of Chumash artifacts, including ornaments and utensils, are also on display. The museum is open Tuesday through Friday and Sunday 1:30 to 4 p.m.; Saturday 11 a.m. to 4 p.m.; closed Monday. Admission is free.

SANTA BARBARA POLO & RACQUET CLUB *3375 Foothill Road, one mile west of Carpinteria (E-24, Santa Barbara and Vicinity city map on the Cities of Santa Barbara street map). (805) 684-8667 (recording), 684-6683.* From April through October, polo games are played here each Sunday beginning at 1 p.m., with the feature match at 3 p.m. Visitors are welcome. For information about matches and schedules, telephone either of the above numbers.

SANTA CLAUS *Santa Claus Lane, off US 101, ½ mile west of Carpinteria (B-1).* Much of the merchandise and decor of this tourist attraction are based on Christmas themes. In addition to a bakery, restaurants and candy kitchen, shops feature toys, dates and gifts. Some visitors enjoy sending mail from Santa Claus, especially in December, because of the postmark. The toy store, date shop, bakery and candy kitchen are open daily from 9 a.m. to 8 p.m. during summer months; 9 a.m. to 6 p.m. Monday through Thursday and until 8 p.m. Friday and Saturday the rest of the year. The hours for other shops vary.

STEWART ORCHIDS *3376 Foothill Road, one mile west of Carpinteria (D-24, Santa Barbara and Vicinity city map on the Cities of Santa Barbara County street map). (805) 684-5448.*

This large nursery is devoted solely to the growing and selling of orchids. More than 80,000 square feet of greenhouse space enclose plants of contrasting shape, size and color. The nursery is open Monday through Friday from 8 a.m. to 4 p.m. and Saturday 10 a.m. to 4 p.m.; closed Sunday and major holidays.

GOLETA

This busy, unincorporated community of more than 72,000 people lies just west of Santa Barbara between the Santa Ynez Mountains and the ocean. Like Carpinteria, agriculture and flower growing play a part in Goleta's economy. More importantly, however, Goleta houses approximately 80 research and development firms in the fields of electronics and space technology. Also located here are the Santa Barbara Municipal Airport and the University of California at Santa Barbara in nearby Isla Vista. Year-round family recreation includes swimming, fishing, boating, surfing, camping, hiking, horseback riding, skin diving, tennis and golf. The community contains several lodgings, numerous restaurants and shops.

In the 1840s this area was the Dos Pueblos land grant on which extensive herds of cattle grazed. By the late 1800s, citrus, walnut and almond orchards became the leading industry of the valley, thanks largely to the pioneering efforts of the Stow family on La Patera Ranch.

Thomas P. Burgnon

Built in 1901, the Goleta Depot was moved in 1981 to its present location and now houses the South Coast Railroad Museum.

All map coordinates refer to the Santa Barbara and Vicinity city map on the *Cities of Santa Barbara County* street map.

SANTA BARBARA ORCHID ESTATE *1250 Orchid Drive (D-10). (805) 967-1284.* Two acres, one under glass and one outdoors, are used to display a multitude of orchids. At any one time, many varieties are in bloom, with each month having its own specialty. Both cut flowers and plants, exclusively orchids, are available to retail buyers as well as wholesalers. Those who wish to simply stroll and enjoy the beauty of the plants are always welcome. The orchid estate is open Monday

through Saturday, 8 a.m. to 5:30 p.m. and Sunday, 10 a.m. to 4 p.m.; closed major holidays.

SOUTH COAST RAILROAD MUSEUM *300 North Los Carneros Road (C-7). (805) 964-3540.* This wooden building, with its distinctive "SP yellow" color, was constructed by the Southern Pacific Railroad Company in 1901, handling freight and passengers until the early 1970s. The station was relocated to its present site, and restoration began in 1981. Antique railroad artifacts, photographs and hands-on exhibits are located in the agency office and passenger waiting rooms. A 400-square-foot, HO-scale model railroad is also on display. An old Southern Pacific

caboose sits on tracks in front of the museum. The museum is open Wednesday through Sunday from 1 to 4 p.m. Admission is free; donations are requested. Rides aboard a miniature train are offered Wednesdays year round, and the second and fourth Saturday each month in summer and the second Saturday the rest of the year.

STOW HOUSE *304 North Los Carneros Road (C-7). (805) 964-4407.* This restored ranch house, built by the Stow family in the 1870s, is a rambling, two-story, Victorian-style structure with some "Carpenter's Gothic" touches. Its wide veranda is shaded by a great Australian primrose tree. Inside, rooms and hallways contain such beautiful period furnishings as chairs, tables, handhooked rugs, clothing and toys. Some of the outbuildings have also been restored and contain antique farm equipment, the Sexton Farm Museum and the Maritime Interpretive Display. Stow House is open 2 to 4 p.m. Saturday and Sunday; special events are held on July 4th, in October during Goleta Valley Days and during the Christmas season. Group tours can be arranged by calling the above number. The house and grounds are closed on rainy days. Donation is $1 for adults.

UNIVERSITY OF CALIFORNIA AT SANTA BARBARA *Two miles south of US 101 via Clarence Ward Memorial*

University of California at Santa Barbara

The University of California at Santa Barbara has occupied its picturesque oceanfront site since 1954.

Boulevard, SR 217 (E-7). (805) 893-8000. Founded in 1891 as a trade school near downtown Santa Barbara, a greatly expanded curriculum brought it into the University of California system in 1944. In 1954 the campus was relocated to its present site—815 acres by the Pacific Ocean in Isla Vista near Goleta.

In addition to traditional programs, UCSB has an extensive Marine Sciences Institute, which uses a large adjacent lagoon as one of its research areas. The major architectural landmark on the campus is 175-foot-high Storke Tower, which houses a 61-bell carillon that is heard twice each hour. The Santa Barbara community is enriched by the university's cultural events presented both on and off campus throughout the year; the fields of music, drama, dance and visual arts are well represented.

Free guided tours of the campus can be arranged all year by contacting the Office of Relations with Schools, 1234 Cheadle Hall, Santa Barbara 93106; or by calling (805) 893-8175 (recording) or 893-2485. Parking is free during evening hours and on weekends and university holidays. On weekdays a $3 pass must be purchased at either entrance gate; the pass includes a map of the campus and visitor parking.

during the late 19th century. They were attracted by the mild climate, mineral hot springs, and mountain and ocean vistas. Many of them decided to establish homes, and the early 20th century saw great houses built on large estates lush with lawns, shrubs and trees. Names prominent in American business had Montecito addresses: Armstrong, Du Pont, Fleischmann, Pillsbury and Stetson.

In the 1920s and '30s Montecito experienced an influx of well-to-do people who chose not to build such elaborate estates. Nevertheless, the community continues to enjoy a reputation for beautiful, lavishly landscaped homes, and some prominent entertainment industry figures have settled here. Unfortunately (for tourists), most of the impressive residences are screened from view by hedges, trees and walls, but the overall beauty of the community makes a sightseeing drive worthwhile.

In the hills above Sycamore Canyon Road, Ganna Walska Lotusland embraces 37 acres of gardens that include a Japanese water garden, dozens of varieties of euphorbia, cactus, ferns, palms and an unparalleled area of cycads. Lotusland is open to the public only by reservation for a guided tour; call (805) 969-9990 at least two months in advance; there is an admission fee.

MONTECITO

Montecito borders the eastern limits of the city of Santa Barbara. This community is an outgrowth of a resort area to which wealthy people flocked

SANTA BARBARA

Long considered one of California's most beautiful communities, Santa Barbara occupies a narrow plain that slopes southward from the rugged

Santa Ynez Mountains to palm-fringed Pacific beaches. With the protection afforded by these mountains and a sea-calming string of offshore islands to the south, Santa Barbara has attained a justifiable reputation for an excellent climate. The benign weather contributes to the natural beauty of the area by supporting a lush growth of subtropical and Mediterranean foliage that provides the city with vivid color and greenery year round.

Enhancing Santa Barbara's natural beauty is an abundance of Spanish-Mediterranean architecture, a suitable outgrowth of the city's Hispanic heritage. This style, with its red-tiled roofs and white walls, is found throughout the city. State Street, the main business thoroughfare, incorporates decorative tile inlaid in concrete drinking fountains, bus benches, newsstands and other public amenities.

The city of Santa Barbara's history is closely tied to that of the entire county. The Chumash Indians were the first inhabitants of the area, and their settlements eventually gave way to the age of Spanish explorers and subsequent building of the presidio and mission. (This era is discussed in detail in the *History* section.)

Following secularization of the missions, America developed an interest in acquiring California. In August 1846, Commodore Robert Stockton landed in Santa Barbara Bay and established a small garrison that was overrun by the Mexicans several weeks later. In December, after entering the town by way of San Marcos Pass, Colonel John C. Frémont's California Battalion established America's authority in Santa Barbara. Although there was little animosity toward the Americans on the part of the townspeople, a few acts of rebellion did occur. One such act involved the disappearance of a small, neglected cannon—for which the town was fined $500. This incident is the basis for the name of a city street, "Canon Perdido," meaning "lost cannon." As American occupation continued, soldiers mustered out of the service in Santa Barbara were absorbed into the community. With settlements throughout the territory, Santa Barbara County was incorporated in 1850, and California was admitted to the Union later that year.

During the second half of the 19th century, Santa Barbara began to assume its present shape. Streets were laid out, and many were given names reflecting the town's Spanish heritage. Americans acquired title to land on which they established farms for raising crops and cattle. One- and two-story frame houses were built in town, often in New England architectural styles.

Santa Barbara's popularity was greatly increased by the discovery of mineral springs that were believed to have medicinal value. From the 1870s into the early 20th century, people came to enjoy the spas built near the springs. One of the most famous was the three-story, 90-room Arlington Hotel, built where Arlington Center for the Performing Arts now stands. Visitors traveled to Santa Barbara by ship or stagecoach, and in 1887 a railroad going northwest from

Saugus reached the town, greatly increasing its accessibility and contributing to a population boom. In 1901 the rail lines were completed to San Francisco, thereby bringing an end to steamer and stagecoach travel.

From the 1880s through the 1920s, Santa Barbara had a sizable community of Chinese, many of whom had worked on the San Marcos Pass road. A small number were merchants, but the majority worked as servants, laundrymen, vegetable growers and vendors. Chinatown, located on Canon Perdido Street between State and Anacapa streets, was the scene of many noisy, exciting New Year's celebrations, but as the Chinese population steadily decreased, Chinatown disappeared.

By 1910 it was evident that Santa Barbara's population was outstripping its water supply. A commission was appointed and a plan developed to dam flood waters in the upper Santa Ynez Valley; the water would be carried to Santa Barbara via a tunnel through the Santa Ynez Mountains north of the city. Successively more ambitious projects were proposed, culminating in the construction of Bradbury Dam and the Cachuma Reservoir in 1953.

One glamorous aspect of Santa Barbara's history was the town's role in movie making. By 1910 the American Film Company had a studio in the center of town, and stars such as Wallace Reid, "Fatty" Arbuckle, Mabel Normand and director D. W. Griffith made celluloid history. For nearly a decade the area's mansions, streets and scenic foothills provided excellent backgrounds, while local residents found work as extras.

The early 1920s brought an awareness that many buildings in the downtown area were unattractive or in need of repair, but it was felt that changes could not be made for many years. Then on June 29, 1925, an earthquake demolished much of central Santa Barbara. Structures were rebuilt, not only with fire and earthquake safety in mind, but also with architecturally harmonious exteriors in the Hispanic style.

The following decades brought growth and prosperity to Santa Barbara. Tourism continued to provide employment in a variety of fields. The University of California, begun in 1891 as Anna S.C. Blake Training School, created a number of jobs and became a catalyst for cultural stimulation. Light industry was brought into the area by several electronic and computer firms. The public school system that began in the late 19th century continued to grow, while special schools like Brooks Institute added prestige to the community.

With the city's growth, cultural and recreational opportunities increased. A resident symphony orchestra was founded in 1953. The visual arts flourished, as small galleries sprang up to house them, and an attractive, comprehensive art museum became a midtown landmark. Theaters like the Arlington and Lobero were adapted to present motion pictures, as well as live entertainment. Stearns Wharf and the breakwater helped make

John Austerman

Pleasure craft amd commercial fishing boats share the protected waters of Santa Barbara Harbor.

provides facilities for fishing, boating and swimming. Throughout the city, special paths are provided for bicycling enthusiasts. Accommodations range from modest motels to deluxe resort hotels. Several bed and breakfast inns, housed in lovely old estates, Victorian showplaces or quaint cottages, provide alternative lodging. Meals in the city encompass everything from the simplest fare to complex ethnic dishes and haute cuisine. Befitting its Latin heritage, Santa Barbara offers a number of top-quality Mexican restaurants. And the city's coastal locale assures fresh fish daily in several good seafood restaurants.

Santa Barbara's harbor safe and convenient for commercial and pleasure boats. Recreational facilities expanded as people developed interests in everything from polo to baseball.

Today Santa Barbara offers a wide selection of things to see and do. High on the list of important historic attractions are Mission Santa Barbara and the restored areas of the presidio. The Museum of Art and the Lobero Theatre are among the places that appeal to those seeking indoor cultural pleasures. Outdoor enjoyment is offered by areas such as the Andree Clark Bird Refuge, the botanic garden, the zoo and a variety of parks. For those who prefer more vigorous activity, the oceanfront

Shopping in Santa Barbara can be as novel as a small handicraft shop or as conventional as a large department store. Probably the most distinctive downtown shopping malls are El Paseo and Paseo Nuevo: El Paseo's one-of-a-kind shops exist in a historical atmosphere, while Paseo Nuevo mirrors the modern scene. Several of the area's inviting antique shops line Brinkerhoff Avenue. A number of fine galleries located throughout the city offer the works of Santa Barbara's resident artists. Popular with both tourists and local shoppers is a small factory outlet district located near Stearns Wharf, between Anacapa and

State streets. The outlets offer goods ranging from handmade ceramic dinnerware to T-shirts and bikinis. For more conventional shopping, there is La Cumbre Plaza, located on Santa Barbara's north side at State Street and La Cumbre Road, where two large department stores adjoin more than 65 shops and restaurants.

Over the past few decades the Santa Barbara area has become a center of activity for serious students in many fields, particularly the arts. A campus of the University of California in nearby Isla Vista and the Music Academy of the West, Santa Barbara City College and the prestigious Brooks Institute of Photography in Santa Barbara all contribute to the city's educational climate.

Within a short drive of downtown Santa Barbara are several smaller

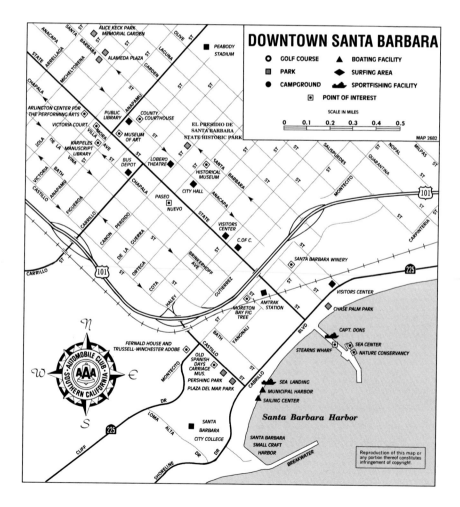

communities which, because of beauty or historical significance—or both—merit a visit. Hope Ranch, an exclusive and beautiful residential area, lies just west of Santa Barbara, on the south side of US 101. This area was originally part of a Mexican land grant called Cañada de Calera. A patent on the land grant was issued to Thomas W. Hope in 1870, and the Spanish designation was changed to Hope Ranch by his heirs. During the early 1900s the land was subdivided and sold in large sections. Few of the fine homes later built on these estates are visible from the street; however, Las Palmas Drive winds through the area and provides a scenic trip leading past the beautiful lake and greens of La Cumbre Golf and Country Club.

The **Automobile Club of Southern California** Santa Barbara district office is located at 3712 State Street, Santa Barbara 93105 (C-14); (805) 682-5811.

All grid coordinates refer to the Santa Barbara and Vicinity city map on the ACSC *Cities of Santa Barbara County* street map.

ALAMEDA PLAZA *bounded by Micheltorena, Garden, Sola and Anacapa streets; bisected by Santa Barbara Street (D-16).* In the square on the east side of Santa Barbara Street are over 70 species of trees, singly or in small groves, that provide an inviting midtown area for picnicking or relaxing. There are benches, picnic tables and children's play equipment, and the park area to the west has a large gazebo used for concerts and speeches.

ALICE KECK PARK MEMORIAL GARDEN *bounded by Arrellaga, Garden, Micheltorena and Santa Barbara streets (D-16).* This inviting park in the midst of the city emphasizes the diverse plant life to be found in Santa Barbara. Plant environments range from marshy to arid, and colors throughout the gardens vary from section to section and season to season. Within the grounds are a pond that hosts a variety of marine plants, two meandering streams, winding pathways, benches and a gazebo.

ANDREE CLARK BIRD REFUGE *1400 East Cabrillo Boulevard (D-18).* This preserve of more than 40 acres includes a lagoon that is dotted with islands and enhanced by well-kept gardens. The refuge provides a sheltered home for many migratory and nonmigratory bird species, including a wide variety of waterfowl. Walkways and bicycle paths border the refuge, and space is provided for free automobile parking off Los Patos Way.

ARTS AND CRAFTS SHOW *along Cabrillo Boulevard, east from State Street (E-17). (805) 962-8956.* On fair-weather Sundays, a stroll eastward from State Street along the beach side of Cabrillo Boulevard leads past an extensive arts and crafts show. Since 1966, artisans of Santa Barbara have been displaying their works here in an outdoor setting that often extends three-quarters of a mile. There is a wide range of artistic taste, style and ability expressed through various media; painting, ceramics, sculpture and photography among them. Everything is for sale, and conversations with the displaying artists are encouraged. The show takes place every Sunday and on holidays throughout the year, 10 a.m. to dusk.

BRINKERHOFF AVENUE *between Cota and Haley streets (E-16)*. Along both sides of this single block are charming old houses which have been converted to antique and gift shops. All sorts of collectible items, from buttons to bathtubs can be found here; browsing is welcome. Most of the shops are open daily 11 a.m. to 5:30 p.m.

BROOKS INSTITUTE OF PHO-TOGRAPHY *(805) 966-3888*. This world-renowned school, established in 1945, occupies three campuses in the foothills above Santa Barbara. The private, coeducational institute offers graduate and undergraduate degrees in all phases of photography, from portraiture to scientific research. Photographs are on display at all three campuses, with the main hallway galleries on the Jefferson and Montecito campuses.

Jefferson Campus *1321 Alameda Padre Serra (C-16)*. This campus houses the institute's illustration/advertising, audio visual and industrial/scientific departments and an advanced electronic imaging lab. The campus, also home to one of the nation's finest photographic libraries, is open Monday through Friday 8 a.m. to 5 p.m. Admission is free.

Media Center *1722 State Street (D-16)*. This facility contains the motion

John Austerman

Outdoor dining is popular among the shoppers at picturesque El Paseo.

picture/video department for the institute. Visitors may tour the center 8 a.m. to 5 p.m. Monday through Friday when school is in session.

Montecito Campus *801 Alston Road (D-19).* This campus contains the institute's portrait and color departments. Conducted tours are given by request daily at 10 a.m. and 2 p.m. when school is in session.

EL PASEO *15 East De la Guerra Street, with access from State, De la Guerra and Anacapa streets (E-16).* Winding walkways, adobe walls and wrought iron railings and balconies evoke a sense of old Spain in this picturesque shopping arcade. A number of shops are housed in Casa de la Guerra, built in 1827 by presidio commandant Don José de la Guerra for his bride. Toys, British imports and fine wines are among the many items in specialty stores, which are generally open Monday through Saturday from 10 a.m. to 5 p.m., with a few open on Sunday from 11 a.m. to 4 p.m. Outdoor dining patios are open year round.

EL PRESIDIO DE SANTA BARBARA STATE HISTORIC PARK *123-126 East Canon Perdido Street (D-16). (805) 966-9719.* The presidio is the birthplace of Santa Barbara, and during the late 18th and early 19th centuries it was the seat of military and civil government for an area extending from Los Angeles to just south of San Luis Obispo. Restoration and reconstruction at the site is ongoing. A 15-minute slide show is presented at the park visitors center.

Cañedo Adobe is the remodeled home of a presidio soldier. The adobe houses the park visitors center and museum exhibits.

Commandant's Quarters include the reconstructed office and a portion of the livingroom from the original commandant's residence. Historically accurate furnishings and decor illustrate the lifestyle of a frontier military and civil official in early California.

El Cuartel is the oldest residence (1788) in Santa Barbara and the second oldest building in California. El Cuartel (Soldier's Quarters) was originally one in a row of buildings that formed the west side of the presidio. Now restored, the structure's furnishings are typical of accommodations for a presidio soldier and his family during the late 18th and early 19th century.

Padre's Quarters is a bedroom and office that was used for visiting padres. It features reproductions of period furnishings and authentically reconstructed architecture. Especially noteworthy are roof tiles made by a 200-year-old method, the 22-inch-thick adobe walls, dirt floor and rawhide cot.

Presidio Chapel, reconstructed on its original foundations, has a colorful interior decor and contains restored 18th-century artifacts.

The park is open daily 10:30 a.m. to 4:30 p.m.; closed New Year's Day, Thanksgiving and Christmas. Admission is free. Visitors may tour the park on their own; for guided group tours call (805) 966-9719.

FERNALD HOUSE AND TRUSSELL-WINCHESTER ADOBE

414 West Montecito Street (E-16). Both open Sunday from 2 to 4 p.m. Reservations for group tours must be made with the Santa Barbara Historical Society; (805) 966-1601. Admission is free.

Fernald House, with its many gables, was built in 1862 and is considered one of the finest remaining examples of Victorian architecture in Santa Barbara. This 14-room house features hand-carved ornamentation and wainscoting. Members of the Fernald family lived in the house continuously for more than 90 years, and many of the furnishings, paintings and personal effects now displayed belonged to Judge and Mrs. Fernald or one of their descendants. Of special interest is the nursery, filled with antique toys and dolls.

Trussell-Winchester Adobe provides a fine example of the transitional architecture that was prevalent between Santa Barbara's Spanish and American periods. The adobe home, constructed in 1854 by sea captain Horatio Trussell, is built of native adobe bricks, as well as salvaged timber and brass from a ship wrecked off Anacapa Island. Occupied for 15 years by the Trussell family, then sold to William Eddy, the house was purchased in 1882 by Sara Winchester. Today 100-year-old furnishings from the Trussell and Winchester families add to the visual interest and historical significance of this house.

HISTORIC ADOBES *Downtown.* In the midst of Santa Barbara's modern business district are a number of "adobes" dating back more than one hundred years (buildings constructed of adobe are often designated by that name). Adobe, as a building material, refers to bricks made of wet, clay-like soil and straw, which are then dried in the sun.

Except as noted, these structures are closed to the public. The best way to see them is on the self-guided "Red Tile Tour" or the guided "Walking Tours Through History" (see separate listings). **Casa Covarrubias** (1817), 715 Santa Barbara Street, may have been used briefly as headquarters by the last Mexican governor of California, Pío Pico. **Casa de la Guerra** (1827), 15 East De la Guerra Street, is now part of El Paseo. **Hill-Carrillo Adobe** (1826), 11 East Carrillo Street, was built by an American for his Spanish bride and contains the town's first wooden floor. **Historic** (Fremont) **Adobe**, adjoining Casa de Covarrubias, was probably built in 1836, and is now standing on its third site. **Orena Adobes**, 27-29 East De la Guerra Street, built between 1849 and 1858, are fine examples of homes built by the city's early wealthy Spanish families. **Rochin Adobe**, 820 Santa Barbara Street, was constructed of bricks from the abandoned presidio. It has since been covered by clapboard except for one square of original wall.

KARPELES MANUSCRIPT LIBRARY MUSEUM, *21 West Anapamu Street (D-16). (805) 962-5322.* Beautifully crafted wooden cases and pedestals are used to display an extensive collection of

original and facsimile manuscripts that includes books, treaties, letters, maps, illustrations and music scores, with many items dating back several centuries. Peter the Great, Wolfgang Amadeus Mozart, Thomas Jefferson, Mark Twain and Leonard Bernstein are among the scores of significant persons whose works are displayed. The museum is open daily 10 a.m. to 4 p.m.; closed Thanksgiving and Christmas. Admission is free.

MISSION SANTA BARBARA *Los Olivos and Laguna streets (C-15). (805) 682-4713.* This beautiful structure of classic Roman and Spanish architecture is considered "Queen of the Missions." The mission was established in December 1786, and construction began the following year. After a series of rebuildings, the mission church acquired its present appearance in 1820. A self-guided tour reveals a simple but imposing church interior. On the west side of the church is a beautifully landscaped patio. The cemetery on the opposite side is the final resting place for some of Santa Barbara's early settlers. Mission rooms display historical items such as illuminated manuscripts, antique musical instruments, embroidered vestments, furnishings, sketches and journals.

A few hundred feet north of the mission across Los Olivos Street are the remains of tanning vats, a pottery kiln and parts of a water system. The latter, built in the early 1880s, was so well constructed that one of its reservoirs is still in use. The mission is open daily 9 a.m. to 5 p.m.; closed Easter, Thanksgiving and Christmas.

Donation is $2 for adults; under 12 free.

MORETON BAY FIG TREE *Chapala and Montecito streets (E-17).* Although not the only Moreton Bay fig tree in Santa Barbara, this is certainly the largest. In fact, it may be the largest in the northern hemisphere. The gnarled, venerable giant began as a seedling in 1876, having been transported from Australia's Moreton Bay. In time the seedling grew into a tree with above-ground roots that cover half a city block and branches that provide over 21,000 square feet of shade. It is not a true fig tree, but a member of the rubber tree family.

NATURE CONSERVANCY *Stearns Wharf, foot of State Street at the harbor (E-17). (805) 962-9111.* Here visitors can obtain information on the Santa Cruz Island Preserve and other conservancy projects throughout the state. Inside the visitor center stands a scale model of Santa Cruz Island (largest of the Channel Islands), a habitat case with an island fox and a mounted peregrine falcon. Video programs on conservancy preserves throughout the nation are also shown. The Nature Conservancy is open Monday through Friday from noon to 4 p.m. and 11 a.m. to 5 p.m. Saturday and Sunday. Admission is free.

OLD SPANISH DAYS CARRIAGE MUSEUM *129 Castillo Street (E-16).* This collection contains scores of carriages, some of which date back more than 200 years. Such transportation as buggies, stagecoaches and army wagons are arranged in rows, seeming to need only horses and drivers to bring them back to life. Once a year some of the carriages do roll down the streets of Santa Barbara during the Old Spanish Days Parade. Two of the more eye-catching vehicles are a bright red steam pumper for fire fighting and a black hearse complete with coffin. On display is a handsome frieze by cowboy artist Edward Borein, and one long wall of the museum is devoted to an extensive collection of saddles. The museum is open every Sunday from 2 to 4 p.m. Special tours at other times may be arranged by calling (805) 962-2353 or 569-2077. Admission is free (donations accepted).

PASEO NUEVO *11 West De la Guerra Street (E-16).* Courtyards, fountains and pleasant winding walkways compose the setting for Nordstrom, The Broadway and 60 other shops and restaurants in this unusual open-air shopping complex. Characterized by distinctive stylized Spanish architecture, the colorful two-square-block center fits comfortably into the heart of downtown Santa Barbara. The center is bounded by State, Chapala, Cannon Perdido and Ortega streets. Shops are open Monday through Friday from 10 a.m. to 9 p.m., Saturday from 10 a.m. to 7 p.m. and Sunday from 11 a.m. to 6 p.m.

RED TILE TOUR, a self-guided walking tour in the downtown area, covers a section roughly bordered by Victoria, Santa Barbara, De la Guerra and State streets. The tour includes historic and cultural landmarks, as well as tucked-away plazas and shopping arcades. Tour maps are available at the Visitor Center (see separate listing).

SANTA BARBARA BOTANIC GARDEN *1212 Mission Canyon Road (B-16). (805) 682-4726.* Native California plant life, including golden poppies, redwoods and cacti, blanket 65 acres in the foothills of the Santa Ynez Mountains. More than five miles of inviting, self-guided trails wind through meadow, desert and manzanita sections, and along the stream that flows through Mission Canyon to the woodland, redwood, canyon and island areas. Also, a new year-round demonstration garden features drought-tolerant plants suitable for residential landscaping. Picnicking is not permitted. The garden is open daily 8 a.m. to dusk. Guided tours are offered daily at 2 p.m. and Thursday, Saturday and Sunday at 10:30 a.m. The Garden Shop, where trail maps are available, is open daily 10 a.m. to 4 p.m., and plants are for sale Tuesday and Thursday through Saturday 10 a.m. to 3 p.m. and Sunday 11 a.m. to 3 p.m. Admission is $3 for adults, $2 for ages 13-17 and seniors, and $1 for children ages 5-12; under 5 free.

SANTA BARBARA COUNTY COURTHOUSE *1100 Anacapa Street (D-16). (805) 962-6464.* More reminiscent of a palace than a courthouse, this beautiful Spanish-Moorish structure has many outstanding features. Specially designed windows, staircases, balconies, turrets and archways reflect the imaginative skill of architect William Mooser, as do the ornately carved doors and imported tiles. On the second floor, murals by Dan Sayre Groesbeck depict Santa

John Austerman

Native California plant life takes center stage at the Santa Barbara Botanic Garden.

Barbara's history. Visitors to the tower can enjoy a good view of the city and seacoast. Beautifully land-scaped grounds include extensive lawns and graceful palms. The court-house is open Monday through

Friday 8 a.m. to 4:45 p.m., Saturday, Sunday and holidays 9 a.m. to 4:45 p.m.; closed Christmas. Free guided tours are given Tuesday through Saturday at 2 p.m. and at 10:30 a.m. Wednesday and Friday. Appointments can be made for groups of at least six on other days.

SANTA BARBARA HARBOR AND CHANNEL CRUISES Telephone for fares, schedules and reservations.

John Austerman

Classical Spanish architecture complements relics of the city's past at the Santa Barbara Historical Museum.

Captain Don's Harbor Cruises *(805) 969-5217.* Harbor, coastal and dinner cruises; sunset and twilight charters also available.

Sailing Center of Santa Barbara *(800) 350-9090; (805) 962-2826.* Harbor, coastal, dinner cruises; coastal island and whale-watching trips also available.

SANTA BARBARA HISTORICAL MUSEUM *136 East De la Guerra Street (E-16). (805) 966-1601.* This handsome structure, which follows classic Spanish colonial lines, contains spacious rooms that house memorabilia from Santa Barbara's multinational past. The adobe bricks used in the museum's construction were made from the soil on which it stands, and the floor tiles were handmade in Mexico. The museum's permanent exhibits include documents, furniture, decorative and fine arts, and costumes from Santa Barbara's Spanish, Mexican and American periods. Among the many works of art in the museum is Edwin Deakin's series of paintings depicting California's 21 missions. The museum also has an extensive research library that specializes in Santa Barbara history. A quiet, shady courtyard, graced by a fountain, is located at the rear of the museum. The museum is open Tuesday through Saturday 10 a.m. to 5 p.m., Sunday noon to 5 p.m.; closed major holidays. Guided tours are given Wednesday, Saturday and Sunday at 1:30 p.m. Admission is free.

SANTA BARBARA MUSEUM OF ART *1130 State Street (D-16). (805) 963-4364; (805) 963-2240 (TDD) for the hearing impaired.* This museum houses within its permanent collections Asian, European and American art, classical antiquities and photography. Displays include touring exhibits from other museums and loans from private collectors. Lectures, films and performance art are also offered. The museum is open Tuesday through Saturday 11 a.m. to 5 p.m., Thursday until 9 p.m., Sunday

noon to 5 p.m.; closed holidays. Guided tours are conducted Tuesday through Sunday at 1 p.m. Admission (charged except Thursday and the first Sunday each month) is $3 for adults, $2.50 for seniors and $1.50 for ages 6-16; under 6 free. For information on current programs, call the museum. **Discount.**

SANTA BARBARA MUSEUM OF NATURAL HISTORY *2559 Puesta del Sol Road (C-15). (805) 682-4711.* This attractively designed complex is located in a lovely natural setting. Within its halls are exhibits on mammals, birds, botany and marine life. A special gallery has changing exhibits, and the Indian Hall provides an excellent introduction to the Chumash culture. The museum's planetarium now includes the

John Austerman

The skeletal remains of a young blue whale greet visitors at the Santa Barbara Museum of Natural History.

59

E.L. Wiegand Space Lab, featuring exhibits of state-of-the-art interactive computer technology. The museum is open Monday through Saturday 9 a.m. to 5 p.m., Sunday and holidays 10 a.m. to 5 p.m. (Space Lab noon to 4 p.m. daily); closed during the Old Spanish Days Parade in August, as well as New Year's Day, Thanksgiving and Christmas. Admission: $3 for adults, $2 for ages 13-17 and 65 and over, and $1 for children under 13.

Planetarium shows are presented at 1:30, 3 and 4 p.m. Saturday and Sunday; admission is included in the museum entrance fee. In addition, an evening show is presented at 8 p.m. Saturday. Admission for the evening show is $3 for adults, $2 for ages 13-17 and 65 and over, and $1 for children under 13.

SANTA BARBARA PUBLIC LIBRARY *40 East Anapamu Street (D-16). (805) 962-7653.* Casual visitors and frequent patrons alike enjoy this spacious and inviting library. Opposite murals of the adventures of Don Quixote in the main lobby, the Faulkner Galleries display works by local artists. The library is open Monday through Thursday 10 a.m. to 9 p.m., Friday and Saturday 10 a.m. to 5:30 p.m., Sunday 1 to 5 p.m.; closed major holidays.

SANTA BARBARA TROLLEY COMPANY *36 State Street. (805) 965-0353.* This shuttle bus, designed to look like an old-fashioned trolley, runs daily on a regularly scheduled route throughout the city of Santa Barbara, connecting visitors with major hotels, shopping areas and local tourist and cultural attractions. The route begins

and ends at Stearns Wharf at the foot of State Street. Fare is $3 for adults and $2 for children 12 and under.

SANTA BARBARA ZOOLOGICAL GARDENS *500 Niños Drive (E-18). (805) 962-6310 (recording), 962-5339.* The zoo, with its charmingly landscaped grounds, is located on land that was once part of a palatial estate. Today an interesting botanical collection and nearly 500 animals from around the world are on view here. A ride on the zoo's miniature train provides views of the park's lush foliage, a portion of the seacoast and the neighboring bird refuge. Picnic grounds, snack bar and a playground add to visitors' enjoyment. The zoo is open daily 9 a.m. to 6 p.m. during summer months; 10 a.m. to 5 p.m. rest of the year; closed Thanksgiving and Christmas. Admission is $5 for adults, $3 for children 2-12 and senior citizens. Train rides are $1 for adults, 50¢ for children. Group rates are available.

SCENIC DRIVE, designated by blue-and-white street signs featuring an arrow and ocean wave, is a do-it-yourself driving tour. The route goes from Montecito's Olive Mill Road to Las Palmas Drive in Hope Ranch, passing beach parks, bluff-top ocean views, Hope Ranch estates, downtown's historic and cultural buildings and Mission Santa Barbara. Scenic Drive maps are available at the Visitor Center (see separate listing).

SEA CENTER *Stearns Wharf, foot of State Street at the harbor (E-17). (805) 962-0885.* Operated by the Santa Barbara Museum of Natural History and the Channel Islands National Marine Sanctuary, this center features life-size models of a California gray whale and her calf, a gray whale skeleton, six aquariums housing many species native to the Santa Barbara Channel and marine photos. Other highlights include a tank where visitors can touch various marine invertebrates, a sea bird display and exhibits on the marine archaeology in the Santa Barbara Channel. Hours for the center vary. Closed January 1, Thanksgiving and December 25. Admission is $2 for adults, $1.50 for seniors and $1 for ages 3-17; under 3 free.

STEARNS WHARF *foot of State Street at the harbor (E-17). (805) 564-5518.* Where State Street ends at Cabrillo Boulevard, Stearns Wharf begins. A Santa Barbara landmark,

the wharf has a long and checkered history. Built in 1872 by John Peck Stearns, it was the site of cargo and passenger activity for many years. In the 1930s, visitors to gambling ships used the wharf as a departure point, and during World War II it served as a naval installation.

Today people can walk or drive onto the wharf to fish, enjoy the restaurants, visit the Sea Center and Nature Conservancy (see separate listings), browse in the specialty shops or purchase fresh fish. Stearns Wharf provides a fine view of the small-craft harbor, as well as a panorama of Santa Barbara and its mountain backdrop. Shops are generally open daily in summer from 10 a.m. to 9

John Austerman

Marine exhibits, interesting shops and several popular restaurants combine to make Stearn's Wharf the hub of tourist activity along the waterfront.

p.m.; in winter, 10 a.m. to 6 p.m.; restaurants have differing hours, with at least one open for breakfast daily all year. Parking is $2 per hour; at least two hours free with validation (depending on which establishment issues the validation).

Marine exhibits, interesting shops and several popular restaurants combine to make Stearns Wharf the hub of tourist activity along the waterfront.

VICTORIA COURT *Victoria and State streets (D-16).* Walkways wind through this two-story complex, which has inviting shops around each turn. A wide range of goods and services is offered, including six restaurants and a post office. Most of the shops are open Monday through Saturday 10 a.m. to 6 p.m., many are open on Sunday; special hours during the December holiday season.

VISITOR CENTERS *One Santa Barbara Street (E-17) and 504 State Street (E-14). (805) 965-3021.* Current information on things to see and do in the city is available at both Chamber of Commerce centers. Housed in a historical building across the street from the beach, the Santa Barbara Street center is open daily from 9 a.m. to 5 p.m. Located downtown, the State Street office is open Monday through Friday from 9 a.m. to 5 p.m.

WALKING TOURS THROUGH HISTORY *18 San Marcos Trout Club. (805) 967-9869.* A local historian conducts guided walking tours of historic Santa Barbara at 10 a.m. and 1:30 p.m.; reservations are required. The one- and two-hour tours, requiring a moderate amount of walking, depart

from the Santa Barbara Courthouse and include visits to El Paseo, the historic adobes, El Presidio de Santa Barbara State Historic Park and the Santa Barbara Historical Museum. The charge is $5 for the one-hour walk and $10 for the two-hour excursion; senior citizens' fees are $4 and $8 respectively; students are $2.50 per hour; children under 10 are free. Group rates are available.

FARMERS MARKETS

Carpinteria

Local farmers set up shop each week at this popular street fair. Fresh fruit, vegetables and flowers share the stage with street musicians, clowns and a barbecue. The market operates Thursday evenings all year along the 800 block of Linden Avenue. Hours are 4 to 7:30 p.m. in summer and 3 to 6:30 the rest of the year. (805) 962-5354.

Goleta

This is the newest market on the Santa Barbara Coast, and also the smallest. Flowers, local honey, fruit, vegetables and live entertainment are featured every Thursday in the 5700 block of Calle Real. The market is open for business from 3 to 7 p.m. (805) 962-5354.

Santa Barbara

Fresh produce, herbs, flowers, local honey, tropical fruit and live entertainment are offered year-round on Saturday from 8:30 a.m. to noon at the corner of Santa Barbara and Cota streets in downtown Santa Barbara.

It also operates every Tuesday in the 500 block of State Street. Hours are 4 to 7:30 p.m. in summer and 3 to 6:30 p.m. the rest of the year. (805) 962-5354.

WINERY

The following winery in the Santa Barbara coastal area offers free tours and tasting. Please call in advance because hours are subject to change.

Santa Barbara Winery *202 Anacapa Street (E-17). (805) 963-3633.* Having opened in 1962, this is the oldest producing winery in Santa Barbara County. A selection of wines can be sampled in the tasting room open daily 10 a.m. to 5 p.m. Guided tours are given daily at 11:30 a.m. and 3:30 p.m.

Rolling hills and grassy rangeland typify much of the Santa Ynez Valley.

Santa Ynez Valley

Northwest of Santa Barbara, the Santa Ynez Valley, bordered by the Santa Ynez and San Rafael mountains, encompasses gently rolling green or golden hills sprinkled with oak trees and stands of eucalyptus. Three highways (US 101, SR 154 and SR 246) and many side roads lead to extensive cattle ranches, horse farms, wineries set amid vineyards, and carefully tended citrus groves and croplands.

Much of the valley's beauty and character, however, remain undiscovered by the many travelers who exit US 101 at Buellton, dine at Pea Soup Andersen's Restaurant and partake in the Danish village atmosphere of Solvang, with its many shops, windmills and pastries. Adventurous visitors leaving the main highway will discover the valley's century-old "country towns," established and still functioning to serve the nearby farming and ranching families; art and antique shops; and a restaurant and a restored hotel housed in former stagecoach stops. Also tucked away in the valley is the smallest county branch library in California; a collection of old-fashioned wagons and carriages; an operating "little red schoolhouse" (circa 1883); one of Southern California's largest, man-made freshwater lakes; and wineries open for tours.

Recently the valley has regained the reputation as a major California wine-producing region that it lost during Prohibition and following years. Its ideal grape-growing climate—warm days and cool nights—contributes to the success of the award-winning wines bottled here since the early 1970s.

Another valley specialty—horse breeding—is evident from the intricate rows of white fences covering acres of green pastures. American Paints, Andalusians, Arabians, Icelandics, Miniatures, Peruvian Pasos, Quarter Horses and Thoroughbreds are all bred here, and most ranches welcome visitors when given advance notice. For the names and phone numbers of the various ranches call the Solvang Chamber of Commerce, (805) 688-3317.

Santa Ynez Valley was first scouted in 1798 when a military party was dispatched from Mission Santa Barbara to find a suitable spot for a mission between Santa Barbara and La Purísima Mission in Lompoc. The site chosen (in what is now Solvang)

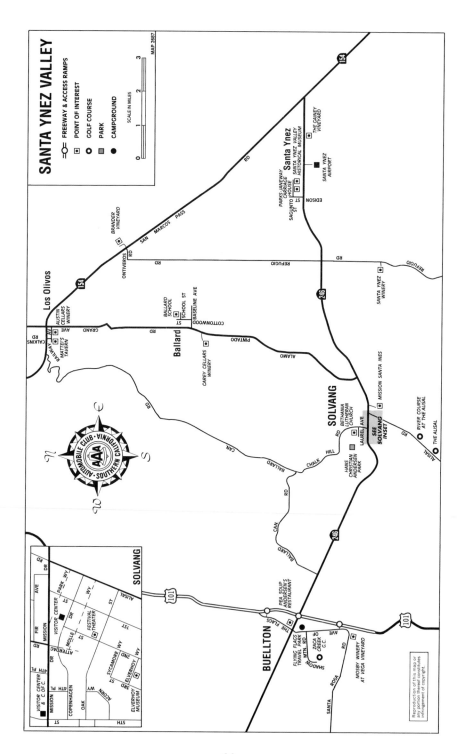

66

became Mission Santa Inés in 1804. A subsequent earthquake in 1812 left the original church and surrounding buildings unsafe; the present church was rebuilt in 1817. Following secularization in 1834, mission lands were divided into land grants that, over decades, were further parceled into rural and town sites. As the century progressed, train and stagecoach lines were routed through the Santa Ynez Valley; one of the hotels and one of the restaurants patronized by their passengers are still in use.

Unless noted otherwise, map coordinates refer to the Santa Ynez Valley city map on the *Cities of Santa Barbara County* street map.

BALLARD

Ballard holds the distinction of being Santa Ynez Valley's oldest (1880) and smallest (250 residents) community. Pioneer George Lewis first built an adobe house on a large ranch in the valley, which was known then as El Alamo Pintado (the painted cottonwood). When Lewis traveled to Mexico, he left his holdings with his friend William Ballard, for whom the town was later named. The township's past can still be seen in two buildings from the 1880s: the 1883 Ballard School (see listing) and the Santa Ynez Valley

Presbyterian Church (1889), now called the Ballard Country Church. One AAA-approved country inn and one AAA-approved restaurant are located in Ballard.

BALLARD SCHOOL *Cottonwood and School streets (D-8)*. Framed by two black walnut trees and topped with a steeple, this "little red schoolhouse" opened its doors in 1883 and has been in continuous use ever since. It currently houses kindergarten through second-grade classes. Grades three through eight are in an adjacent building.

BUELLTON

Located at the junction of US 101 and SR 246, Buellton's convenient location attracts travelers to the town's

John Austerman

Still in use today, Ballard School has been open for more than 100 years.

many motels, restaurants, service facilities, trailer parks and gift shops. Buellton is best known as "the home of split pea soup," in reference to Pea Soup Andersen's Restaurant (see listing). It also boasts an expansive parkway with eight large American flags flying from 50-foot-high poles. Just east of Buellton along SR 246, drivers pass several thoroughbred and Arabian horse-breeding ranches on the way to Solvang and other Santa Ynez Valley towns.

Buellton had its beginnings in 1867 when a portion of a Mexican land grant was deeded to Rufus Thompson Buell and his brother Alonzo. The brothers developed a highly successful cattle ranch until a drought in 1890 forced the sale of 10,000 acres of land to the Santa Ynez Land Development Company. In 1920 part of that acreage became Buellton.

The town contains several AAA-approved lodgings and restaurants and one AAA-approved campground.

PEA SOUP ANDERSEN'S RESTAU-RANT *on SR 246, one block west of junction with US 101 (G-2).* The restaurant which began in 1924 as a very small cafe owned and operated by Anton and Juliette Andersen now encompasses several dining rooms, a coffee shop, a wine cellar and a gift shop. The restaurant is open in summer Monday through Thursday 5:30 a.m. to 10 p.m., Friday to 11 p.m., Saturday 7 a.m. to 11 p.m., Sunday to 10 p.m.; in winter 6:30 a.m. to 10 p.m. daily.

LOS ALAMOS

Although not formally a part of the Santa Ynez Valley, Los Alamos shares historic and geographic traits with, and is easily reached from, the valley. What is now Los Alamos Valley, 13 miles north of Buellton off US 101, was originally split into two land grants—Rancho Los Alamos and Rancho La Laguna—following Mexico's independence from Spain in 1821. The acreage, used extensively for cattle grazing, was first subdivided in 1878 when two men from San Francisco bought 28,000 acres and established a town. Visitors began arriving in the valley by stage-coach following the opening of the Union Hotel in 1880 (see listing). By 1882, rail passengers had also gained access with the arrival of the Pacific Coast Railroad.

Today Los Alamos (population 950) maintains strong ties with its western heritage and continues to serve the neighboring farming and ranching families. The town celebrates "Old Days" the last weekend of September with entertainment, a parade, barbecue and roping demonstrations. Old-time residents use this as an opportunity to reminisce. Throughout the year, visits to antique stores and art galleries are a popular pastime, as are picnics beneath oak and maple trees at Los Alamos County Park.

UNION HOTEL *362 Bell Street (V-2, Santa Barbara County map). (805) 344-2744.* Built in 1880 as a stage-coach stop, the Union Hotel has been restored in a manner as authentic as possible, even to the boardwalk which fronts the street. Architecture, interior design and furnishings all reflect the late 19th century. Adjacent is a restored 1864 Victorian house known as the "Victorian Mansion," with six thematically decorated rooms. The hotel is open Friday through Sunday; the mansion is open daily. The restaurant is open for dinner at 5 p.m. Friday through Sunday. Dining is family style with a selection of 10 entrees. Restaurant reservations are suggested for parties of more than six. Hotel reservations are required. For further information and reservations, call the above number or write Union Hotel, P.O. Box 616, Los Alamos, CA 93440.

LOS OLIVOS

A small-town, country charm exudes from this community set amid oak-studded rolling hills off SR 154, three miles east of US 101. From the flag-pole at the center of town, erected in 1918 to honor America's war veterans, to the water tower beside the century-old stagecoach stop, Los Olivos hearkens back to an earlier era. Recently artists have discovered the attraction of this hamlet of about 350, and more than a dozen galleries are now open.

The community traces its roots to the opening of Mattei's Tavern in 1886 (see listing). With the arrival of the stagecoach and later the narrow-gauge Pacific Coast Railroad, the town prospered. Besides Mattei's tavern and hotel, Los Olivos (meaning "the olives") contained

several stores, livery stables and blacksmith shops, a post office and a public school. At the turn of the century, however, decisions were made to bypass Los Olivos and to route the first major north-south railroad and highway (now US 101) along the coast and west of town. This precluded major development in Los Olivos and helped preserve the rural atmosphere it retains today. The town has a AAA-approved lodging and two AAA-approved restaurants.

MATTEI'S TAVERN *Railway Avenue, one-half block west of SR 154 and Grand Avenue junction (B-7). (805) 688-4820.* In 1886 Felix Mattei, a Swiss immigrant, built a combination hotel and restaurant to accommodate the railroad and stagecoach passengers stopping in Los Olivos. Now more than 100 years later, the restaurant is still in operation. Among the charms of this rambling structure is that each dining area is decorated differently. The restaurant opens Monday through Thursday at 5:30 p.m., Friday through Sunday at noon; closing times vary. Reservations are advised.

SANTA YNEZ

Visitors to Santa Ynez can readily see the pioneer flavor of the town being kept alive by several false-front, old-west-style buildings in the business district. Located about three miles east of Solvang off SR 246, the community once served as a principal stagecoach stop between the Santa Ynez Valley and Santa Barbara.

At the time of its incorporation in 1882, Santa Ynez was the social and economic center of the valley, housing many stores, saloons, Chinese laundries, and even more important, the impressive two-story College Hotel. The hotel, built in 1891 for $30,000, was considered one of the finest accommodations in all of California until a fire destroyed it in 1935.

PARKS-JANEWAY CARRIAGE HOUSE *3596 Sagunto Street (G-10). (805) 688-7889.* Opened in 1978, the carriage house contains one of the West's finest collections of horse-drawn vehicles and accessories. The more than 35 vehicles range in age from a covered freight wagon built around 1860 to a 1940 jog cart. An overland mail stage (circa 1898), one of the largest in the country carrying as many as 15 people, boasts a restored interior and the original paint and gilt exterior. Besides the coaches, the collection also includes buggies and phaetons and a Sicilian donkey cart. In addition, the museum houses an extensive saddle exhibit, including works by famed silversmith Edward Bohlin. Hours are Tuesday through Thursday from 10 a.m. to 4 p.m. and Friday through Sunday from 1 to 4 p.m. Admission is free, but donations are accepted.

SANTA YNEZ VALLEY HISTORI-CAL MUSEUM *3596 Sagunto Street (G-10). (805) 688-7889.* Articles made or used by area residents are housed in this seven-room museum. A gallery devoted to Chumash Indian culture features a diorama, baskets and tools. Other galleries depict the lifestyle of

valley residents in the late 19th century with clothing, furnishings and other items. A 1907 two-cylinder "car" plus old farm machinery and equipment are also on display. The museum is open Friday through Sunday from 1 to 4 p.m. Admission is free, but donations are accepted.

On Sagunto Street, near the museum, stands the county's first (1912)— and one of the state's smallest— public library. Open Friday from 2 to 5 p.m.

WINDHAVEN GLIDER RIDES *Santa Ynez Airport (G-10). (805) 688-2517.* Passengers soar high above the Santa Ynez Valley's hills, towns and vineyards in aircraft flown by commercial glider pilots. Rides are offered daily 10 a.m. to 5 p.m., June 15 through September 15; Tuesday through Sunday 10 a.m. to 5 p.m. the rest of the year, weather permitting; closed December 24 and 25. Fares are $55 for the 15-20 minute Scenic Flight at 2500 feet; $110 for the 25-30 minute Mountain Adventure Flight at 4000 feet; $135 for the 35-40 minute Mile-High Flight at 5280 feet. Reservations are suggested for weekend flights.

SOLVANG

Tourists from all parts of the world congregate in Solvang to take in the Danish-village atmosphere, complete with gas streetlights from Copenhagen, working windmills, a horse-drawn streetcar and 19th-century timber and plaster architecture. Located 45 miles northwest of

Santa Barbara on SR 246, Solvang has a permanent population of about 4800 people. But each day, thousands more partake in the village's fresh Danish pastries and its wide assortment of merchandise in the many shops and galleries: imported Danish handicrafts of wood or cloth, pewter and ceramic kitchenware and porcelain dinnerware, prints and original artworks, jewelry, clocks and unusual holiday decorations.

Every year during the third weekend in September, the city celebrates Danish Days with entertainment, dancing, special foods and a parade. Each December is highlighted by Winterfest, featuring a Christmas parade, as well as tree-lighting ceremonies, special shop window displays and caroling.

Solvang was established in 1911 when a group of Danish educators chose the Santa Ynez Valley as the ideal place to build a college and establish a colony. Soon they were joined by others from the midwest and Denmark, and by 1914, with the building of Atterdag College, Solvang became a cultural center and gathering place for Danes on the West Coast. The college is no longer in existence, but the AAA-approved Bit O'Denmark Restaurant on Alisal Road occupies the site of the original two-story school.

Originally, Solvang developed as an agricultural community serving the needs of the neighboring farmers. It wasn't until 1947, after an article appeared in the *Saturday Evening Post* describing the people of Solvang and

John Austerman

Spectators line Alisal Road in Solvang for the community's annual Danish Days Parade.

71

the Danish-style structures, that tourism became a major economic factor.

Today, two nearby county parks provide recreation for the area's residents and visitors, Lake Cachuma and Nojoqui Falls. Numerous AAA-approved accommodations and four AAA-approved restaurants are located in Solvang.

BETHANIA LUTHERAN CHURCH *603 Atterdag Road (H-6). (805) 688-4637.* Built in 1928, this church is a fine example of 14th-century Danish architecture. The interior is noted for its hand-carved pulpit and carefully detailed miniature sailing ship that is suspended from the ceiling. The presence of the ship is a Danish tradition; it represents a soul on life's sea guided by God. The doors of the church are open Monday through Saturday 8 a.m. to 4 p.m.

ELVERHOY MUSEUM *1624 Elverhoy Way (C-1). (805) 686-1211.* The museum is housed in a typical 18th-century Danish farm house located on a residential street. Danish artifacts and memorabilia, as well as various types of art, are housed in rooms devoted to Solvang's history, Danish heritage and an art gallery. Hours are 1 to 4 p.m. Wednesday through Sunday, and by appointment. Admission is free (donations are accepted).

HANS CHRISTIAN ANDERSEN PARK *off Atterdag Road, three blocks north of Mission Drive (H-5).* Beautiful trees, including coast live oak and valley oak, grace this park. An Old World-style entrance leads to a 50-acre site offering barbecue and picnic facilities, tennis courts and a children's playground. The park is open daily 8 a.m. to dusk. Admission is free.

THE HONEN *(805) 686-0022.* These horse-drawn replicas of early 20th-century streetcars in Copenhagen, Denmark offer guided tours of downtown Solvang daily in summer 11:30 a.m. to 5 p.m. The rest of the year tours are conducted Friday through Monday, on holidays and during festivals; hours vary. Excursions aboard the bright yellow and brown cars depart from the Conference & Visitors Bureau office on Copenhagen Drive and last about 15 to 20 minutes. Also, one car operates Wednesday through Sunday between the Visitors Bureau and the Elverhoy Museum. Fare is $2.50 for adults, $2 for seniors and $1.50 for children under 12.

LAKE CACHUMA COUNTY PARK *off SR 154 (G-9, Santa Barbara County map). (805) 688-4658.* This man-made lake takes its name from a Chumash village, called either Juichama or Juichuneas, that once stood on the land now covered by the waters of Cachuma Bay. Fishermen are challenged by the lake's population of bass, crappie, catfish, bluegill and trout. Rental boats and motors are available, and fishing licenses can be purchased at a bait and tackle shop. In addition to fishing and boating, there are sites for picnicking and camping (see *Recreation*). Although swimming in the lake is prohibited, two pools within the recreational area are open during the summer. A snack bar, general store, service station and rental bicycles are also in the park. Day-use admission fee is $3.50 per vehicle.

Lake Cachuma Boat Cruises, a two-hour view of the lake's wildlife and bird populations, begins at the park marina. Cruises are offered Friday through Sunday in summer. November to March cruises to observe the American bald eagle depart Wednesday through Sunday. Call ahead for exact times; reservations are recommended. Adults $8; children under 12, $5. For information, call (805) 568-2460.

MISSION SANTA INES *1760 Mission Drive (H-6). (805) 688-4815.* This mission was founded in 1804, and the reconstructed campanario (bell tower) and authentically restored church sanctuary reflect its original beauty. The mission complex is currently being restored to its original configuration. Rooms open to the public contain mission furnishings and artifacts dating back to the early 19th century. A side door of the church leads to a quiet, attractively landscaped garden. Tours of the mission are given Monday through Saturday 9:30 a.m. to 4:30 p.m., Sunday 1:30 to 4:30 p.m.; closed New Year's Day, Easter, Thanksgiving and Christmas. Donation is $2; under 16 free.

NOJOQUI FALLS COUNTY PARK *Seven miles southwest of Solvang on Alisal Road (H-6, Santa Barbara County map).* This 82½-acre site offers barbecue and picnic areas, as well as softball diamonds, volleyball courts, horseshoe pits and children's play areas. The park is named for the

164-foot-high falls that, after a sufficient rainy season, cascades over a moss-covered limestone cliff. Legend tells of an Indian maiden and her lover leaping to their deaths from the top of the fall. A pleasant, non-strenuous trail up to the fall winds beside a creek and is bordered by live oak, sycamore and California bay trees. The park is open daily 8 a.m. to dusk. Admission is free.

THEATERFEST From June through September, the Pacific Conservatory of the Performing Arts (PCPA), based at Allan Hancock College in Santa Maria, presents music and drama in repertory at Solvang's Festival Theater, 420 2nd Street (B-3). The productions, which range from musicals to classic drama, are noted for their quality. (This is an outdoor theater; patrons should dress accordingly.) Information about schedules and ticket prices is available at Auto Club district offices or by calling (805) 922-8313 or (800) 549-7272.

WINERIES

Tours

The following wineries in the Santa Ynez Valley offer free tours and tasting. Wineries should be contacted in advance because hours are subject to change.

Brander Vineyard *Two miles southeast of Los Olivos off SR 154 at 2401 Refugio Road (C-9). (805) 688-2455.* The 40-acre vineyard was planted in 1975, and the winery was built in 1980. Today 8000 cases of estate-bottled varietals are shipped annually, with emphasis on Sauvignon Blanc. The tasting room is open daily from 10 a.m. to 5 p.m. Guided tours are given by appointment only.

Carey Cellars *Three miles north of Solvang off SR 246 at 1711 Alamo Pintado Road (E-7). (805) 688-8554.* The winery began operations in 1978, and today vintage-dated varietals, including Sauvignon Blanc, Chardonnay, Merlot and Cabernet Sauvignon, are produced in a renovated barn. Tours and tasting are offered daily from 10 a.m. to 4 p.m. Visitors are welcome to use a shaded picnic area.

Firestone Vineyard *Zaca Station Road, near Los Olivos, two miles north of US 101 and Zaca Station Road junction (F-7, Santa Barbara County map). (805) 688-3940.* The winery sits on a hill in the midst of its vineyards and is housed in a modern wooden structure that blends beautifully with the landscape. Today bottlings include Riesling, Gewürztraminer, Sauvignon Blanc, Chardonnay, Merlot, Cabernet Sauvignon and a rosé. Tours and tasting occur daily from 10 a.m. to 4 p.m.

The Gainey Vineyard *One mile east of Santa Ynez on SR 246 (G-11). (805) 688-0558.* This modern winery features informative tours covering all phases of winemaking. The adjacent 65-acre vineyard produces much of the fruit for the winery's 12,000-case-per-year, five-varietal output. Tours and tasting are offered daily from 10 a.m. to 5 p.m.; last tour 3:30 p.m. Picnic facilities are on the grounds.

Mosby Winery *9496 Santa Rosa Road (H-1). (805) 688-2415.* Once part of a 19th-century land grant, the winery was founded in 1979 in a restored carriage house. Today Chardonnay, Riesling, Gewürztraminer, Pinot Noir and Italian-style varietals, including Nebbiolo and Pinot Grigio, are produced from estate-grown and purchased grapes. Tasting is available daily from 10 a.m. to 4 p.m. Guided tours are given by appointment only. Picnic facilities are located on the grounds.

Santa Ynez Winery *343 North Refugio Road (H-9). (805) 688-8381.* In 1969 this family-owned winery began converting dairy land into vineyards and remodeled a barn to house its winemaking facilities. Today 17,000 cases are shipped annually, and the emphasis is on white varietals, including Sauvignon Blanc, Chardonnay and Riesling, all from the winery's 105-acre vineyard. Tasting is offered daily 10 a.m. to 5 p.m.; self-guided tours (groups should make advance reservations for tours).

Zaca Mesa Winery *Foxen Canyon Road, eight miles north of US 101 and Zaca Station Road junction (E-7, Santa Barbara County map). (805) 688-3310.* In 1973 Zaca Mesa Ranch converted 213 acres of grazing land to vineyard, and a new winery was completed in time for the 1978 harvest. Zaca Mesa offers a full line of estate-bottled varietal wines. Tours and tasting are conducted daily from 10 a.m. to 4 p.m. The winery has an adjacent, shaded picnic area.

Tasting Only

The following wineries have tasting rooms on the premises, but do not offer tours.

Austin Cellars *2923 Grand Avenue, Los Olivos (B-7). (805) 688-9665.* Open daily 11 a.m. to 5 p.m.

Sanford Winery *Five miles west of Buellton at 7250 Santa Rosa Road (G-5,* Santa Barbara County *map). (805) 688-3300.* Open daily 11 a.m. to 4 p.m.

*Mission life and architecture of the early 1800s are featured at
La Purísima Mission.*

Lompoc Valley

Located between the Santa Ynez Mountains on the south and the Purísima Hills on the north, the Lompoc Valley lies about 55 miles northwest of Santa Barbara. Its diverse economy ranges from oil and space exploration to flower seed production.

Massive oil reserves below the valley floor yield several thousand barrels daily. Diatomaceous earth (fossilized remains of microscopic plants that grew beneath the prehistoric ocean floor) is mined just below the surface and then processed into a fine, powdery substance used as a filter for items such as swimming pools and pharmaceutical products. Vandenberg Air Force Base, the western base for all military space launches, hosts many divisions, and leading aerospace companies provide launch and support facilities. The area is also known as "The Valley of Flowers" with its rich soil contributing to the cultivation of more than a dozen varieties of flowers grown for seed. A colorful salute to this industry is held in Lompoc on the last full weekend in June. Rounding out the valley's commodities are prize Herefords, Black Angus and dairy cattle that roam the grassy rangelands.

Lompoc Valley's history can be traced to the Chumash people who settled in the valley hundreds of years before the first European settlers. In 1787, La Purísima Mission, number 11 of 21 Franciscan Missions of Spanish California, was dedicated in a location called "Algascapi" by the natives. (American settlers later changed the name to Lompoc.) Completed in 1791, the mission attracted many converts and prospered until an earthquake in 1812 destroyed it. Following the earthquake, torrential rainstorms inundated the valley floor making it impossible for the padres to rebuild the mission on the same site. A location was selected four miles northeast of the original, and the new mission was built in record time using a then-innovative design to resist the threat of future earthquakes. The edifice was buttressed with stone, and its walls were built of adobe 4½ feet thick. The mission again flourished until 1821 when Mexico declared independence from Spain.

In 1824 a revolt by the Native American population at nearby Mission Santa Inés in Solvang spread to La Purísima. Indians took command of La Purísima, and soldiers from the army garrison at Monterey were called in to reclaim it. Ten years later this mission was closed permanently, and the padres moved to Mission Santa Inés. The buildings fell into disrepair and were finally auctioned off in 1845. The land was used for sheep ranching and farming until the early 1900s when the property was purchased by the Union Oil Company. In 1933, the mission's renovation began with property donations by the Union Oil Company, the Catholic Church, Santa Barbara County and the State of California. Work by the National Park Service and the Civilian Conservation Corps restored the mission to its status of the early 1800s, and it opened to the public in 1941.

LOMPOC

With a population of more than 38,800, Lompoc (lŏm´ pōk) is the largest community in the valley and the third largest city in the county. Its mild climate and long, rainless summers are ideal for flower-seed harvest. The community contains a number of AAA-approved accommodations, fine restaurants, shopping areas and recreational facilities.

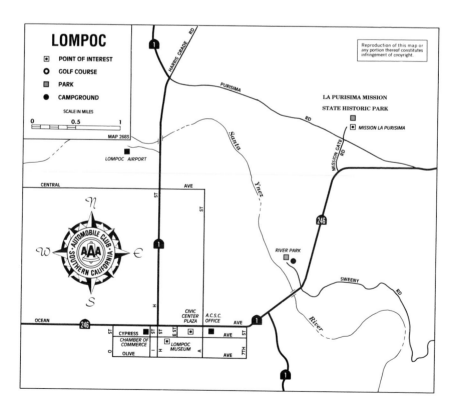

Thomas P. Burgnon

Blossoms grown in the Lompoc Valley adorn the entry to the modern Civic Center Plaza.

The **Automobile Club of Southern California** district office is located at 816 East Ocean Avenue, Lompoc 93436 (H-3); (805) 735-2731.

Unless noted otherwise, map coordinates refer to the Lompoc city map on the *Cities of Santa Barbara County* street map.

JALAMA BEACH COUNTY PARK *20 miles southwest of Lompoc off SR 1 and Jalama Road (H-2,* Santa Barbara County *map). (805) 736-6316 (recording), 736-3504.* Originally a Chumash Indian settlement, the park's name comes from the Spanish spelling of the Indian village, "Halam." This 28-acre park just north of Point Conception offers surf fishing for perch, cabezon, kelp bass and halibut, as well as sailboarding, surfing at nearby Tarantula Point, beachcombing, picnicking, barbecues and camping. Whales can be spotted in February and March and from September through November, while bird watching and rockhounding can be enjoyed all year. Strong ocean winds can be expected at this park, and swimming is not recommended because of severe riptides. A general store sells tackle, bait and camper supplies; other amenities include a snack bar, horseshoe pits and two play areas for children. Day-use admission is $3.50 per vehicle.

LA PURISIMA MISSION STATE HISTORIC PARK *Three miles northeast of Lompoc, off SR 246 (D-4). (805) 733-3713.* Extensive restoration work has been done on this handsome mission built in the early 1800s, and today La Purísima represents one of California's most complete and authentic examples of mission life and architecture. The imposing colonnade of the residence building is especially noteworthy, as is the simple beauty of the chapel. The primitive but effective water system has been restored, complete with picturesque fountain. The mission is open daily from 10 a.m. to 5 p.m. The rest of the year it is open daily 9 a.m. to 4:30 p.m. The mission and park are closed New Year's Day, Thanksgiving and Christmas. The park area around the mission has gardens, riding and hiking trails and picnic facilities. Admission is $5 per car. Guided tours for groups can be arranged by calling (805) 733-1303.

LOMPOC FLOWER FIELDS *SR 246; SR 1; Central Avenue; Sweeney Road.* With its soil and climate ideal for raising flowers, the Lompoc area produces a prodigious amount of the flower seeds sold in the entire world. From early June through mid-July, 1000 acres bloom with more than 200 varieties of flowers. To aid in identifying the blossoms, a visit to the labeled display garden in Lompoc's Civic Center Plaza at the corner of Ocean Avenue and C Street is recommended. Among the flowers that grow in Lompoc's fields are marigolds, sweet peas, asters, larkspur, calendula, lavender, lobelia and cornflowers. A map of the flowerfields drive is available at the Chamber of Commerce, 111 South I Street; (805) 736-4567. The Lompoc Flower Festival is held each year in June (see *Annual Events*).

LOMPOC MUSEUM *200 South H Street (H-3). (805) 736-3888.* Converted from one of the nation's few remaining Carnegie Library buildings, this attractive museum houses an extensive collection of Native American artifacts. Emphasis is on the Chumash, and exhibits include basketry, weapons and the shells that were used for money and ornamentation. The downstairs gallery contains models, photographs and displays that portray Lompoc's history from the founding of La Purísima Mission through

Thomas P. Burgnon

Chumash artifacts and Lompoc area historical exhibits are found in the Lompoc Museum.

Thomas P. Burgnon

Located at the northern end of the Lompoc Valley, this gate serves as entryway to Vandenberg Air Force Base.

the development of Vandenberg Air Force Base. A public research library includes volumes on local archaeology and history. The museum also hosts temporary exhibits and offers public lectures and film presentations. The museum is open Tuesday through Friday from 1 to 5 p.m., Saturday and Sunday from 1 to 4 p.m.; closed major holidays. Group tours can be arranged by telephone. Admission and tours are free (donations welcome).

VANDENBERG AIR FORCE BASE TOUR *Santa Maria gate off SR 1, seven miles northwest of Lompoc (F-2, Santa Barbara County map).* Free guided tours give visitors an overview of the military's west coast space operations facilities the first Tuesday of each month at 8:45 a.m. Tours last approximately five hours and involve a minimum amount of walking. It is recommended that tour guests be at least 12 years old. For further information and reservations, contact the Lompoc Valley Chamber of Commerce or the Santa Maria Valley Chamber of Commerce (see *Area Chambers of Commerce/Tourism Offices*).

FARMERS MARKET

Lompoc

A variety of fresh produce, flowers, honey and herbs are sold every Friday from 3 to 7 p.m. at Ocean Avenue (SR 246) and I Street. (805) 343-2135.

Santa Maria City Hall exemplifies the Spanish-Mediterranean architecture found throughout the county.

Santa Maria Valley

The flat, fertile Santa Maria Valley extends some 20 miles from the brush-covered foothills of the Sierra Madre Mountains to the sand dunes bordering the Pacific Ocean. The valley's early-morning fog and afternoon sunshine are instrumental in the growth of the flowers and plants that give the area its nickname, "Valley of Gardens."

Today's Santa Maria Valley looks completely different from when Gaspar de Portolá's expedition passed through in 1769 in search of the elusive Monterey Bay. The Spanish explorers saw nothing more than a windswept desert with scant vegetation and a dry riverbed. Prior to the expedition's visit the only settlement, by Chumash Indians, had occurred along the slopes of the Sierra Madre Mountains where moisture could gather in the canyons permitting the growth of oak and sycamore trees. Portolá's party eventually chose mission sites both north and southwest of Santa Maria. These missions later contributed to the development of the Santa Maria Valley.

Following secularization of mission lands in 1834, individual citizens were entitled to own property. William Benjamin Foxen and his family purchased Rancho Tinaquaic in 1837 and lived there for many generations. Real development didn't begin until after the Civil War when veterans were given free land in the valley as a result of the Homestead Act. The first settlers planted grain and beans on land they found to be fertile and easy to plow. Swiss dairymen and farmers from a variety of countries soon moved there, giving the valley a multinational population. The first town was established in 1868 near present-day Orcutt, just south of Santa Maria.

Today agriculture, the dairy industry and cattle raising continue to be the major economic forces in the valley, with oil exploration, business interests and the expanding wine industry lending strong support.

SANTA MARIA

Santa Maria got its start in 1874 when four land owners, whose property bordered the corner of present-day Broadway and Main Street, donated acreage where their properties adjoined. Originally called "Central City," the name was changed in 1882 to Santa Maria because so much mail intended for residents was being sent by mistake to Central City, Colorado.

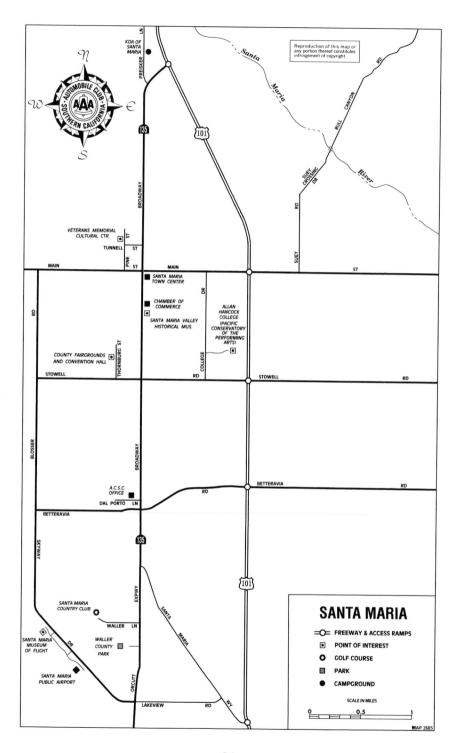

SANTA MARIA

Also in 1882, the narrow-gauge Pacific Coast Railroad from San Luis Obispo County arrived to help move the valley's produce to markets outside the area. Nineteen years later the Southern Pacific Railroad from the north was built through the lower part of the valley en route to Los Angeles.

Diversity is the key to the present city of Santa Maria. In addition to being the agricultural and business hub of the Santa Maria Valley, the city boasts a mild year-round climate that encourages participation in a number of outdoor events. Golf and tennis are popular in the city, while nearby beaches, lakes and mountain recreation areas foster such activities as deep-sea and surf fishing, boating, swimming, bicycling, hiking and hunting.

Cultural activities within the community focus on the Marian Performing Arts Center at Allan Hancock College. Plays, musical programs, lectures and concerts are presented during the school year, and the theater hosts the Pacific Conservatory of Performing Arts (PCPA) programs (see listing).

Several AAA-approved lodgings and restaurants can be found in Santa Maria. And no visit to the city would be complete without sampling a Santa Maria-style barbecue (see listing), served at many eating establishments and public gatherings.

John Austerman

Santa Maria Town Center features two large department stores and more than 60 retail outlets in a two-level, enclosed mall.

Shopping opportunities range from small specialty shops to large department stores. The Santa Maria Town Center is the largest indoor shopping plaza in Santa Barbara County. The two-level mall, with more than 90 specialty stores and restaurants, is anchored by Gottschalk's, May Company and Sears department stores. A pedestrian bridge links the center with Town Center West, an open-air shopping center that includes a Mervyn's store, Thrifty Drug and Big 5 Sporting Goods.

Major annual events in Santa Maria include the Elks Rodeo and Parade in June and the Santa Barbara County Fair, which is held during the last week of July (see *Annual Events*).

The Santa Maria district office of the **Automobile Club of Southern California** is located at 2033-B South Broadway, Santa Maria 93454 (H-5); (805) 922-5731.

Map coordinates refer to the Santa Maria city map on the *Cities of Santa Barbara County* street map.

PACIFIC CONSERVATORY OF THE PERFORMING ARTS (PCPA)
Allan Hancock College, 800 South College Drive (F-6). (805) 922-8313, (800) 549-7272. This professional theater group performs high-caliber productions ranging from musicals to classic drama year-round in the Marian Performing Arts Center at Allan Hancock College and from June through September in Solvang at the Festival Theater (see *Theaterfest* under Solvang). Call for a current schedule and ticket prices.

SANTA MARIA MUSEUM OF FLIGHT, *3015 Airpark Drive (K-4). (805) 922-8758.* Within an aircraft hangar are displayed such airplanes as the P-38 and the Stinson V77-Reliant. An extensive collection of model planes depicts aviation history from the Wright brothers' pioneering effort to the "flying wing" Stealth bomber. Also on view is the once highly secret Norden bombsight and its accessories. Picnic tables are available. The museum is open Friday through Sunday, 9 a.m. to 5 p.m. April through November; 10 a.m. to 4 p.m. the rest of the year; closed New Year's Day and Christmas. Donations are appreciated.

SANTA MARIA-STYLE BARBECUE
originated in the 1800s during the time of the vast valley ranchos. At round-up time, ranchers would assist neighbors with the gathering and branding of new calves. Following this, the host ranch would provide a feast under the oak trees, where beef was barbecued over the coals of a red oakwood fire and then served with bread, beans and salad. Today's menu has changed very little, and the barbecue can be enjoyed at many restaurants, public gatherings and annual events in the Santa Maria Valley. The meat, the top block of choice grade sirloin known as tri-tip, is seasoned only with salt, pepper and garlic salt. Chefs cut the beef into three-inch thick pieces of about 3 to 5 pounds each and prepare it the original way. Tri-tip is served with a Santa Maria Valley exclusive—the little, pink pinquito bean—sautéed with onion, garlic and chili sauce. A tossed green salad, salsa, macaroni and

cheese and sweet French bread complete the menu.

SANTA MARIA VALLEY HISTORICAL SOCIETY MUSEUM *616 South Broadway (F-5). (805) 922-3130.* Changing displays, which include artifacts from the Chumash Indian, Spanish rancho and American pioneer eras, depict the early history of the valley. Museum hours are noon to 5 p.m. Tuesday through Saturday; closed Sunday, Monday and major holidays. Admission is free (donations are accepted).

WALLER COUNTY PARK *Orcutt Expressway and Waller Lane (K-4). (805) 937-1302.* The 100-acre park, covered with Monterey and other pines, serves as home for numerous domestic ducks and geese. It features vast expanses of lawn, a lake with fountains and waterfalls, a fishing area, several play areas, basketball courts, baseball diamonds, group and family picnic areas with barbecue equipment, pony rides, and volleyball and horseshoe areas.

VANDENBERG AIR FORCE BASE TOUR (see listing under *Lompoc Valley*).

FARMERS MARKET

Santa Maria

Fresh produce, flowers, honey and herbs are sold every Wednesday from 2 to 6 p.m. in the Mervyn's parking lot at Westside Town Center, located at the corner of Broadway and Main streets. (805) 343-2135.

WINERIES

Map coordinates refer to the *Santa Barbara County* map.

Tours

The following wineries in the Santa Maria Valley offer free guided tours and tasting.

Byron Vineyard & Winery *12 miles southeast of Santa Maria at 5230 Tepusquet Road (D-6). (805) 937-7288.* Since its first crush in 1984 the winery has emphasized the production of Chardonnay and Pinot Noir, while also turning out limited quantities of Cabernet Sauvignon and Sauvignon Blanc. All of the grapes used by the winery are estate grown or purchased from vineyards in the Santa Maria and Santa Ynez valleys. Tours and tasting are offered daily 10 a.m. to 4 p.m.; groups of 10 or more should call for reservations. A landscaped picnic area is on the grounds.

Rancho Sisquoc Winery *18 miles southeast of Santa Maria via US 101, Betteravia and Foxen Canyon roads; on Foxen Canyon Road (D-6). (805) 934-4332.* The owners of Rancho Sisquoc, a large cattle ranch in the foothills of the San Rafael Mountains, turned over a small portion of land to grapes, with the first crush in 1972. Now the winery bottles more than 4000 cases of varietals yearly. Tours and tasting are offered daily from 10 a.m. to 4 p.m. A landscaped picnic area is provided for visitors.

Cold Spring Arch Bridge, a 700-foot single span, crosses Cold Spring Canyon along SR 154.

Los Padres National Forest

A major portion of Santa Barbara County's backcountry lies within Los Padres National Forest, the second largest national forest in California. The Los Padres boundaries enclose nearly two million acres of five counties—Kern, Monterey, San Luis Obispo, Ventura and Santa Barbara.

Los Padres National Forest is composed largely of rugged mountains and deep, remote valleys. This is particularly true of the forest in Santa Barbara County, a major portion of which comprises the roadless San Rafael and Dick Smith wilderness areas. Within Santa Barbara County, the forest's highest peaks are in the wilderness, culminating in 6828-foot Big Pine Mountain. Although not high by most standards, the mountain ranges of Los Padres begin near sea level, resulting in an elevation difference between high and low points roughly similar to the Tetons.

Considering the enormous population of Southern California, surprisingly few roads enter Los Padres National Forest, especially in Santa Barbara County. In fact only one road—Sierra Madre—ventures far into the county's Los Padres backcountry: it is unpaved, dusty, frequently rough and should not be attempted in poor weather.

Several paved and dirt roads provide access to picnic areas and camp-grounds at the edge of the forest. Notable are Gibraltar Road and Camino Cielo near Santa Barbara, Figueroa Mountain and Happy Canyon roads above the Santa Ynez Valley and Tepusquet Road east of Santa Maria. All of these require slow, careful driving. Pavements are narrow and, in places, rough; curves are sharp and frequent. In wet weather Gibraltar Road may be closed to motor vehicles.

There's a plus side to these tortuous roads—the lack of traffic. At midweek, even in summer, motorists may travel miles without meeting another car. (State Routes 154 and 166 are the only heavily traveled roads within the forest and together total less than 20 miles inside forest boundaries.) Other benefits for users of the lightly traveled roads are the likelihood of observing wildlife and the opportunity to view spectacular mountain, canyon and ocean scenery from numerous roadside overlooks.

The lower slopes of Los Padres alternate between grassland and oak

89

forest. Middle elevations are chaparral covered, and higher altitudes are forested with pines and firs. These varied environments provide habitats for nearly 500 species of animals and birds, including black bear, fox, deer, golden eagle and peregrine falcon. The endangered California condor, North America's largest bird, has recently been reintroduced in Los Padres National Forest, its last natural habitat.

Summers are long, warm and dry in Los Padres, with little rain falling from May to October except for an occasional afternoon thundershower near the higher peaks. Winter is generally cool and wet, although many winter days are sunny and mild. Snow sometimes dusts the highest summits but invariably melts quickly. The forest is at its most appealing in the spring, when wildflowers sprout from newly green hillsides and streams tumble at their liveliest. Fall also provides beauty in the form of autumn color at higher elevations.

In addition to enjoying the scenery and solitude, the most popular activities within the forest are camping and picnicking. Other favorites include hiking, fishing and horseback riding. For information about these and other recreational pursuits, turn to *Recreation*.

Map coordinates refer to the *Santa Barbara County* map.

SAN MARCOS PASS AREA

CHUMASH PAINTED CAVE STATE HISTORIC PARK *two miles north-* *west of Santa Barbara via SR 154 and Painted Cave Road (H-11)*. This park consists of a shallow cave and surrounding terrain. On the cave walls the Chumash long ago left their mark in brightly colored designs. These pictographs are a fine example of Native American art and are thought to have played a part in Chumash religion. A locked, metal screen protects the designs but allows a view of the interior. The road leading to the cave is narrow and winding; parking near the cave consists of pulling off onto a narrow shoulder.

COLD SPRING ARCH BRIDGE *best seen ¼ mile below Cold Spring Tavern on Stagecoach Road (H-10)*. This graceful steel structure leaps Cold Spring Canyon in one 700-foot span, providing a spectacular sight for travelers on Stagecoach Road 400 feet below. Completed in 1963, the bridge was constructed so that motorists on SR 154 may avoid the twisting route through Cold Spring Canyon.

COLD SPRING TAVERN *½ mile southwest of SR 154 on Stagecoach Road, 14 miles northwest of Santa Barbara (H-10)*. (805) 967-0066. After completion of the San Marcos Pass toll road in the 1880s, a small restaurant was opened here to accommodate stagecoach passengers. Travelers today also can enjoy food and drink in the tavern, which still occupies the original structure. Another building set in this tree-shaded spot formerly served as a bottling plant for the spring water and now houses the Wagon Wheel Back Bar. Cold Spring Tavern is open for lunch and dinner daily from 11 a.m. to 3 and 5 to 9 p.m.; on Friday and Saturday until

John Austerman

At the end of a rough dirt road, tiny Zaca Lake offers an isolated setting where one can get "away from it all."

10 p.m. Breakfast is served from 8 to 11 a.m. Saturday and Sunday. The Wagon Wheel Back Bar is open Friday from 5 p.m. to midnight, and Saturday and Sunday from noon to midnight.

ZACA LAKE

ZACA LAKE *off Zaca Station Road, 12 miles northeast of US 101 and Zaca Station Road junction (E-8).* This small, privately owned lake is virtually hidden away amidst tree-covered hills in Los Padres National Forest. Public access is along ¾ mile of paved road followed by 4½ miles of a rough dirt and gravel road that fords several streams and can be hazardous after winter rainstorms.

Zaca Lake offers picnicking facilities, swimming and rental boats; fishing and motorized craft are prohibited. Overnight accommodations consist of 18 rustic cabins at the east end of the lake. The lodge dining room serves breakfast from 8 to 10:30 a.m., lunch from noon to 2:30 p.m. and dinner from 6 to 8 p.m. (reservations required). Day-use fees, payable at the lodge, are $5 for adults and $3 for children. For overnight rates and reservations call (805) 688-4891, or write P.O. Box 187, Los Olivos 93441.

*Scenic Cabrillo Bikeway in Santa Barbara passes Andree Clark Bird Refuge and
continues along the ocean.*

Recreation

Santa Barbara County offers something for everyone in the way of recreation. Whether it's water sports, hiking, golfing, tennis or camping, outdoors is a good place to be almost anytime of the year.

BEACHCOMBING

Carpinteria State Beach proves to be a good area for collecting shells and pebbles, while shells and driftwood are abundant after winter storms at Jalama Beach and Ocean Beach county parks and at Point Sal State Beach. Tidepool explorers can see several species of starfish, as well as mussels, clams, crabs, sea urchins, sand dollars, hermit crabs and anemone in the rocky pools at Carpinteria State Beach, Arroyo Burro County Beach (known to the locals as Hendry's Beach), Coal Oil Point (just north of the University of California at Santa Barbara), Gaviota State Beach, Jalama Beach County Park and Point Sal State Beach. Remember, marine life may be observed—but not collected.

BICYCLING

The county's wide valleys and gently rolling hills make bicycling both enjoyable and challenging. Marked routes have been implemented in the communities of Goleta, Lompoc, Los Alamos, Montecito and Santa Barbara, and most state highways are wide enough to accommodate cyclists along with motor vehicles. The routes listed, except for the ones in the city of Santa Barbara, are generally Class II, with a difficulty rating of "B."

Class I paths have been constructed exclusively for use by cyclists and offer the most pleasant recreational riding. Class II bikeways share an existing right-of-way with automobiles. A lane of the roadway is marked for bicycle use by a painted stripe, offering limited protection from automobile traffic. A difficulty rating of "A" indicates that the ride is level throughout. "B" denotes a partially or moderately hilly route, not too strenuous for the average cyclist.

Santa Barbara Coast

Santa Barbara's climate and terrain readily lend themselves to enjoyable bicycling during much of the year. Map coordinates refer to the Santa Barbara and Vicinity city map on the *Cities of Santa Barbara County* street map.

Atascadero Recreational Trail, *Goleta*. Length, 7⅛ miles; Class I and II; Difficulty Rating, A.

This point-to-point route offers a leisurely trip along Atascadero Creek in Goleta. The trail begins at the corner of Encore Drive and Modoc Road (C-12) and follows residential streets for about ½ mile before entering the Atascadero Creek levee. It then travels southwest past stables and rural acreage, with wooden bridges crossing the creek at several points. The route officially terminates at Goleta Beach County Park, but cyclists can continue on a Class I spur to the University of California at Santa Barbara campus.

Cabrillo Beachway, *Santa Barbara*. Length 2¾ miles; Class I; Difficulty Rating, A.

John Austerman

Santa Barbara's scenic beach-front bike path is popular with cyclists, joggers, roller skaters and strollers.

This point-to-point trail runs along the north side of Cabrillo Boulevard from the Andree Clark Bird Refuge (D-18) to Milpas Street. Then it follows the shoreline of the Santa Barbara Channel to a small-craft harbor just east of Leadbetter Beach. Signs are placed every ¼ mile, and route maps are posted at three locations.

Goleta Valley Bikeway, *Goleta.* Length, 9½ miles; Class II; Difficulty Rating, B.

This route follows Cathedral Oaks Road between San Marcos Pass Road (B-12) and Alameda Avenue. The bikeway passes through both suburban and semi-rural areas, making the ride alternately lively and tranquil. A spur heading south along Turnpike Road connects the Goleta Valley Trail with the Atascadero Recreational Trail, a Class I bikeway paralleling Atascadero Creek. Additional east-west branches run along Calle Real and Hollister Avenue, and a spur runs to Goleta Beach County Park near the University of California at Santa Barbara.

RENTALS

Beach Rentals 8 *West Cabrillo Boulevard, Santa Barbara (E-17). (805) 963-2524.* This establishment rents bicycles, roller skates, in-line skates and four-wheel surreys. Open daily 8 a.m. to dusk.

Cycles 4 Rent, Inc. *three locations: 101 State Street (E-17), (805) 966-3804; 633 East Cabrillo Boulevard in Fess Parker's Red Lion Resort (E-17), (805) 564-4333, extension 444; and 1111 East Cabrillo Boulevard in the Sheraton Santa Barbara Hotel & Spa (E-18), (805) 963-0744.* The outlets rent bicycles, in-line skates and four-wheel surreys (locks and helmets provided). Open 8 a.m. to 8 p.m. daily in summer; for hours the rest of the year call (805) 652-0462.

Santa Ynez Valley

Beginners as well as experienced riders are challenged by this region with its wide, flat valley floor and hilly grades. The valley also offers cyclists a chance to explore turn-of-the-century towns, shop in the Danish-American city of Solvang, take a winery tour, picnic and fish at Lake Cachuma or visit art galleries in Los Olivos. The valley's two state highways—SR 246 and SR 154—have wide shoulders, but riders should be careful because both carry a lot of traffic. Most of the north-south connecting roads carry substantially less traffic and can be pedaled at a more leisurely pace. The roads in the Santa Ynez Valley are level throughout; however, cyclists will encounter some grades on SR 246 near Solvang and Santa Ynez, and along SR 154 from the junction of SR 246 to Lake Cachuma County Park.

RENTALS

Cachuma Bicycle Rentals *Lake Cachuma County Park off SR 154, Santa Barbara (G-9, Santa Barbara County map). (805) 688-6286.* Open daily Memorial Day weekend through Labor Day weekend.

Lompoc Valley

The 36-mile loop trip between Lompoc and Buellton takes riders through some scenic terrain and offers pleasant places to stop for sightseeing and recreational activities. The route begins in Lompoc at Ocean Avenue (SR 1) and H Street (G-3, Lompoc city map on *Cities of Santa Barbara County* street map), goes east on Ocean to the junction with SR 1/SR 246 and then proceeds south on SR 1 for about 1½ miles to Santa Rosa Road. Cyclists then turn left on Santa Rosa and travel about 16½ miles to Buellton in the Santa Ynez Valley. The road passes over gently rolling hills, skirting a few vineyards and paralleling the Santa Ynez River much of the way. At the halfway point, Santa Rosa County Park offers picnic sites, barbecue pits, a volleyball court, horseshoe pits and a small play area for children. To return from Buellton, ride west on the wide shoulders of SR 246 through the rolling Santa Rita Valley and back into Lompoc where the highway becomes Ocean Avenue (SR 1). SR 246 passes within a mile of La Purísima Mission State Historic Park just northeast of Lompoc.

Santa Maria Valley

This level valley invites cyclists of all abilities to explore the region. A flat 13-mile ride goes from the junction of SR 135 (Broadway) and SR 166 (Main Street) in Santa Maria (F-5, Santa Maria city map on the *Cities of Santa Barbara County* street map) west on SR 166 to Rancho Guadalupe Dunes County Park on the Pacific Ocean. Riders can stop and explore the sand dunes or surf fish at the county park. The road from the city of Guadalupe to the park is rough and potholed, but it carries very little traffic. More experienced cyclists might like to pedal over the Casmalia Hills on SR 1 from the Santa Maria

gate at Vandenberg Air Force Base to the SR 1/SR 135 junction (F-2, *Santa Barbara County* map). This 6⅓-mile ride along SR 1, a two-lane, divided highway, is very steep, but it provides some spectacular views of the Santa Maria Valley, and the highway is wide enough to accommodate both cyclists and motorists.

BOATING AND WATERSKIING

Santa Barbara County offers numerous boating opportunities, whether in a pedal boat at Lake Cachuma County Park or aboard a yacht plying the waters off the Santa Barbara coast. The following listings indicate where boats can be launched or moored. Entries include each establishment's location and phone number and give additional information on rental equipment, fuel, boat repairs and other facilities and services available nearby.

For waterskiers, the city of Santa Barbara offers a good area off East Beach, away from harbor traffic. Waterskiing is not permitted in either of the county's two freshwater lakes.

Santa Barbara

Map coordinates refer to the Santa Barbara and Vicinity city map on the *Cities of Santa Barbara County* street map, unless noted otherwise.

Gaviota State Park *off US 101, 32 miles west of Santa Barbara (J-6,* Santa Barbara County *map). (805)* 968-3294. Open daily all year.

Opportunities for boating abound in Santa Barbara County.

Facilities: hoist. No rentals. Miscellaneous: bait, groceries, ice (available daily during summer months; weekends rest of year), picnic area.

Goleta Pier *5905 Sandspit Road, Goleta (E-9). (805) 967-1300.* Open daily all year. Facilities: sling hoist. No rentals. Miscellaneous: bait, snack bar, restaurant, picnic area.

Sailing Center of Santa Barbara *in the harbor at the public launch ramp, Santa Barbara (E-17). (800) 350-9090; (805) 962-2826.* Open daily except New Year's Day, Thanksgiving and Christmas. Rentals: rowboats, motorboats (13 to 24 ft.), sailboats (21 to 51 ft.). Miscellaneous: sailing school, boat charters, whale-watch trips, dinner cruises and sailing excursions aboard a 50-ft. catamaran.

Santa Barbara Municipal Harbor *132-A Harbor Way on the breakwater; Santa Barbara (E-17). (805) 564-5520.* Open 24 hours daily all year.

Facilities: paved launching ramp (fee), slips. Concessionaire facilities: hull repairs, hoist launching, marine fuel. Rentals: see Sailing Center of Santa Barbara. Miscellaneous: bait, ice, snack bars, restaurants, groceries, harbor cruise.

Union Marine Station *on the breakwater, Santa Barbara (E-17). (805) 962-7186.* Open daily except New Year's Day, Thanksgiving and Christmas. Facilities: marine fuel, marine waste station. No rentals.

Santa Ynez Valley

LAKE CACHUMA
(Also see *Lake Cachuma County Park* on page 72.)

Cachuma Lake Boat Rentals, Inc. *on south shore, one mile north of SR 154, Solvang (G-9, Santa Barbara County map). (805) 688-4040.* Open daily all year. $3.50 day-use fee.

Facilities: paved ramp, temporary mooring, slips, dry storage, boat fuel. Rentals: rowboats, motorboats (4.5 to 9 hp), pedal boats, pontoon boats, fishing tackle. Miscellaneous: marine hardware, bait, groceries, ice, snack bar, picnic area, lake tours.

Los Padres National Forest

ZACA LAKE

(Also see listing on page 73.)

Zaca Lake Resort *on east shore, Los Olivos (E-8*, Santa Barbara County map). *(805) 688-4891*. Open daily all year. Facilities: graded ramp (free). Rentals: rowboats, pedal boats, canoes. Miscellaneous: ice, restaurant, rustic lodging, picnic area.

CAMPING

Seaside, mountain and valley camping can all be enjoyed in Santa Barbara County. Fees shown are for one night's camping, usually for two people plus a recreational vehicle. Electricity, water and sewer hookups are indicated by the letters E, W and S. The private campgrounds listed have been inspected by an Automobile Club representative and meet current AAA quality standards. The ⦿ symbol preceding a listing identifies that establishment as a AAA Official Appointment; it indicates that the campground has expressed a particular interest in serving AAA members. All rates are subject to change. For a detailed listing of additional public and private campgrounds, see the Auto Club's *Central and Southern California Camping* map.

Map coordinates refer to the *Santa Barbara County* map, unless noted otherwise.

RESERVATIONS

In making campground reservations, be aware that in addition to the camping fee, reservation and cancellation fees are usually charged. Policies vary regarding reservation and cancellation notices, reservation hours and accepted forms of payment.

Reservations for state park campsites must be made through **MISTIX** as follows: Charge reservations by phone with American Express, DiscoverCard, MasterCard or VISA by calling (800) 444-7275. The TTD/TTY number for hearing- or speech-impaired is (800) 274-7275.

Reservations for those few campgrounds in Los Padres National Forest that take reservations, must be made with **National Forest Reservation Center** as follows: Charge reservations by phone with Discovercard, MasterCard or VISA by calling (800) 280-2267. The TTD/TTY number for hearing- or speech-impaired is (800) 879-4496.

For other campgrounds, reservations usually can be made with the campground directly or, in some cases, reservations are not accepted. Automobile Club members can make reservations for private campgrounds that accept them through any Club office. In many cases reservations are accepted only during a campground's peak season. If this is the case, campsites are available on a first-come, first-served basis during the remainder of their open period.

John Austerman

Campers rise to a damp, foggy morning at Carpinteria State Beach.

Santa Barbara Coast

PRIVATE

El Patio RV Park *Santa Barbara, 4040 Calle Real, 1 blk. E. of jct.* US 101 *and SR 154; San Marcos Pass exit (C-13, Santa Barbara and Vicinity map on the* Cities of Santa Barbara County *street map). (805) 687-7614.* 90 RV spaces, 90 EWS, cable TV, piped water, flush toilets, coin laundry, showers; 3 beaches and fishing within 5 mi. Open all year. $23 per night for 2 persons; $1 per night for each additional person. Small pets only.

STATE

Reservations can be made through MISTIX for these state park campgrounds and are required during the busy summer months. Camping fees are $16 per night from April 1 through October 30 and $14 the rest of the year, unless otherwise noted. A fee of $1 per night is charged for pets. Dogs are not allowed on the beaches.

Carpinteria State Beach *in Carpinteria off US 101 via SR 224 (D-3, Carpinteria city map on the* Cities of Santa Barbara County *street map). (805) 684-2811.* 262 tent or RV spaces, 30-ft. RV max. length, 85 EWS, sanitary disposal station, piped water, flush toilets, pay showers, fire pits, tables; fishing, swimming; propane, groceries, restaurant, laundromat within ½ mi. $14-$21 without hookups, $18-$25 with hookups.

El Capitan State Beach *12 mi. W. of Goleta off US 101 (J-8). (805) 968-1033.* 140 tent or RV spaces, 3 group tent sites, 30-ft. RV max. length, no hookups, sanitary disposal station, piped water, flush toilets, pay showers, fire pits, tables; limited groceries; fishing and swimming.

Gaviota State Park *23 mi. W. of Goleta off US 101 (J-6). (805) 968-1033.* 18 tent and 36 RV spaces, no hookups, flush toilets, showers, fire pits and tables at tent sites only; fishing and swimming. Reservations are not accepted.

Refugio State Beach *15 mi. W. of Goleta off US 101 (J-7). (805) 968-1033.* 85 tent or RV spaces, 1 group tent site, 30-ft. RV max. length, no hookups, piped water, flush toilets, showers, fire pits, tables, playground; limited groceries; fishing and swimming.

Santa Ynez Valley

COUNTY

Lake Cachuma County Park *eight mi. E. of Santa Ynez off SR 154 (G-9). (805) 688-4658.* 125 RV spaces, 500 tent or RV spaces, 25 EW, 100 EWS, sanitary disposal station, piped water, flush toilets, showers, coin laundromat, playground; boat and bicycle rentals; swimming during summer months, fishing; propane and groceries available. Open all year. $12 per night without hookups, $16 per night with EW and $17 per night with EWS. Individual campsites on a first-come, first-served basis. Fee for group reservations. Pets are permitted for an additional fee of $1 per night.

PRIVATE

⊕ Flying Flags Travel Park *Buellton on Av of Flags (G-2, Santa Ynez Valley city map on the* Cities of Santa Barbara County *street map). (805) 688-3716.* 303 tent or RV spaces, 250 EW, 220 S, sanitary disposal station, piped water, flush toilets, showers, grills, tables; swimming pool, 2 whirlpools, playground, arcade games, fee for cable TV; coin laundry, propane, groceries. Golf course adjacent. Open all year. $14.50-20.50 per night for 2 persons; $2 per night for each additional person. Reservations are accepted, deposit required. Pets are permitted for an additional fee of 50¢ per night.

Lompoc Valley

CITY

River Park Lompoc, *SR 246 and Sweeney Rd. junction, E. side of Santa Ynez River (G-4, Lompoc city map on the* Cities of Santa Barbara County *street map). (805) 736-6565.* 36 RV spaces (EWS), disposal station ($2), area for tents and bicyclists, flush toilets, tables, playground; fishing pond; propane, groceries, laundromat within 5 mi. Open all year. First-come, first-served. $12 per night per motor vehicle, $8 for tent sites, $3 per night per bicyclist or hiker. Pets are permitted for an additional fee of $1 per night.

COUNTY

Jalama Beach County Park *20 mi. S.W. of Lompoc off SR 1 on Jalama Rd (H-2). (805) 736-6316 (recording), 736-3504.* 110 tent or RV spaces, potable water, flush toilets, showers, tables, playground; fishing; groceries; snack bar. Open all year. $12 per night without hookups and $16 with hookups. Pets, with proof of rabies inoculation, are permitted at an additional cost of $1 per night. Individual campsites on first-come, first-served basis. Fee for group reservations; call (805) 934-6211.

Santa Maria Valley

PRIVATE

Santa Maria Pines Campground
2210 Preisker Ln, 1 blk. W. of US 101, exit Broadway (Santa Maria city map on the Cities of Santa Barbara County *street map, C-5). (805) 922-7214.* 43 tent or RV spaces (EWS), flush toilets, hot showers, coin laundry, groceries, swimming pool open May 15-Oct. 15. $25.95 for 2 persons, $4 for each additional person. Pets are permitted.

Los Padres National Forest

U.S. FOREST SERVICE

Numerous campgrounds are located in the portion of Los Padres National Forest that lies in Santa Barbara County. Unless noted, these campgrounds are open all year and are all accessible by car, usually from SR 154, Tepusquet Road or SR 166.

While these campsites do not have electric, water or sewer hookups, many are equipped with piped water, and a few have flush toilets. Each site has a table and fire pit. There are no showers, and sanitary disposal stations are not available. Fees for one night vary, depending upon facilities, and with the exception of Paradise campground and Figueroa and Sage Hill group camps (National Forest Reservation Center), reservations are not accepted. Pets are allowed at no extra fee but must be kept on a leash or physically controlled at all times.

Changes in campground information may occur, depending upon road and weather conditions and campground maintenance. Fishing and swimming are seasonal. For further information, contact your nearest Auto Club district office or Los Padres National Forest Headquarters at 6144 Calle Real, Goleta 93117; (805) 683-6711.

Aliso *8 mi. S.W. of New Cuyama off SR 166 (D-11).* El. 3200 ft. 11 tent or RV spaces, 22-ft. RV max. length, no water, pit toilets. No fee.

Ballinger *17 mi. S.E. of New Cuyama off SR 33 (D-15).* El. 3000 ft. 20 tent or RV spaces, 32-ft. RV max. length, no water, pit toilets. No fee.

Barrel Springs *17 mi. N.E. of Sisquoc via Tepusquet and Colson Canyon rds. (D-7).* El. 1000 ft. 6 tent spaces, piped water, chemical toilets. No fee.

Bates Canyon *18 mi. W. of New Cuyama on Cottonwood Canyon Rd. (C-10).* El. 2900 ft. 4 tent or RV spaces, 16-ft. RV max. length, no water, chemical toilets. No fee.

Cachuma *16 mi N.E. of Santa Ynez off SR 154 on Happy Canyon Rd. (F-10).* El. 2200 ft. 6 tent spaces, no water, pit toilets. No fee.

Colson *12 mi. N.E. of Sisquoc via Tepusquet and Colson Canyon rds. (C-7).* El. 2080 ft. 9 tent or RV spaces, 22-ft. RV max. length, piped water, chemical toilets. No fee.

Davy Brown *37 mi. N.E. of Santa Barbara off SR 154 via Armour Ranch and Happy Canyon rds. (F-9).* El. 2200 ft. 13 tent or RV spaces, 22-ft. RV max. length, piped water, pit toilets; fishing. $6.

Figueroa Group Camp *12 mi. N.E. of Los Olivos on Figueroa Mountain Rd. (F-9).* El. 4000 ft. 33 tent or RV spaces, 22-ft. RV max. length, piped water, pit toilets. $6. National Forest Reservation Center.

Fremont *19 mi. N.W. of Santa Barbara off SR 154 (H-11).* El. 1000 ft. Open 4/1-10/15. 15 tent or RV spaces, 22-ft. RV max. length, piped water, flush toilets; fishing and groceries available within 5 mi. $8; $2 for additional vehicles.

Juncal *31 mi N.E. of Santa Barbara off SR 154 via E. Camino Cielo Rd. or off Gibraltar Rd. via Juncal Rd. (J-14).* El. 1800 ft. 6 tent spaces, no water, pit toilets. No fee.

Los Prietos *19 mi N.W. of Santa Barbara off SR 154 (H-11).* El. 1000 ft. Open 4/1-10/15. 38 tent or RV spaces, 32-ft. RV max. length, piped water, flush toilets; fishing within 5 mi. $8; $2 for additional vehicles.

Middle Santa Ynez *34 mi N.E. of Santa Barbara off SR 154 via E. Camino Cielo and Juncal Rd. or off Gibraltar Rd. via Juncal Rd. (H-13).* El. 1800 ft. 12 tent spaces, no water, pit toilets; fishing within 5 mi. No fee.

Mono *37 mi. N. of Santa Barbara off SR 154 via E. Camino Cielo and Juncal Rd. or off Gibraltar Rd. via Juncal Rd. (H-13).* El. 1500 ft. 9 tent spaces, no water, pit toilets; fishing within 5 mi. No fee.

Nira *22 mi. N.E. of Santa Ynez off SR 154 via Happy Canyon and Sunset Valley rds. (E-9).* El. 2100 ft. 12 tent or RV spaces, 22-ft. RV max. length, no water, pit toilets; fishing within 5 mi. No fee.

Paradise *18 mi. N.W. of Santa Barbara off SR 154 via Paradise Rd. (H-11).* El. 1000 ft. 15 tent or RV spaces, 22-ft. RV max. length, piped

water, flush toilets; fishing and groceries available within 5 mi. $8; $2 for additional vehicles. National Forest Reservation Center.

P-Bar Flat *35 mi. N.E. of Santa Barbara off SR 154 via E. Camino Cielo and Juncal Rd. or off Gibraltar Rd. via Juncal Rd. (H-13).* El. 1800 ft. 4 tent spaces, no water, pit toilets; fishing within 5 mi. No fee.

Sage Hill Group Camp *20 mi. N.W. of Santa Barbara off SR 154 via Paradise Rd. (H-11).* El. 1100 ft. Piped water, flush toilets; swimming within 1 mi., fishing within 5 mi. $25 per group site. Reservations are accepted and may be made up to 3 months in advance. National Forest Reservation Center.

Santa Ynez *26 mi. N.W. of Santa Barbara off SR 154 via Paradise Rd. (H-12).* El. 1100 ft. Open 4/1-10/15. 34 tent or RV spaces, 22-ft. RV max. length, piped water, pit toilets; swimming within 1 mi., fishing within 5 mi. $8; $2 for additional vehicles.

Upper Oso *22 mi. N.W. of Santa Barbara off SR 154 via Paradise Rd. (H-11).* El. 1200 ft. 27 tent or RV spaces, 22-ft. RV max. length, piped water, flush toilets; fishing within 5 mi. $8; $2 for additional vehicles.

Wagon Flat *21 mi. N.E. of Sisquoc via Tepusquet, Colson and La Brea Canyon rds. (C-7).* El. 1400 ft. 5 tent or RV spaces, 16-ft. RV max. length, no water, chemical toilets. No fee.

FISHING

Freshwater Fishing

Lake Cachuma offers good fishing year round for bass, crappie, catfish,

John Austerman

Lake Cachuma is one of Southern California's largest man-made freshwater lakes.

bluegill and trout; a California State Fishing License is required for anyone over age 16. Children's fishing areas can be found at River Park in Lompoc and Waller County Park in Santa Maria.

Santa Ynez Valley

Lake Cachuma *12 mi. E. of Solvang off SR 154 (G-9,* Santa Barbara County *map). (805) 688-4658.* $3.50 day-use fee.

Los Padres National Forest

Fishing in Los Padres National Forest is best in the spring months following the stocking of catchable-sized trout at Davy Brown and Manzana creeks. Catches along the Santa Ynez River are also good in late winter and early spring. Fishing conditions in the summer and fall months are considered poor because of the warm water temperatures and low surface flows.

Ocean Fishing

Pier fishermen can catch halibut, bonito, mackerel, barracuda, calico bass and white sea bass at Stearns Wharf in Santa Barbara Harbor and at Goleta Pier, end of Sandspit Road, Goleta. These piers have floodlights for night fishing. Those who prefer deep-sea fishing can find albacore, barracuda, white sea bass, bonito, halibut, calico bass, lingcod, mackerel, rockfish, sculpin, sheephead and silver salmon in the waters off Santa Barbara.

Surf fishermen along the Santa Barbara County coastline can snag a variety of fish that includes four species of surf perch, cabezon, kelp bass and halibut. Arroyo Burro Beach, Goleta Beach, Isla Vista Beach, Jalama Beach, Lookout Park, Ocean Beach, Rancho Guadalupe Dunes and Rincon Beach are all considered good spots for surf fishing.

Harbor cruises and charters leave from the Santa Barbara Small Craft Harbor.

Surface fishing is usually best from April through October; good bottom fishing is enjoyed all year. Although pier fishing does not require a license, a valid California sportfishing license is required for surf or deep-sea fishing.

SPORTFISHING CHARTERS

Map coordinates refer to the Santa Barbara and Vicinity city map on the *Cities of Santa Barbara County* street map.

Captain Don's Deep-Sea Fishing *on Stearns Wharf opposite Moby Dick's restaurant (look for large blue flag), Santa Barbara (E-17). (805) 969-5217.* The company offers half-day, full-day and multiple-day charters year round, specializing in trips for groups of six or fewer passengers.

Sea Landing Sport Fishing *Cabrillo Blvd. at Bath St., Santa Barbara (E-17). (805) 963-3564.* This establishment offers half-day, three-quarter-day and all-day fishing trips year round.

GOLFING

Santa Barbara County's temperate climate helps to make golfing a year-round pleasure. Following is information on public, semi-private and private courses, listed by area and community. Each golf course listing includes name, location, mailing address, phone number and facilities, plus yardage, par and slope and USGA ratings (all from men's white tees). Unless otherwise stated, each course is open daily all year. The abbreviation N/A means the information was not available. Package plan indicates a special rate combining hotel or resort rooms and golfing fees. Greens fees are given for weekday and weekend play during peak season. Many courses have senior citizen rates. Military golf courses show greens fees that apply to civilian guests of military personnel.

The listings have been made as complete as possible; a few courses, however, have been intentionally omitted at the request of the owners.

All semi-private and private courses have restrictions on public play ranging from members and guests only to liberal reciprocal agreements with members of other courses. It is impossible to list all of the restrictions for each course, so please telephone the course directly if in doubt. Reservations are advised at most courses; some country clubs require reservations months in advance.

Each golf course listing gives general street directions from the nearest freeway. For detailed directions refer to Automobile Club of Southern California street maps.

Santa Barbara Coast

Map coordinates refer to the Santa Barbara and Vicinity city map on the *Cities of Santa Barbara County* street map, unless noted otherwise.

GOLETA

Ocean Meadows Golf Club (Public)
(805) 968-6814
½ mi s of US 101 off Storke Rd at 6925 Whittier Dr (E-6); PO Box 8708, 93118.

The course is 9 holes; 3001 yards; N/A rating. Rates: $11 (9 holes), $15 (18 holes) weekdays; $12 (9 holes), $20 (18 holes) weekends. Clubhouse, golf shop, professional, power and hand carts, rental clubs, driving range; restaurant, coffee shop, snack bar, beer, wine.

Sandpiper Golf Course (Public)
(805) 968-1541
South of US 101 off Winchester Canyon Rd at 7925 Hollister Av, 93117 (D-4).

The course is 18 holes; 6670 yards; par 72; 126 slope; 72.5 rating. Rates: $50 weekdays, $70 weekends. Clubhouse, golf shop, professional, power and hand carts, rental clubs, driving range; coffee shop, snack bar, beer, wine.

Twin Lakes Golf Course (Public)
(805) 964-1414
¼ mi s of US 101 off Fairview Av at 6034 Hollister Av, 93117 (C-8).

The course is 9 holes; 1292 yards; par 29; 73 slope; 53.6 rating. Rates: $6.50 (9 holes) weekdays, $7.50 (9 holes) weekends. Clubhouse, golf shop, professional, hand carts, rental clubs, lighted driving range; snack bar, beer.

SANTA BARBARA

Birnam Wood Golf Club (Private)
(805) 969-0919
North on Sheffield Dr from US 101 to 2031 Packing House Rd, 93108 (D-22). Closed Dec 25.

The course is 18 holes; 6020 yards; par 70; N/A slope; 68.7 rating. Rates: $75 weekdays, $100 (mandatory golf cart included) weekends. Clubhouse, locker room, golf shop, professional, power and hand carts, rental clubs, driving range; tennis, swimming; restaurant, cocktails.

Hidden Oaks Country Club (Semi-private)
(805) 967-3493
1½ mi s of US 101 off Hollister and Puente Dr at 4760 Calle Camarada, 93110 (D-11).

The course is 9 holes; 1118 yards; par 27; N/A rating. Rates: $7 (9 holes), $10 (18 holes) weekdays; $9 (9 holes), $12 (18 holes) weekends. Clubhouse, golf shop, professional, hand carts, rental clubs; tennis, swimming; coffee shop.

La Cumbre Golf & Country Club (Private)
(805) 682-3131
¼ mi s of US 101 off Las Palmas Dr at 4015 Via Laguna, 93110 (D-13). Closed Dec 25.

The course is 18 holes; 6140 yards; par 71; 122 slope; 69.8 rating. Rates: $97 (mandatory golf cart included) weekdays and weekends. Clubhouse, locker room, golf shop, professional, power and hand carts, rental clubs, driving range; tennis, swimming; restaurant, snack bar, cocktails.

Santa Barbara Golf Club (Public)
(805) 687-7087
1 mi n of US 101 off Las Positas Rd at 3500 McCaw Av, 93105 (D-14). Closed Dec 25.

The course is 18 holes; 5777 yards; par 70; 101 slope; 66.1 rating. Rates: $18 weekdays, $20 weekends. Clubhouse, golf shop, professional, power and hand carts, rental clubs, driving range; coffee shop, snack bar, cocktails.

Valley Club of Montecito (Private)
(805) 969-2215, 969-4681
1 mi n of US 101 off Sheffield Dr at 1901 E Valley Rd; PO Box 5640, 93105 (D-21).

The course is 18 holes; 6400 yards; par 72; 122 slope; 70 rating. Rates:

$100 weekdays, N/A weekends. Clubhouse, locker room, golf shop, professional, power and hand carts, rental clubs, driving range; tennis.

Santa Ynez Valley

BUELLTON

Zaca Creek Golf Course (Public)
(805) 688-2575
¼ mi w of US 101 via Buellton Pkwy at 223 Shadow Mountain Dr, 93427 (G-1).

The course is 9 holes; 1544 yards; par of 29; N/A rating. Rates: $5 weekdays, $6 weekends. Clubhouse, golf shop, professional, power and hand carts, rental clubs, driving range; tennis; coffee shop, snack bar, beer, wine.

SOLVANG

The Alisal (Private)
(805) 688-4215
2 mi s at 1054 Alisal Rd, 93463 (H-3). Package plan.

The Ranch course is 18 holes; 6396 yards; par 72; 114 slope; 68.5 rating. Rates: $65 weekdays and weekends. Clubhouse, locker room, golf shop, professional, power and hand carts, rental clubs, driving range; tennis, swimming; restaurant, coffee shop, snack bar, cocktails.

The Alisal (Public)
(805) 688-6042
1 mi s at 150 Alisal Rd, 93463 (H-3). Package plan.

The River course is 18 holes; 6451 yards; par 72; 120 slope; 70.6 rating. Rates: $35 weekdays, $45 weekends. Clubhouse, golf shop, professional, power and hand carts, rental clubs, driving range; restaurant, cocktails.

Lompoc Valley

LOMPOC

La Purísima Golf Course (Public)
(805) 735-8395
5 mi e at 3455 E Hwy 246, 93436.
Package plan.

The course is 18 holes; 6657 yards; par 72; 132 slope; 72.8 rating. Rates: $40 weekdays, $50 weekends. Clubhouse, golf shop, professional, power and hand carts, rental clubs, driving range; coffee shop, beer, wine.

Village Country Club (Private)
(805) 733-3537
5 mi n via SR 1 and Burton Mesa Bl at 4300 Clubhouse Rd, 93436 (A-3).
Closed Jan 1 and Dec 25.

The course is 18 holes; 6269 yards; par 72; 118 slope; 69.6 rating. Rates: $30 weekdays, $40 weekends. Clubhouse, locker room, golf shop, professional, power and hand carts, rental clubs, driving range; tennis, swimming; restaurant, coffee shop, snack bar, cocktails.

VANDENBERG
AIR FORCE BASE

Marshallia Ranch Golf Course
(Semi-private)
(805) 734-4764
4 mi n of main gate off Lompoc Casmalia Rd; PO Box 5938, 93437.
Closed Mon, Jan 1 and Dec 25.

The course is 18 holes; 6388 yards; par 72; 122 slope; 71.1 rating. Rates: $30 weekdays, $50 weekends. Clubhouse, locker room, golf shop, professional, power and hand carts, rental clubs, driving range; snack bar.

Santa Maria Valley

SANTA MARIA

Rancho Maria Golf Club (Public)
(805) 937-2019
5 mi w of US 101 off Clark Rd at 1950 Casmalia Rd (SR 1), 93455 (N-1).

The course is 18 holes; 6150 yards; par 72; 109 slope; 68.7 rating. Rates: $18 weekdays, $24 weekends. Golf shop, professional, power and hand carts, rental clubs, driving range; coffee shop, cocktails.

Santa Maria Country Club (Private)
(805) 937-2027
1½ mi w of US 101 off Santa Maria Wy at 505 W Waller Ln, 93455 (J-4).
Closed Mon.

The course is 18 holes; 6270 yards; par 72; 122 slope; 70 rating. Rates: $50 weekdays and weekends. Clubhouse, locker room, golf shop, professional, power and hand carts, rental clubs, driving range; tennis, swimming; restaurant, coffee shop, snack bar, cocktails.

HIKING

The foothills and canyons in Santa Barbara County are inviting areas for hikers, and the trails listed here are among those that afford moderate to challenging hikes. The Los Padres chapter of the Sierra Club (covering both Santa Barbara and Ventura counties) sponsors group hikes planned for differing abilities and can provide further hiking information; call (805) 966-6622.

For those interested in more extensive hiking and backpacking, contact Los Padres National Forest headquarters at 6144 Calle Real, Goleta 93117, (805) 683-6711; Santa Barbara Ranger District, Star Route, Santa Barbara 93105, (805) 967-3481; or Santa Maria Ranger District, 1616 North Carlotti Drive, Santa Maria 93454, (805) 925-9538. Fire permits are issued on an annual basis and are required for backcountry camping during fire season.

Los Padres National Forest

Map coordinates refer to the *Santa Barbara County* map, unless noted otherwise.

Aliso Canyon Self-guided Nature Trail *begins about five miles east of Paradise Road and SR 154 junction behind Sage Hill Group Camp (H-11).* The trail is a three-mile, self-guided loop, with a moderately steep grade. Developed by 11- to 14-year-old students, the trail offers beautiful views and is a good introduction to local natural history.

Cold Springs Trail *begins about ½ mile east of Cold Springs Road and Mountain Drive junction (B-19, Santa Barbara and Vicinity city map on the* Cities of Santa Barbara County *street map).* The trail runs 4½ miles to East Camino Cielo. The grade is moderate to steep, with a starting elevation of 750 feet and an elevation gain of 2650 feet. At the lower level the trail borders a creek that is filled most of the year and has lovely pools.

Davy Brown Trail *begins off Figueroa Mountain Road near the Figueroa campground (F-9).* The steep trail follows a creek the length of Fir Canyon, passing an old mine shaft and remnants of a miner's cabin.

Hikers are advised to start at Figueroa Mountain Road and walk downhill to Davy Brown campground (meet transportation there). The trail winds through large stands of big cone fir, pine and sycamore, so it is well shaded even in summer. Davy Brown Trail connects with Munch Canyon Trail.

Jesusita Trail *begins just north of Cater Water Filtration Plant on San Roque Road, north of Foothill Road (B-15, Santa Barbara and Vicinity city map on the* Cities of Santa Barbara County *street map).* The trail runs three miles to Inspiration Point and another mile to intersect with Tunnel Trail. The grade is moderate, with a starting elevation of 400 feet and an elevation gain of 642 feet. At lower levels are large, old trees; upper levels present views of the city and Channel Islands.

Little Pine Mountain Trail *begins at Upper Oso campground, 22 miles northwest of Santa Barbara off SR 154 (H-11).* The five-mile trail gains 3260 feet of elevation from its start on a dirt road at the northeast end of Upper Oso campground to its summit next to a large, outstanding pine tree. Follow the dirt road for ¾ mile until it turns right. At the turn, continue straight to a sign reading "Santa Cruz Trail." From the sign, parallel Oso Creek for one mile through a canyon to the junction with a side trail to Nineteen Oaks Camp. Keep to the left, cross the stream and take switchbacks up a brush-covered slope. At ⅘ mile farther, the trail comes to a grassy meadow and follows a ridge line, then goes along the side of a rocky overhanging wall. After curving into a side canyon, the trail switchbacks up to another section of the brush-covered slope. Just short of 4 miles, the route intersects a path leading up to a spring. Continuing past the spring, the trail climbs through a large grassy area, then levels off to reach a junction and several trail signs. Turn right at the signs. Several hundred yards farther, the trail joins an old roadbed. Turn right upon reaching a wire fence, follow a small path to a meadow of deep grass and head straight across the area to the large pine tree.

McKinley Trail *begins at Cachuma Saddle, junction of Figueroa Mountain Road and Happy Canyon Road (F-9).* This trail follows an administrative road 10 miles past Cachuma Peak to a saddle west of McKinley Mountain, tracing the southern edge of the San Rafael Wilderness. The route offers good views of the Manzana drainage and Hurricane Deck to the north, and the Santa Ynez drainage to the south. Hikers should carry water because the only reliable source is at McKinley Spring trail camp, nine miles from Cachuma Saddle.

McPherson Peak Trail *begins at Aliso campground, 8 miles southwest of New Cuyama off SR 166 via Aliso Canyon Road (D-11).* The six-mile trail goes to the summit of McPherson Peak and involves an elevation gain of 3000 feet. Hikers should carry their own water because the only source, at Hog Pen Spring campground, is undependable and sometimes impure. The route begins at the southwest edge of Aliso campground and follows an old jeep road up a canyon for 2⅕ miles to Hog Pen Spring. Here a small tank may contain the only water on the mountain. Just beyond a boundary fence, a trail leads left (south) and begins

climbing chaparral-covered slopes. After the second switchback, the trail forks; the left branch is the best route up the mountain. At 4½ miles, the trail meets a fire road. Turn right and continue past a locked metal gate and some corrals. From this point, there are two options: continue northwest on the fire road for 1½ miles to a junction with a spur road, which leads to the right for about ¾ mile to the summit; or, climb directly up the ridge line from the corrals on a rutted old road past an abandoned campground for 1⅕ miles to the top.

Munch Canyon Trail *begins off Sunset Valley Road just east of Davy Brown campground (F-9).* Evidence of old mine excavations can be seen along this four-mile trail that was constructed as a mining access road. The trail connects with the Sunset Valley and Davy Brown trails.

Piño Alto Self-guided Nature Trail *begins two miles off Figueroa Mountain Road at the Pino Alto picnic area (F-9).* This easy, ½-mile trail forms a loop requiring 30 to 45 minutes to walk. A trail guide providing information about observation points along the way is available at the picnic area.

Rattlesnake Trail *begins at the bridge on Las Canoas Road, just north of Skofield Park (B-17, Santa Barbara and Vicinity city map on the* Cities of Santa Barbara County *street map).* The trail runs two miles to Tin Can Junction, then branches west to meet Tunnel Trail and east to Gibraltar Road; either fork is approximately three-quarters of a mile long. The grade is moderate, with starting elevation of 900 feet and an elevation gain of 1550 feet. During the spring a variety of wildflowers bloom along this trail. Note: It is advisable to carry drinking water.

Sulphur Springs Trail *begins at Cedros Saddle about 5½ miles north of Figueroa Mountain Road near Sulphur Spring (E-8)*. The two-mile trail to the south goes to Zaca Lake. The steep four-mile trail to the north travels from Cedros Saddle to Manzana Creek in the San Rafael Wilderness. The route drops 2100 feet as it passes through oak woodlands and areas of pine. A spring is located halfway between Cedros Saddle and Manzana Creek.

Sunset Valley Trail *parallels Sunset Valley Road from Sunset Valley southeast to Fish Creek Divide (F-9)*. The short, two-mile trail meanders through oak and pine trees and chaparral. The trail begins off the Munch Canyon Trail just south of Sunset Valley Road.

Tunnel Trail *begins at the locked gate at the north end of Tunnel Road (B-15, Santa Barbara and Vicinity city map on the* Cities of Santa Barbara County *street map)*. The trail runs five miles to East Camino Cielo; 1⅒ miles west on Camino Cielo is La Cumbre Peak Lookout. The grade is moderate to steep with a starting elevation of 900 feet and an elevation gain of 3000 feet. La Cumbre Peak, at an elevation of 3981 feet, is the highest point in the area immediately behind Santa Barbara. Note: Hikers should carry water and prepare for full sun since there is almost no shade along the trail.

Zaca Peak Trail *begins off Zaca Ridge Road about 4½ miles north of Figueroa Mountain Road (E-8)*.

The trail follows a ridge west for two miles from Zaca Ridge Road, with the west end of the trail dropping down to Zaca Lake. Good views of the Santa Ynez Valley and Zaca Lake basin are found along this route.

HORSEBACK RIDING

Santa Barbara County has a number of interesting trails for horseback riding. The following stables rent horses; call for rates and reservations. Pony rides for children are available at Waller County Park in Santa Maria.

Circle Bar B Ranch Stables *1800 Refugio Road 3½ miles north of US 101 (J-8, Santa Barbara County* map*)*. *(805) 968-3901*. Guides lead riders along mountain and canyon trails on Circle Bar B Ranch. Open daily.

San Ysidro Stables *900 San Ysidro Lane (C-21, Santa Barbara and Vicinity city map on the* Cities of Santa Barbara *street map)*. *(805) 969-5046*. Escorts take riders on trails through the mountains. Open daily. Saturday is reserved for ranch guests only, but there may be some cancellations.

PICNICKING

All of the parks listed offer picnic tables; other amenities are noted. No fees are charged.

Santa Barbara Coast

Map coordinates refer to the Santa Barbara and Vicinity city map on the *Cities of Santa Barbara County* street map.

CARPINTERIA

Rincon Beach County Park *about 2 miles south of Carpinteria, off US 101 at the Santa Barbara and Ventura county lines (K-15,* Santa Barbara County *map).*

GOLETA

Goleta Beach County Park *adjacent to the Santa Barbara Municipal Airport and the University of California at Santa Barbara (E-8).* Fishing pier. Children's play area.

Lake Los Carneros County Park *off Los Carneros Road north of US 101 (C-7).* Includes South Coast Railroad Museum and Stow House.

Stow Grove County Park *borders La Patera Lane running south from Cathedral Oaks Road (C-8).* Barbecues. Children's play area.

MONTECITO

Manning County Park *one mile north of US 101 off San Ysidro Road (D-20).* Barbecues. Children's play area.

SANTA BARBARA

Arroyo Burro Beach County Park *½ mile southwest of Las Positas Road and Cliff Drive junction (F-13).*

Bohnett Park *600 West Anapamu Street (E-15).* Barbecues.

Chase Palm Park *Cabrillo Boulevard, foot of Santa Barbara Street (E-17).*

Dwight Murphy Field *Punta Gorda Street and Los Niños Drive junction (E-18).*

East Beach *Cabrillo Boulevard, foot of Por la Mar Drive (E-18).* Barbecues.

Eastside Neighborhood Park *junction Soledad and Yanonali streets (D-17).* Barbecues.

Franceschi Park *1510 Mission Ridge Road (C-16).* Good city view.

Hilda Ray Park *1400 Kenwood Road (E-15).* Barbecues.

Leadbetter Beach *West Cabrillo Boulevard and Loma Alta Drive (F-16).* Barbecues.

MacKenzie Park *corner State Street and Las Positas Road (C-14).* Barbecues.

Oak Park *300 West Alamar Avenue (D-15).* Barbecues. Children's wading pool open during summer.

Ortega Park *600 East Ortega Street (D-17).* Barbecues. Children's wading pool open during summer.

Rocky Nook County Park *Mission Canyon Road just north of Mountain Drive near the Santa Barbara Museum of Natural History (C-16).* Barbecues. Children's play area.

San Antonio Canyon County Park *San Antonio Creek Road just north of Cathedral Oaks Road (B-11).* Children's play area.

Shoreline Park *junction La Marina and Shoreline Drive (F-16).* Barbecues.

Skofield Park *1819 Las Canoas Road (B-16).* Barbecues.

Stevens Park *258 Canon Drive (B-14).* Barbecues.

West Beach *Cabrillo Boulevard, foot of Chapala Street (E-17).* Children's wading pool open during summer.

Willowglen Park *600 Willowglen Road (C-14).*

SUMMERLAND

Lookout Beach County Park *on the edge of Summerland between US 101 and the ocean (E-22).* Barbecues.

Santa Ynez Valley

Listings for Hans Christian Andersen Park, Lake Cachuma County Park, Nojoqui Falls County Park and Zaca Lake can be found in the *Points of Interest* section.

Many wineries in the valley also have picnic tables. Map coordinates refer to the Santa Ynez Valley city map on the *Cities of Santa Barbara County* street map, unless noted otherwise.

Los Alamos County Park *off Drum Canyon Road in Los Alamos (F-5, Santa Barbara County map).* Barbecues. Children's play area.

Los Olivos Park *center of town (B-7). Santa Ynez County Park off SR 246 on Cuesta Road (G-10).* Barbecues. Children's play area.

Lompoc Valley

A listing for Jalama Beach County Park can be found in the *Points of Interest* section.

Formerly a hideout for bandits in the early 1800s, Los Alamos County Park today lies amidst oak and maple trees and offers picnicking and other activities.

Map coordinates refer to the Lompoc city map on the *Cities of Santa Barbara County* street map.

Beattie Park *Olive Avenue and 5th Street (H-4).*

Johns-Manville Park *Chestnut Avenue and A Street (G-3).*

Miguelito County Park *3½ miles south of Lompoc on Miguelito Road (G-3). Barbecues. Children's play area.*

Ocean Beach County Park *13 miles northwest of Lompoc on Vandenberg Air Force Base at end of Ocean Avenue (F-1).*

Pioneer Park *Pine Avenue and 5th Street (G-4). Barbecues.*

Ryon Memorial Park *Ocean Avenue and O Street (H-2). Barbecues. Children's play area.*

Santa Rosa County Park *8½ miles west of Buellton off Santa Rosa Road (G-5). Children's play area.*

Santa Ynez River Park *SR 246 and River Park Road (F-4). Barbecues. Children's fishing pond.*

Spaceport Museum Park *north end of Lompoc off SR 1 (D-2). Barbecues.*

Thompson Park *College Avenue and R Street (G-2). Barbecues.*

Westvale Park *West Fir Avenue between T and U streets (H-1).*

Santa Maria Valley

A listing for Waller County Park can be found in the *Points of Interest* section.

Map coordinates refer to the Santa Maria city map on the *Cities of Santa Barbara County* street map.

Adam Park *600 West Enos Drive (G-4). Barbecues.*

Armstrong Park *1120 East Fesler Street (E-6). Barbecues. Children's play area.*

Atkinson Park *1000 North Railroad Avenue (E-4). Barbecues. Children's play area.*

Buena Vista Park *300 West Park Avenue (F-5). Barbecues. Children's play area.*

Joe White Park *500 Palisade Drive (F-6). Barbecues. Children's play area.*

Le Roy County Park *just north of Guadalupe on Eleventh Street (C-2).*

Memorial Park *Pine and Tunnell streets (E-4). Barbecues. Children's play area.*

Oakley Park *1220 West Harding Avenue (E-4). Barbecues. Children's play area.*

Preisker Park *2301 North Broadway (C-5). Barbecues. Children's play area.*

Rice Park *700 East Vickie Avenue (E-6). Barbecues. Children's play area.*

Russell Park *200 South Russell Avenue (F-4). Children's play area.*

Simas Park *500 South McClelland Street (F-5). Children's play area.*

Tunnell Park *1151 North Palisade Drive (E-6). Barbecues. Children's play area.*

Los Padres National Forest

Richardson County Park *off SR 166 in New Cuyama (C-12).* Barbecues. Children's play area.

Toro Canyon County Park *northeast of Summerland off Toro Canyon Road (D-25, Santa Barbara and Vicinity city map on the* Cities of Santa Barbara County *street map).* Barbecues. Children's play area.

SKIN AND SCUBA DIVING

The most popular skin and scuba diving areas along Santa Barbara County's coastline are off Arroyo Burro County Beach, Carpinteria, Refugio State Beach, Shoreline Park and at the foot of Butterfly Lane. A valid California sportfishing license is required to spearfish in the waters off the mainland and the islands.

RENTALS

Rental equipment, air refills and information on water conditions are available at the establishments listed below. Map coordinates refer to the Santa Barbara and Vicinity city map on the *Cities of Santa Barbara County* street map.

Bob's Diving Locker *500-B Botello Road, Goleta (D-8). (805) 967-4456.* Open Monday through Saturday 10 a.m. to 6 p.m. Closed major holidays.

Divers Den *22 Anacapa Street, Santa Barbara (E-17). (805) 963-8917.* Open Monday through Friday 9 a.m. to 6 p.m., Saturday and Sunday 10 a.m. to 5 p.m.; closed New Year's Day, Thanksgiving and Christmas.

Santa Barbara Aquatics *5370 Hollister Avenue, Goleta (D-10). (805) 964-8680.* Open Monday through Friday 10 a.m. to 6:30 p.m., Saturday and Sunday 9 a.m. to 5:30 p.m. Closed major holidays.

Underwater Sports *at the Breakwater, Santa Barbara (F-17). (805) 962-5400.* Open Monday through Friday 9 a.m. to 6 p.m., Saturday and Sunday 8 a.m. to 5:30 p.m. Closed New Year's Day, Thanksgiving and Christmas.

SURFING

Surfing in the Santa Barbara Coast area is best at Rincon Point, three miles south of Carpinteria. This spot is particularly good during the winter, when surf averages from two to four feet with swells to 12 feet during storms. A designated surfing zone at Refugio State Beach usually has winter surf from three to six feet. Surfing is also possible at El Capitan State Beach and Arroyo Burro Beach. Farther north, surfing is good at Tarantula Point, ½ mile south of Jalama Beach County Park near Lompoc and at Rancho Guadalupe Dunes County Park, west of Santa Maria.

SWIMMING

Calm waters off the county's south-facing beaches provide good ocean swimming, but west-facing shores north of Point Conception receive high winds and severe riptides that make swimming dangerous. Daily lifeguard service in summer is provided at East, West and Leadbetter beaches in the city of Santa Barbara; at state park beaches along the coast; at Arroyo Burro, Goleta and Lookout Park county beaches; and at Carpinteria City Beach (no lifeguard at Isla Vista and Rincon Beach county parks). Day-use fee at all state park beaches is $6 per vehicle. Swimming in Lake Cachuma is prohibited; but two swimming pools are open in summer (see listing).

East Beach Fitness Center *1118 E. Cabrillo Boulevard (E-18, Santa Barbara and Vicinity city map on the* Cities of Santa Barbara County *street map). (805) 965-0509*. This facility has showers, dressing rooms, a weight-lifting room and lockers available for a daily fee. Beach equipment rentals are available; the center provides access to 14 beach volleyball courts. Snack bar. Hours are Monday through Friday 8 a.m. to 5 p.m.; Saturday, Sunday and holidays 10 a.m. to 5 p.m. during the summer and 11 a.m. to 4 p.m. rest of year.

Public Swimming Pools

Santa Barbara Coast

Los Baños del Mar Pool *401 Shoreline Drive (E-17, Santa Barbara and Vicinity city map on the* Cities of Santa Barbara County *street map). (805) 966-6110*. This public pool is open for recreational swimming during summer months only, Monday through Friday 1:45 to 3:45 p.m.; Saturday, Sunday and holidays 1:15 to 5 p.m. Fees are $2 adults, $1 ages 17 and under. Adults can swim laps daily year-round; call for hours.

Santa Ynez Valley

Lake Cachuma County Park *off SR 154 (G-9, Santa Barbara County map). (805) 688-4658*. Although swimming in the lake is prohibited, two pools within the recreational area are open during the summer. Admission to the recreational area is $3.50 per vehicle per day.

Lompoc

Lompoc Municipal Pool *Ocean Avenue and C Street (G-3, Lompoc city map on the* Cities of Santa Barbara County *map). (805) 735-5050*. This indoor pool is open for recreational swimming on Monday, Wednesday and Friday from 7:30 to 8:45 p.m.; Saturday and Sunday from 1 to 3:45 p.m.; and Saturday evening from 7 to 8:45 p.m. Fee is $2 adults, $1 children.

Santa Maria

Map coordinates refer to the Santa Maria city map on the *Cities of Santa Barbara County* street map.

Allan Hancock College *800 South College Drive (F-6). (805) 922-6966, ext. 3227*. The swimming pool is open daily for public use in the summer months; call for schedule.

Paul Nelson Municipal Pool *516 South McClelland Street (F-5). (805) 925-0951, ext. 248*. The pool is open for public swimming Monday through Friday during summer and for lap swimming all year Monday through Saturday. Hours are limited in spring and fall; call for schedule.

TENNIS

The following tennis courts are open all year and do not require permits or fees for public use, unless otherwise noted. Play at all courts is on a first-come, first-served basis when players are waiting, with a limit of 30 minutes for an individual, one hour for singles and 1½ hours for doubles.

Santa Barbara Coast

Map coordinates refer to the Santa Barbara and Vicinity city map on the *Cities of Santa Barbara County* street map, unless noted otherwise.

MONTECITO

Manning County Park *one mile north of US 101 off San Ysidro Road (D-20).* One court.

SANTA BARBARA

A $2 daily permit is required for each player 18 years of age and over to use the following public tennis facilities in the city of Santa Barbara. Permits can be purchased at the courts.

Las Positas Courts *1002 Las Positas Road (E-14).* Six lighted tennis courts.

Municipal Tennis Center *1414 Park Place (D-18).* 12 courts.

Pershing Park *100 Castillo Street at Cabrillo Boulevard junction (E-16).* Eight courts.

The following facility in the city of Santa Barbara does not require a permit.

Oak Park *300 W. Alamar Avenue at Quinto Street (D-15).* Two courts.

Santa Ynez Valley

SOLVANG

Hans Christian Andersen Park *off Atterdag Road, three blocks north of Mission Drive (H-5, Santa Ynez Valley city map on the* Cities of Santa Barbara County *street map).* Four tennis courts.

Lompoc Valley

LOMPOC

Ryon Memorial Park *Ocean Avenue and O Street (H-2, Lompoc city map on the* Cities of Santa Barbara County *street map).* Two lighted tennis courts.

Santa Maria Valley

SANTA MARIA

Map coordinates refer to the Santa Maria city map on the *Cities of Santa Barbara County* street map.

Allan Hancock College *800 South College Drive (F-6).* (805) 922-6966, ext. 3227. Six lighted tennis courts are open daily in summer, weekends only the rest of year, with limited access at night during the school term. Call for availability.

Atkinson Park *1000 North Railroad Avenue (E-4).* Four lighted tennis courts.

Minami Community Center *600 West Enos Drive (G-4).* Six lighted tennis courts.

Lodgings and Restaurant Listings

The lodging and restaurant properties listed in these pages have been inspected at least once in the past year by a trained representative of the Automobile Club of Southern California. In surprise inspections, each property was found to meet AAA's extensive and detailed requirements for approval. These requirements are reflective of current industry standards and the expectations of the traveling public. Less than two-thirds of the lodging establishments open for business are listed in AAA publications.

Virtually all listings include AAA's esteemed diamond rating, reflecting the overall quality of the establishment. Many factors are considered in the process of determining the diamond rating. In lodging properties, the facility is first classified according to its physical design—is it a motel, a hotel, a resort, an apartment, etc. Since the various types of lodging establishments offer differing amenities and facilities, rating criteria are specific for each classification. For example, a motel, which typically offers a room with convenient parking and little if any recreational or public facilities, is rated using criteria designed only for motel-type establishments—it is not compared to a hotel with its extensive public and meeting areas, or to a resort with its wide range of recreational facilities and programs. The diamonds do, however, represent standard levels of quality in all types of establishments.

There is no charge for a property to be listed in AAA publications. Many lodgings and restaurants, however, choose to advertise their AAA approval by displaying the ⬥ emblem on the premises and using it in their advertising. These properties are especially interested in serving AAA members.

Properties are listed alphabetically under the nearest town, with lodging facilities first and restaurants second. The location is given from the center of town or from the nearest major highway.

Nearly all lodging and restaurant facilities accept credit cards as forms of payment for services rendered. The following symbols are used to identify the specific cards accepted by each property.

AE	American Express
CB	Carte Blanche

DI	Diner's Club International
DS	Discover
ER	En Route (European)
JCB	Japanese Credit Bureau
MC	MasterCard
VI	VISA

Some lodgings and restaurants listed in Auto Club publications have symbols indicating that they are accessible to individuals with disabilities. The criteria used in qualifying these listings are consistent with, but do not represent the full scope of, the Americans with Disabilities Act of 1990. AAA does not evaluate recreational facilities, banquet rooms or convention and meeting facilities for accessibility. Individuals with disabilities are urged to phone ahead to fully understand an establishment's facilities and accessibility.

In accommodations, a 🚷 indicates that at least one fully accessible guest room exists and that an individual with mobility impairments will be able to park and enter the building, register, and use at least one food and beverage outlet. For restaurants, the symbol indicates that parking, dining rooms and rest rooms are accessible.

The 🚷 at the end of a lodging listing means that the following elements are provided: closed captioned decoders; text telephones; visual notification for fire alarms, incoming phone calls and door knocks; and, phone amplification devices.

LODGING

The following accommodations classifications appear in this book.

Bed & Breakfast—Usually a small establishment emphasizing personal attention. Individually decorated guest rooms provide an at-home feeling and may lack some amenities such as TVs, phones, etc. Usually owner-operated with a common room or parlor where guests and owners can interact during evening and breakfast hours. May have shared bathrooms. A continental or full hot breakfast is included in the room rate.

Complex—A combination of two or more kinds of lodgings.

Cottage—Individual bungalow, cabin or villa, usually containing one rental unit equipped for housekeeping. May have a separate living room and bedroom(s). Parking is usually at each unit.

Country Inn—Similar in definition to a bed and breakfast. Offers a dining room reflecting the ambience of the inn. At a minimum, breakfast and dinner are served.

Hotel—A multi-story building usually including a coffee shop, dining room, lounge, room service, convenience shops, valet, laundry and full banquet/meeting facilities. Parking may be limited.

Lodge—Typically two or more stories with all facilities in one building. Located in vacation, ski, fishing areas, etc. Usually has food and beverage service. Adequate on-premises parking.

Motel—Usually one or two stories; food service, if any, consists of a limited facility or snack bar. Often has a pool or playground. Ample parking, usually near the guest room door.

Motor Inn—Usually two or three stories, but may be a high-rise. Generally has recreation facilities, food service and ample parking. May have limited banquet/meeting facilities.

Apartment—Usually four or more stories with at least half the units equipped for housekeeping. Often in a vacation destination area. Units typically provide a full kitchen, living room and one or more bedrooms, but may be studio-type rooms with kitchen equipment in an alcove. May require a minimum stay and/or offer discounts for longer stays. This classification may also modify any of the other lodging types.

Condominium—A destination property located in a resort area. Guest units consist of a bedroom, living room and kitchen. Kitchens are separate from bedrooms and are equipped with a stove, oven or microwave, refrigerator, cooking utensils and table settings for the maximum number of people occupying the unit. Linens and maid service are provided at least twice weekly. This classification may also modify any of the other lodging types.

Historic—Accommodations in restored, pre-1930 structures, reflecting the ambience of yesteryear and the surrounding region. Rooms may lack some modern amenities and have shared baths. Usually owner-operated and provides food service. Parking is usually available. This classification may also modify any of the other lodging types.

Resort—May be a destination in itself. Has a vacation atmosphere offering extensive recreational facilities for such specific interests as golf,

tennis, fishing, etc. Rates may include meals under American or Modified American plans. This classification may also modify any of the other lodging types.

Suite—Units have one or more bedrooms and a living room, which may or may not be closed off from the bedrooms. This classification may also modify any of the other lodging types.

A property's **diamond rating** is not based on the room rate or any one specific aspect of its facilities or operations. Many factors are considered in calculating the rating, and certain minimum standards must be met in all inspection categories. If a property fails approval in just one category, it is not listed in Club publications. The inspection categories include housekeeping, maintenance, service, furnishings and decor. Guest comments received by AAA may also be reviewed in a property's approval and rating process.

These criteria apply to all properties listed in this publication:

- Clean and well-maintained facilities

- Hospitable staff

- Adequate parking

- A well-kept appearance

- Good quality bedding and comfortable beds with adequate illumination

- Sturdy locks on all doors and windows

- Comfortable furnishings and attractive decor

- Smoke detectors

- Adequate towels and supplies

- At least one comfortable easy chair with adequate illumination
- A desk or other writing surface with adequate illumination

Lodging ratings range from one to five diamonds and are defined below:

◆—Good but unpretentious. Establishments are functional. Clean and comfortable rooms must meet the basic needs of privacy and cleanliness.

◆◆—Shows noticeable enhancements in decor and/or quality of furnishings over those at the one-diamond level. May be recently constructed or an older property. Targets the needs of a budget-oriented traveler.

◆◆◆—Offers a degree of sophistication with additional amenities, services and facilities. There is a marked upgrade in services and comfort.

◆◆◆◆—Excellent properties displaying high levels of service and hospitality and offering a wide variety of amenities and upscale facilities, inside the room, on the grounds and in the common areas.

◆◆◆◆◆—Renowned for an exceptionally high degree of service, striking and luxurious facilities and many extra amenities. Guest services are provided in a flawless manner. Guests are pampered by a very professional, attentive staff. The property's facilities and operations set standards in hospitality and service.

Occasionally a property is listed without a rating, such as when an establishment is under construction or renovations are in progress and a rating cannot be determined.

Room rates shown in the listings are provided by each establishment's management for publication by the Auto Club. During special events or holiday periods rates may exceed those published and special discounts or savings programs may not be honored. High-season rates are always shown; off-season rates are listed if they are substantially lower than the rest of the year. Rates are for typical rooms, not special units, and do not include taxes.

Three **rate options** are listed. Listings stating *Rates Subject to Change* mean that the published rates may be changed by the establishment during the life of the publication. The two other rate options are available only to AAA members who identify themselves as such upon registration and request the listed rate option. Where a listing says *Rates Guaranteed*, the management has agreed to honor the published rates for AAA members. The third rate option, *AAA Special Value Rates*, gives AAA members at least 10 percent off the published rates. Some properties offer discounts to senior citizens, or special rate periods such as weekly or monthly rentals. Inquiries as to the availability of any special discounts should be made at the time of registration. Typically, a property will allow a guest to take advantage of only one discount during their stay (i.e., a guest staying at a property offering both the *AAA Special Value Rates* and Senior Discount may choose only one of the two savings plans).

Each rate line gives the dates for which the rates are valid, and the rates for one person (abbreviated 1P), two persons with one bed (2P/1B), two persons with two beds (2P/2B), and the rate for each extra person (XP) not included in the family rate. Figures following these abbreviations are the price(s) for the specified room and occupants. Most rates listed are European plan, which means that no meals are included in the rate. Some lodgings' rates include breakfast [BP] or continental breakfast [CP]. At a few properties you will find the American Plan [AP] which includes three meals, or a Modified American Plan [MAP] which offers two meals, usually breakfast and dinner.

All baths have a combination tub and shower bath unless noted otherwise. Since nearly all establishments have air conditioning, telephones and color TV, only the absence of any of these items is noted in the listing. Check-in time is shown only if it is after 3 p.m.; check-out time is shown only if it is before 10 a.m. Service charges are not shown unless they are $1 or more, or at least five percent of the room rate. If the pet acceptance policy varies within the establishment, no mention of pets is made. By U.S. and Canada laws, pet restrictions do not apply to guide dogs. A heated pool is heated when it is reasonable to expect use of a pool. Outdoor pools may not open in winter.

Reservations are always advisable in resort areas and may be the only way to assure obtaining the type of accommodations you want. Deposits are almost always required. Should your plans change and you need to cancel your reservation, be aware of the amount of notice required to receive a refund of your deposit.

Many properties welcome children in the same room with their parents at no additional charge; individual listings indicate if there is an age limit. There may be charges for additional equipment, such as roll-aways or cribs. Some properties offer a discount for guests ages 60 and older— be aware that the Senior Discount cannot usually be taken in conjunction with other discounts.

Fire warning and protection equipment are indicated by the symbols D (all guest rooms have smoke detectors) and S (all guest rooms have sprinklers). Many properties have reserved rooms for non-smokers; look for the ⊘ symbol in the listing and be sure to request a non-smoker room both when you make a reservation and upon registration.

RESTAURANTS

Restaurants listed in this publication have been found to be consistently good dining establishments. In metropolitan areas, where many restaurants are above average, we select some of those known for the superiority of their food, service and atmosphere and also those offering a selection of quality food at moderate prices (including some cafeterias and family restaurants). In smaller communities the restaurants considered to be the best in the area may be listed.

The type of cuisine featured at a restaurant is used as a means of classification for restaurants. You will find listings for steakhouses and continental cuisine as well as a range of ethnic foods, such as Chinese, Japanese, Italian and yes, American. Special menu types, such as early bird, a la carte, children's or Sunday brunch, are also listed. We have tried to indicate something about each restaurant's atmosphere and appropriate attire. The availability of alcoholic beverages is shown, as well as entertainment and dancing.

Price ranges are indicated for an average, complete dinner without alcoholic beverage; taxes and tips are not included.

Restaurant ratings are applied to two categories of operational style—full-service eating establishments, and self-service, family-dining operations such as cafeterias or buffets.

◆—Good but unpretentious dishes. Table settings are usually simple and may include paper placemats and napkins. Alcoholic beverage service, if any, may be limited to beer and wine. Usually informal with an atmosphere conducive to family dining.

◆◆—More extensive menus representing more complex food preparation and, usually, a wider variety of alcoholic beverages. The atmosphere is appealing and suitable for either family or adult dining. Service may be casual, but host or hostess seating can be expected. Table settings may include tablecloths and cloth napkins.

◆◆◆—Extensive or specialized menus and a more complex cuisine preparation requiring a professional chef contribute to either a formal dining experience or a special family meal. Cloth table linens, above-average quality table settings, a skilled service staff and an inviting decor should all be provided. Generally, the wine list includes representatives of the best domestic and foreign wine-producing regions.

◆◆◆◆—An appealing ambience is often enhanced by fresh flowers and fine furnishing. The overall sophistication and formal atmosphere visually create a dining experience more for adults than for families. A wine steward presents an extensive list of the best wines. A smartly attired, highly skilled staff is capable of describing how any dish is prepared. Elegant silverware, china and correct glassware are typical. The menu includes creative dishes prepared from fresh ingredients by a chef who frequently has international training. Eye-appealing desserts are offered at tableside.

◆◆◆◆◆—A superb operation with even more luxury and sophistication than four-diamond restaurants. A proportionally large staff, expert in preparing tableside delicacies, provides flawless service. Tables are set with impeccable linens, silver and crystal glassware.

Santa Barbara Coast

CARPINTERIA

Lodging

Best Western Carpinteria Inn    Motor Inn   ◆◆
(805) 684-0473; FAX (805) 684-4015   *Rates Subject to Change*

10/2-4/30	1P 85.00 -105.00	2P/1B 89.00 -109.00	2P/2B 89.00 -109.00	XP ..10
5/1-10/1	1P 99.00 -119.00	2P/1B 109.00 -129.00	2P/2B 109.00 -129.00	XP ..10

Adjacent to US 101; northbound exit Santa Monica Rd, southbound exit Reynolds Av. 4558 Carpinteria Av (93013). 144 rooms; 3 stories; interior corridors; meeting rooms. Many rooms with patio or balcony surrounding landscaped garden area. Some smaller rooms. Cable TV. Fee for VCP. Small heated pool, whirlpool. Pets, $25 deposit required. Reservation deposit required in summer. AE, CB, DI, DS, ER, MC, VI. Dining room 7-10 am & 5-9:30-pm; $9-$18; cocktails.   D S ⊘

SANTA BARBARA

Lodging—Beach Area

Ambassador By The Sea    Motel   ◆◆
(805) 965-4577; FAX (805) 965-9937   *Rates Subject to Change*

10/2-4/30 [CP]	1P ...	2P/1B 58.00 -128.00	2P/2B 58.00 - 98.00	XP ..10
5/1-10/1 [CP]	1P ...	2P/1B 88.00 -158.00	2P/2B 88.00 -128.00	XP ..10

3 blks s of US 101, between Bath & Chapala sts. 202 W Cabrillo Bl (93101). 32 rooms; 2 stories; exterior corridors. 4 2-bedroom units. Kitchens, $20 extra. 2 sun decks with beach view. Across from beach. Shower or combination baths. Some refrigerators. No A/C. Heated pool. No pets. Reservation deposit required. AE, DI, DS, ER, MC, VI.   D ⊘

Best Western-El Patio Beachside Inn    Motor Inn   ♦♦
(805) 965-6556; FAX (805) 966-6626   *AAA Special Value Rates*

9/5-5/29	1P 71.00 -117.00	2P/1B 77.00 -133.00	2P/2B 97.00 -143.00	XP 8
5/30-9/4	1P 80.00 -126.00	2P/1B 86.00 -142.00	2P/2B 106.00 -152.00	XP 8

4 blks s of US 101. 336 W Cabrillo Bl at Castillo St (93101). 60 rooms. 3 stories; exterior corridors. Some smaller rooms; 3 2-bedroom units. Across from beach, yacht harbor & city park. Cable TV, free movies; coffeemakers; shower or combination baths. Some refrigerators. Fee for valet service. Heated pool. No pets. Children 12 and under stay free. Weekly & monthly rates available. Credit card guarantee. AE, CB, DI, DS, ER, JCB, MC, VI. Complimentary breakfast Mon.-Fri. Restaurant, see *Andria's Harborside Restaurant.* **(See ad below.)**   D ⊘

Coast Village Inn   Motel   ♦♦
(805) 969-3266   *Rates Subject to Change*

Fri-Sat 5/15-9/14 [CP]	1P 89.00 - 99.00	2P/1B 89.00 - 99.00	2P/2B 95.00 -105.00	XP 5
Sun-Thurs 5/15-9/14 & Fri-Sat 9/15-5/14 [CP]	1P 80.00 - 95.00	2P/1B 80.00 - 95.00	2P/2B 85.00 - 95.00	XP 5
Sun-Thurs 9/15-5/14 [CP]	1P 70.00 - 85.00	2P/1B 70.00 - 85.00	2P/2B 75.00 - 85.00	XP 5

In Montecito; adjacent to US 101, exit Olive Mill Rd. 1188 Coast Village Rd (93108). 25 rooms; 2 stories; exterior corridors. 2 kitchens. Smoke-free premises. Cable TV; shower or combination baths. No A/C. Heated pool. No pets. Children 12 and under stay free. Senior discount. Reservation deposit required. AE, MC, VI. Restaurant nearby. **(See ad below.)**   D ⊘

Fess Parker's Red Lion Resort

Motor Inn ♦♦♦♦

(805) 564-4333; FAX (805) 564-4964. *Rates Subject to Change*

All year [EP]   1P 195.00 -255.00   2P/1B 195.00 -295.00   2P/2B 195.00 -295.00   XP ..15

Check in 4 pm. 3 blks off US 101 via Milpas St. 633 E Cabrillo Bl (93103). 360 rooms; 3 stories; interior/exterior corridors; conference facilities; meeting rooms. Across from beach on spacious landscaped grounds. Balconies or patios. Cable TV, free & pay movies; bars, coffeemakers. Coin laundry. Heated pool, sauna, whirlpool, exercise room. Basketball court, shuffleboard; putting green; rental bicycles. Fee for 3 lighted tennis courts. Services: Airport transportation. Pets, $50 deposit. Children 17 and under stay free. Reservation deposit required. AE, DI, DS, ER, MC, VI. Coffee shop 6:30 am-11 pm; $7-$12; cocktails. **(See ad below.)**   D S ⊘

SANTA BARBARA: NOW 20% LESS OUTRAGEOUS.

Four Seasons Biltmore   Resort Complex   ◆◆◆◆
(805) 969-2261; FAX (805) 969-4212   *Rates Subject to Change*
All year   1P 290.00 -360.00   2P/1B 290.00 -360.00   2P/2B 290.00 -360.00   XP ..30
In Montecito; ½ mi s of US 101, exit Olive Mill Rd. 1260 Channel Dr (93108). 234 rooooms; 2 stories; interior/exterior corridors; meeting rooms. Large rooms in lodge & cottages. An elegant oceanfront resort on spacious, beautifully landscaped grounds. Spanish architecture. Garden or ocean views. Cable TV, free movies; bars; safes; no A/C. Secretarial services; valet laundry. 24-hour room service. 2 heated pools, saunas, whirlpools; exercise room; putting green; croquet court; shuffleboard court; bicycles. Beach. Fee for 3 lighted tennis courts; health club. Children's program. Pets in cottages only. Reservation deposit required. AE, DI, ER, JCB, MC, VI. Afternoon tea; entertainment. 2 dining rooms, restaurant; 6:30 am-10 pm, Fri & Sat to 11:30 pm; $14-$40; cocktails. **(See ad below.)**   Ⓓ ⊘

Franciscan Inn   Motel   ◆◆◆
(805) 963-8845; FAX (805) 564-3295   *Rates Subject to Change*

5/15-9/15
& Fri-Sat
9/16-5/14 [CP]   1P   65.00 - 85.00   2P/1B   75.00 -115.00   2P/2B   90/00 -145.00   XP 8
Sun-Thur
9/16-5-14 [CP]   1P   55.00 - 85.00   2P/1B   60.00 - 89.00   2P/2B   70.00 -145.00   XP 8

2½ blks s of US 101. 109 Bath St (93101). 53 rooms; 1-2 stories; exterior corridors. 4 2-bedroom units; 24 efficiencies. 1 blk to beach. Guest rooms have attractive country decor. 30 refrigerators; 13 A/C; cable TV, free movies; shower or combination baths. Fee for VCPs. Coin laundry. Heated pool, whirlpool. No pets. Weekly & monthly rates available. AE, CB, DI, ER, MC, VI. **(See ad below.)**   Ⓓ ⊘

Harbor View Inn ⊛   Motel   ◆◆◆
(805) 963-0780; FAX (805) 963-7967.   *Rates Subject to Change*
All year [CP]   1P   85.00 -215.00   2P/1B   85.00 -215.00   2P/2B 100.00 -165.00   XP ..15
3 blks s of US 101, ½ blk w of State St. 28 W Cabrillo Bl (93101). 64 rooms; 2-3 stories; interior/exterior corridors. 6 large ocean-view rooms with balcony, $200-$215. 2 2-bedroom units. Across from beach & Stearn's Wharf. Variety of room sizes; spacious, beautifully furnished rooms in newer wing. Cable TV; shower or combination baths. Some A/C; refrigerators. Heated pool; whirlpool. No pets. Reservation deposit required. AE, CB, DI, ER, MC, VI. Complimentary beverages each evening. Restaurant nearby. **(See ad below.)**   Ⓓ Ⓢ ⊘

Harbour Carriage House   Bed & Breakfast   ◆◆
(805) 962-8447   *AAA Special Value Rates*
All year [BP]   1P ...   2P/1B   85.00 -185.00   2P/2B 155.00   XP ..20
½ blk w of Castillo St. 420 W Montecito St (93101). 9 rooms; 2-3 stories; interior/exterior corridors. Smoke-free premises. Rooms in 1895 French country-style home & new carriage house. Shower or combination baths; no phones. Some A/C; whirlpools. No TVs. Many rooms with wood-burning fireplace. No pets. 2-day minimum stay weekends. Reservation deposit required; 5-day refund notice. AE, MC, VI. Complimentary beverages each evening.   Ⓓ ⊘

Kings Inn of Santa Barbara 🅐🅐   Motel   ◆◆
(805) 963-4471; FAX (805) 962-2633   *Rates Subject to Change*

6/15-9/30	1P 74.00 - 88.00	2P/1B 74.00 - 94.00	2B/2B 74.00 - 94.00 XP 6
10/1-6/14	1P 50.00 - 70.00	2P/1B 54.00 - 74.00	2B/2B 54.00 - 74.00 XP 6

1½ blks s of US 101. 128 Castillo St (93101). 45 rooms; 3 stories; interior/exterior corridors. Many rooms with patio or balcony. 2 blocks from beach; across the street from city park. Cable TV, free movies. Some refrigerators. Heated pool, saunas, whirlpool. No pets. Weekly & monthly rates available. Reservation deposit required. AE, CB, DI, MC, VI. **(See ad below.)**   Ⓓ ⊘

Marina Beach Motel 🅐🅐   Motel   ◆◆
(805) 963-9311; FAX (805) 564-4102   *Rates Subject to Change*

Fri-Sat 5/15-9/15 [CP]	1P 75.00 -135.00	2P/1B 75.00 -140.00	2P/2B 80.00 -200.00
Fri-Sat 9/16-5/14 [CP]	1P 55.00 -125.00	2P/1B 55.00 -125.00	2P/2B 55.00 -185.00
Sun-Thurs 5/15-9/15 [CP]	1P 55.00 - 95.00	2P/1B 55.00 -100.00	2P/2B 60.00 -145.00
Sun-Thurs 9/16-5/14 [CP]	1P 43.00 - 85.00	2P/1B 43.00 - 95.00	2P/2B 50.00 -130.00

21 Bath St (93101). 31 rooms; exterior corridors. 1 2-bedroom unit. ½ block to beach. 3 efficiencies; 15 kitchens. Cable TV; no A/C; coffeemakers; shower or combination baths. Some refrigerators; whirlpools. Bicycles. No pets. Senior discount. Children stay free. Weekly & monthly rates available. 2-night minimum stay weekends 5/15-9/15. Credit card guarantee. AE, CB, DI, DS, MC, VI.   Ⓓ ⊘

Mason Beach Inn ⒶⒶ
(805) 962-3203

Motel ♦♦

Rates Subject to Change

2/1-5/14 & 9/5-10/31	1P ...		2P/1B	58.00 -105.00	2P/2B	58.00 -105.00	XP	6
5/15-9/4	1P ...		2P/1B	68.00 -125.00	2P/2B	68.00 -125.00	XP	6
11/1-1/31	1P ...		2P/1B	55.00 - 95.00	2P/2B	55.00 - 95.00	XP	6

2 blks s of US 101; southbound exit Castillo St; northbound exit Cabrillo Bl, then n to Castillo St. 324 W Mason St (93101). 44 units; 2 rooms; interior corridors. 3 suites with microwave and refrigerator, $95-$145. 1 blk from beach. Contemporary decor. Cable TV. Some microwaves & refrigerators. Heated pool, whirlpool. No pets. Children 6 and under stay free. Weekly & monthly rates available. Credit card guarantee. AE, DI, DS, MC, VI. Ⓓ Ⓢ ∅

Montecito Inn ⒶⒶ
(805) 969-7854; FAX (805) 969-0623

Historic Hotel ♦♦♦

Rates Guaranteed

5/16-9/4 [CP]	1P 150.00 -165.00	2P/1B 150.00 -165.00	2P/2B 185.00
9/5-5/14 [CP]	1P 130.00 -145.00	2P/1B 130.00 -145.00	2P/2B 175.00

In Montecito; adjacent to US 101, exit Olive Mill Rd. 1295 Coast Village Rd (93108). 52 rooms; 4 stories; interior corridors; meeting rooms. Charming historic inn built in 1928. Located in center of town. Cable TV, free movies; shower or combination baths. Some refrigerators. No A/C. Heated pool, sauna, whirlpool; exercise room. Bicycles. Services: Valet laundry; valet parking. No pets. Reservation deposit required. AE, DI, DS, ER, MC, VI. Restaurant; 11:30 am-2:30 & 5:30-10 pm; $7-$14; cocktails. Ⓓ Ⓢ ∅

Old Yacht Club Inn ⒶⒶ
(805) 962-1277; FAX (805) 962-3989

Bed & Breakfast ♦♦

Rates Subject to Change

Fri-Sun & Mon-Thurs 6/1-9/30 [BP]	1P 85.00 -140.00	2P/1B 85.00 -145.00	2P/2B ...		XP ..30
Mon-Thurs 10/1-5/31 [BP]	1P 70.00 -115.00	2P/1B 75.00 -115.00	2P/2B ...		XP ..30

½ blk n of Cabrillo Bl. 431 Corona del Mar (93103). 9 rooms; 2 stories; interior/exterior corridors. 1 room with whirlpool tub & semi-private deck, $125-$135. 1912 California Craftsman and 1920 Early California homes in a residential area. Smoke-free premises. 2 blocks to beach. Shower or combination bath. No TVs; no A/C. Bicycles. 5-course gourmet dinner served most Saturday evenings; additional charge. No pets. Senior discount. 2-night minimum stay weekends. Package plans available. Reservation deposit required; 3-day refund notice. AE, DI, DS, MC, VI. Complimentary beverages each evening. Ⓓ ∅

Radisson Hotel Santa Barbara ⓐⓐ

Motor Inn ◆◆◆

(805) 963-0744; FAX (805) 962-0985 — *Rates Subject to Change*

5/27-10/10	1P 140.00 -215.00	2P/1B 140.00 -215.00	2P/2B 180.00 -215.00 XP ..20
2/6-5/26 & 10/11-11/20	1P 120.00 -195.00	2P/1B 120.00 -195.00	2P/2B 160.00 -195.00 XP ..20
11/21-2/5	1P 110.00 -180.00	2P/1B 110.00 -180.00	2P/2B 145.00 -180.00 XP ..20

2 blks e of Milpas St; southbound US 101 exit Milpas St; northbound exit Cabrillo Bl; 1111 E Cabrillo Bl (93103). Formerly Sheraton Santa Barbara Hotel. Check in 4 pm. 174 rooms; 3 stories; interior corridors; meeting rooms. Many ocean or mountain-view rooms. Few smaller rooms. 8 kitchens. Across from beach. Cable TV, fee for movies; bars; shower and combination baths. Heated pool. Fee for health club & message. Services: Valet laundry. No pets. Children 17 and under stay free. Senior discount. Reservation deposit required; 3-day refund notice. AE, CB, DI, DS, JCB, MC, VI. Restaurant; 6:30 am-10:30 pm; $11-$20; cocktails. Ⓓ Ⓢ ⊘

Santa Barbara Inn ⓐⓐ

Motor Inn ◆◆◆

(805) 966-2285; FAX (805) 966-6584 — *AAA Special Value Rates*

4/2-10/30	1P 149.00 -189.00	2P/1B 149.00 -189.00	2P/2B 149.00 -189.00 XP ..15
10/31-4/1	1P 99.00 -139.00	2P/1B 99.00 -139.00	2P/2B 99.00 -139.00 XP ..15

3 blks s of US 101, exit Milpas St. 901 Cabrillo Bl (93103). 71 rooms; 3 stories; interior/ exterior corridors; meeting rooms. 6 rooms with kitchen, $10 extra. Across from beach. Spacious rooms with ocean or mountain views. 3rd floor sun deck with ocean view. Refrigerators; cable TV; coffeemakers, refrigerators. Some A/C. Heated pool, whirlpool. Services: Valet laundry; valet parking. No pets. Children 16 and under stay free. Monthly & weekly rates available. AE, CB, DI, DS, MC, VI. Restaurant, see *Citronelle Restaurant*. Ⓓ Ⓢ ⊘

Summerland Inn ⓐⓐ

Motel ◆◆◆

(805) 969-5225 — *Rates Subject to Change*

Fri-Sat [CP]	1P 90.00 -120.00	2P/1B 100.00 -140.00	2P/2B 120.00 -140.00 XP ..15
Sun-Thurs [CP]	1P 55.00 - 90.00	2P/1B 65.00 - 90.00	2P/2B 80.00 - 90.00 XP ..15

Adjacent to US 101, northbound exit Evans St, southbound exit Summerland. 2161 Ortega Hill Rd (PO Box 1209, Summerland 93067). 11 rooms; 2 stories; interior/exterior corridors. Smoke-free premises. 2 units with gas fireplace. Charming country-inn decor. Cable TV; shower or combination baths. Some A/C. No pets. Senior discount. 2-night minimum stay weekends. Reservation deposit required; 3-day refund notice. AE, DI, DS, MC, VI. Ⓓ ⊘

Travelodge Santa Barbara Beach ⓐⓐ

Motel ◆◆

(805) 965-8527; FAX (805) 965-6125 — *Rates Subject to Change*

5/1-9/15	1P 70.00 -120.00	2P/1B 80.00 -120.00	2P/2B 95.00 -150.00 XP ..10
9/16-4/30	1P 60.00 - 95.00	2P/1B 65.00 - 95.00	2P/2B 75.00 -125.00 XP ..10

3 blks s of US 101. 22 Castillo St (93101). 19 rooms; exterior corridors. 4 rooms with patios. ½ blk from beach; across from city park. Cable TV, free movies; coffeemakers. No pets. Senior discount. Reservation deposit required. Restaurant nearby. AE, DI, DS, MC, VI. Ⓓ

Tropicana Harborside Inn 🅐🅐🅐   Motel   ♦♦
(805) 963-7851; FAX (805) 962-9428   *Rates Subject to Change*

5/27-9/30 [CP]	1P 75.00 - 99.00	2P/1B 75.00 - 99.00	2P/2B 85.00 -109.00	XP 5
10/1-1/31 [CP]	1P 72.00 - 96.00	2P/1B 72.00 - 96.00	2P/2B 82.00 -106.00	XP 5
2/1-5/26 [CP]	1P 65.00 - 89.00	2P/1B 65.00 - 89.00	2P/2B 75.00 - 99.00	XP 5

2 blks sw of US 101, 1 blk w of Castillo St. 433 W Montecito St (93101). Formerly Polynesian Inn. 41 rooms; 2 stories; exterior corridors. Smoke-free premises. 22 kitchens, $10
extra. Attractive country decor. 3 blocks to beach; within walking distance of city park.
Cable TV. No A/C. Coin laundry. Heated pool; whirlpool. No pets. Weekly & monthly
rates available. Reservation deposit required. AE, CB, DI, DS, MC, VI.   Ⓓ ⊘

Tropicana Inn & Suites 🅐🅐🅐   Motel   ♦♦♦
(805) 966-2219; FAX (805) 962-9428   *Rates Subject to Change*

5/27-9/30 [CP]	1P 92.00 -142.00	2P/1B 92.00 -142.00	2P/2B 102.00 -199.00	XP 5
10/1-1/31 [CP]	1P 88.00 -138.00	2P/1B 88.00 -138.00	2P/2B 98.00 -190.00	XP 5
2/1-5/26 [CP]	1P 82.00 -132.00	2P/1B 82.00 -132.00	2P/2B 92.00 -170.00	XP 5

Southbound US 101 exit Castillo St; northbound exit Cabrillo Bl, 3 mi w to Castillo St,
then 2½ blks n. 223 Castillo St (93101). 31 rooms. Smoke-free premises. 1 2-bedroom
unit. 1 large 2-bedroom suite with kitchen & dining room, $140-$199 for up to 8 persons.
Cozy country decor; park-like landscaping. 2 blocks to beach & harbor; adjacent to city
park. Cable TV; shower & combination baths; refrigerators. No A/C. Heated pool, whirlpool. No pets. Weekly & monthly rates available. AE, CB, DI, DS, MC, VI.   Ⓓ ⊘

Villa Rosa 🅐🅐🅐   Bed & Breakfast   ♦♦
(805) 966-0851; FAX (805) 962-7159   *Guaranteed Rates*

Fri-Sat & 7/1-9/30 [CP]	1P 90.00 -190.00	2P/1B 90.00 -190.00	2P/2B ...
Sun-Thurs 10/1-6/30 [CP]	1P 80.00 -160.00	2P/1B 80.00 -160.00	2P/2B ...

15 Chapala St. (93101) 18 rooms; 2 stories; interior corridors; meeting rooms. 2 rooms
with kitchenette & fireplace, $160-$190; without fireplace, $160-$165. Designated
smoking area. A classic 1930s Spanish-style building. 1 blk from beach. Rooms decorated in attractive southwest theme. No A/C; no phones. Some cable TV; efficiencies; refrigerators. Pool, whirlpool. Services: valet laundry. No pets. Children 14 and under stay
free. 2-night minimum stay weekends. Reservation deposit required; 5-day refund notice.
AE, MC, VI. Complimentary beverages each evening.   Ⓓ ⊘

West Beach Inn 🏧   Motel   ♦♦♦
(805) 963-4277; FAX (805) 564-4210   *Rates Subject to Change*

6/10-9/5 [CP]	1P 108.00 -158.00	2P/1B 108.00 -158.00	2P/2B 128.00 -158.00	XP ..15
2/1-6/9 [CP]	1P 79.00 -155.00	2P/1B 79.00 -155.00	2P/2B 99.00 -155.00	XP ..15
9/6-11/3 [CP]	1P 81.00 -155.00	2P/1B 81.00 -155.00	2P/2B 101.00 -155.00	XP ..15
11/4-1/31 [CP]	1P 81.00 -121.00	2P/1B 81.00 -121.00	2P/2B 101.00 -121.00	XP ..15

4 blks s of US 101. 306 W Cabrillo Bl at Bath St (93101). Check in 4 pm. 44 rooms; 2-3 stories; exterior corridors. 1 2-bedroom unit. 2 deluxe 1-bedroom apartments with kitchen, $147-$185 for up to 4 people. 1 2-bedroom apartment with fireplace & refrigerator, $187-$235 for up to 6 people. Across from yacht harbor & beach. Some patios or balconies. A/C; cable TV, free movies; refrigerators. Coin laundry. Heated pool, whirlpool. Services: Data ports. No pets. Weekly & monthly rates available. Reservation deposit required; 3-day refund notice. AE, CB, DI, MC, VI.   Ⓓ ⊘

Lodging—Inland Area

Bath Street Inn   Bed & Breakfast   ♦♦
(805) 682-9680   *AAA Special Value Rates*

Sun-Thurs 10/1-6/30 [BP]	1P 70.00 -125.00	2P/1B 75.00 -125.00	2P/2B 90.00	XP ..20
Fri-Sat All year & Sun-Thurs 7/1-9/30 [BP]	1P 90.00 -145.00	2P/1B 95.00 -150.00	2P/2B 115.00	XP ..20

2½ blks s of Mission St. 1720 Bath St (93101). 10 rooms. 3 stories; interior corridors. Smoke-free premises. 1 unit with fireplace & whirlpool bathtub. 1873 Queen Anne Victorian house in residential area. Shower or combination baths; refrigerators. Some cable TV, radios; phones; fee for whirlpools. No A/C. Bicycles. No pets. 2-night minimum stay weekends. Reservation deposit required; 3-day refund notice. AE, MC, VI. Complimentary beverages each evening.   Ⓓ ⊘

Bayberry Inn   Bed & Breakfast   ♦♦
(805) 682-3199; FAX (805) 962-0103   *Rates Subject to Change*

All year [BP]	1P 85.00 -135.00	2P/1B 85.00 -135.00	2P/2B ...

Corner of Valerio and Chapala sts. 111 W Valerio St (93101). 8 rooms. 2-stories; interior corridors. Smoke-free premises. 4 units with wood-burning fireplace. 1886 Federal-style house in residential area. No TV, no phones; shower or combination baths; some whirlpools. No A/C. Some cable TV hookups & telephone jacks. Bicycles. Small pets only. Weekly rates; 2-night minimum stay weekends. Reservation deposit required; 7-day refund notice. AE, DS, MC, VI.   Ⓓ ⊘

Best Western Encina Lodge ⓐⓐ   Motor Inn   ◆◆◆
(805) 682-7277; FAX (805) 563-9319   *AAA Special Value Rates*

All year   1P 102.00 -134.00   2P/1B 108.00 -138.00   2P/2B 108.00 -138.00   XP 6

½ mi n of US 101; exit Mission St. 1 blk s of Santa Barbara Cottage Hospital. 2220 Bath St (93105). 121 rooms. 33 1- & 2-bedroom kitchen apartments, 3 bi-level. Some patios & balconies. Spacious grounds. Cable TV, free movies; refrigerators; shower and combination baths; some A/C. Coin laundry. Heated pool, sauna, whirlpool. Services: Airport transportation. No pets. Reservation deposit required. AE, CB, DI, DS, ER, JCB, MC, VI. Restaurant; 7:30 am-9:30 pm; $11-$19; cocktails.   Ⓓ ⊘

Best Western Pepper Tree Inn ⓐⓐ   Motor Inn   ◆◆◆
(805) 687-5511; FAX (805) 682-2410   *Rates Subject to Change*

5/27-9/6 [CP]   1P 102.00 -124.00   2P/1B 102.00 -130.00   2P/2B 102.00 -130.00   XP 6
9/7-1/31 [CP]   1P 102.00 -120.00   2P/1B 102.00 -126.00   2P/2B 102.00 -126.00   XP 6
2/1-5/26 [CP]   1P 96.00 -114.00   2P/2B 96.00 -120.00   2P/2B 96.00 -120.00   XP 6

3½ mi nw, ½ mi e of jct US 101. 3850 State St (93105). 150 rooms; 2 stories; exterior corridors; meeting rooms. Attractively decorated rooms with patio or balcony. Located across from large shopping mall. Cable TV, free movies; refrigerators, coffeemakers; safes. Coin laundry. 2 heated pools, sauna, whirlpools. Services: Airport transportation. No pets. Reservation deposit required. AE, CB, DI, DS, ER, JCB, MC, VI. Restaurant; 6 am-9:30 pm; Fri & Sat to 11 pm; $9-$16; cocktails.   Ⓓ ⊘

Best Western South Coast Inn   Motel   ◆◆◆
(805) 967-3200; FAX (805) 683-4466   *Rates Subject to Change*

All year [CP]   1P 89.00 -150.00   2P/1B 94.00 -150.00   2P/2B 94.00 -150.00   XP ..10

Adjacent to US 101; between Patterson & Fairview avs exits. 5620 Calle Real (Goleta, 93117). 121 rooms; 2 stories; exterior corridors; meeting rooms. Rooms with 2 beds somewhat crowded. Nicely landscaped. Cable TV, free & pay movies. Some microwaves, refrigerators; radios; VCPs. Heated pool, whirlpool; ping pong table. No pets. Children 18 and under stay free. Credit card guarantee. AE, CB, DI, DS, MC, VI. Complimentary beverages each evening.   Ⓓ Ⓢ ⊘

Blue Quail Inn ⓐⓐ   Bed & Breakfast   ◆◆◆
(805) 687-2300   *Rates Subject to Change*

5/16-10/31
& Fri-Sun
11/1-5/15 [BP]   1P ...   2P/1B 82.00 -165.00   2P/2B ...   XP ..20
Mon-Thurs
11/1-5/15 [BP]   1P 66.00 -132.00   2P/1B 74.00 -149.00   2P/2B 86.00 -149.00   XP ..20

From US 101, northbound exit Arrellaga St; southbound exit Mission St. 1908 Bath St (93101). 9 rooms; interior/exterior corridors. Smoke-free premises. Attractively furnished rooms in main house & cottages on nicely landscaped grounds. No TV; no A/C; no phones. No pets. 2-night minimum stay weekends. Reservation deposit required; 3-day refund notice. AE, DI, DS, MC, VI. Complimentary beverages each evening.   Ⓓ ⊘

Cathedral Oaks Lodge 🆎   Motel   ◆◆◆
(805) 964-3511; FAX (805) 964-0075.   *Rates Subject to Change*
All year [CP]   1P 74.00 -110.00   2P/1B 84.00 -110.00   2P/2B 88.00 -110.00   XP ..10
5 mi nw on US 101; exit Turnpike Rd, 1 blk n. 4770 Calle Real (93110). 126 rooms; 2
stories; interior corridors; meeting rooms. 1 2-bedroom unit. Many rooms with balconies
or patios. Surrounding garden & lagoon area populated by Koi fish & ducks. Cable TV,
free movies; coffeemakers. Some refrigerators. Coin laundry. Heated pool, whirlpool. No
pets. Children 12 and under stay free. Reservation deposit required. AE, CB, DI, MC, VI.
Restaurant nearby.   D ⊘

The Cheshire Cat   Bed & Breakfast   ◆◆◆
(805) 569-1610   *Rates Subject to Change*
Fri-Sun [BP]   1P 119.00 -195.00   2P/1B 119.00 -249.00   2P/2B ...   XP ..25
Mon-Thurs [BP] 1P 75.00 -179.00   2P/1B 79.00 -190.00   2P/2B ...   XP ..25
Corner Chapala & Valerio sts. 36 W Valerio St (93101). 14 rooms. Smoke-free premises.
Large unit with separate living room, efficiency & large whirlpool tub $190-$249. 1800
Queen Anne & Victorian homes located in residential area. 3 fireplaces. Shower & comb
baths; no A/C. Some cable TV, radios; efficiencies, refrigerators; whirlpools. No pets. 2-
night minimum stay weekends. Reservation deposit required; 7-day refund notice. MC,
VI. **(See ad below.)**   D ⊘

Eagle Inn ⏺   Apartment Motel   ◆◆
(805) 965-3586; FAX (805) 966-1218   *Guaranteed Rates*

Fri-Sat 6/11-9/30 [CP]	1P 85.00 -110.00	2P/1B 85.00 -110.00	2P/2B 90.00 -120.00	XP 5
Fri-Sat 10/1-6/10 [CP]	1P 75.00 - 85.00	2P/1B 75.00 - 85.00	2P/2B 85.00 -110.00	XP 5
Sun-Thurs 6/11-9/30 [CP]	1P 65.00 - 70.00	2P/1B 65.00 - 70.00	2P/2B 70.00 - 95.00	XP 5
Sun-Thurs 10/1-6/10 [CP]	1P 50.00 - 60.00	2P/1B 50.00 - 60.00	2P/2B 60.00 - 75.00	XP 5

3 blks s of US 101. 232 Natoma Av at Bath St (93101). 17 rooms; 2 stories; interior corridors. Most apartments with fully equipped kitchens; 4 smaller units without kitchen have microwave, refrigerator & coffeemaker. 1½ blks to beach. Cable TV, free movies; no A/C; shower or combination baths; coffeemakers. Some microwaves, refrigerators. Coin laundry. No pets. Children 15 and under stay free. Senior discount. Weekly and monthly rates available. Reservation deposit required; 3-day refund notice. AE, DI, DS, MC, VI. Ⓓ

El Prado Motor Inn ⏺   Motel   ◆
(805) 966-0807; FAX (805) 966-6502   *Rates Subject to Change*

6/1-9/15 [CP]	1P 55.00 - 90.00	2P/1B 60.00 - 90.00	2P/2B 60.00 -100.00	XP 5
9/16-5/31 [CP]	1P 50.00 - 80.00	2P/1B 55.00 - 80.00	2P/2B 55.00 - 90.00	XP 5

1601 State St (93101). 66 rooms; 1-3 stories; meeting rooms. 6 2-bedroom units; 2 efficiencies, refrigerators. Some smaller rooms. Downtown location within walking distance of shops, restaurants & theaters. Cable TV, free movies; shower or combination baths. Valet laundry. Heated pool. No pets. Children 18 and under stay free. AE, DI, DS, MC, VI.   Ⓓ ⊘

The Glenborough Inn ⏺   Bed & Breakfast   ◆◆
(805) 966-0589; FAX (805) 564-2369   *Rates Subject to Change*

5/21-9/5 & Fri-Sat 9/6-5/20 [BP]	1P 70.00 -170.00	2P/1B 75.00 -170.00	2P/2B ...	XP ..25
Sun-Thurs 9/6-5/20 [BP]	1P 70.00 -140.00	2P/1B 70.00 -140.00	2P/2B ...	XP ..25

1327 Bath St (93101). 11 rooms; 2 stories; exterior corridors. 3 suites with fireplace. Smoke-free premises. 3 homes built in 1880s & early 1900s. Located in residential area. No TVs; no A/C. Whirlpool; bicycles. No pets. 2-night minimum stay weekends. Reservation deposit required; 3-day refund notice. AE, CB, DI, MC, VI. Complimentary beverages each evening.   Ⓓ ⊘

Hacienda Motel ⏺   Motel   ◆
(805) 687-6461   *Rates Subject to Change*

6/16-9/14	1P 54.00 - 69.00	2P/1B 54.00 - 74.00	2P/2B 64.00 - 79.00	XP 5
9/15-6/15	1P 44.00 - 54.00	2P/1B 44.00 - 64.00	2P/2B 49.00 - 69.00	XP 5

3643 State St (93105). 31 rooms. 2 stories; exterior corridors. On busy commercial strip. Pleasantly decorated rooms, most with large closets & bathrooms. 26 refrigerators. 5 kitchens. Cable TV, free movies; shower or combination baths; some refrigerators. No A/C. No pets. Senior discount. Reservation deposit required. AE, DS, MC, VI.   Ⓓ

Holiday Inn-Santa Barbara/Goleta   Motor Inn   ♦♦
(805) 964-6241; FAX (805) 964-6241   *Rates Subject to Change*
All year   1P 86.00 -125.00   2P/1B 96.00 -135.00   2P/2B 96.00 -135.00   XP ..10
7 mi nw adjacent to US 101; between Patterson & Fairview avs exits. 5650 Calle Real
(Goleta 93117). 154 rooms; 2 stories; exterior corridors; meeting rooms. Cable TV, fee for
movies. Heated pool. Services: Valet laundry; airport transportation. Pets. AE, DI, DS,
MC, VI. Dining room; 6 am-2 & 5-10 pm; $8-$15; cocktails.   Ⓓ ⊘

Inn on Summer Hill 🅰🅰   Bed & Breakfast   ♦♦♦♦
(805) 969-9998; FAX (805) 969-9998   *Rates Subject to Change*
All year   1P 160.00- 275.00   2P/1B 160.00 -275.00   2P/2B 170.00 -195.00   XP ..20
N side of US 101; northbound exit Evans St; southbound exit Summerland then ½ mi e.
2520 Lillie Av (Summerland 93067). 16 rooms; 2 stories; exterior corridors. Beautifully
decorated rooms in an English country motif. Ocean view. Smoke-free premises. Gas
fireplaces. Cable TV, VCPs; whirlpools; refrigerators. Whirlpool. No pets. Senior discount. 2-night minimum stay weekends. Reservation deposit required; 5-day refund
notice. AE, MC, VI. Complimentary beverages each evening.   Ⓓ ⊘

Mountain View Inn 🅰🅰   Motel   ♦♦
(805) 687-6636   *Rates Subject to Change*

Fri-Sat 6/15-9/15 [CP] 1P 83.00	2P/1B 85.00	2P/2B 87.00	XP 5
Sun-Thurs 6/15-9/15 [CP] 1P 68.00	2P/1B 70.00	2P/2B 72.00	XP 5
Fri-Sat 9/16-6/14 [CP] 1P 61.00	2P/1B 67.00	2P/2B 69.00	XP 5
Sun-Thurs 9/16-6/14 [CP] 1P 46.00	2P/1B 52.00	2P/2B 54.00	XP 5

1 mi e of US 101, exit Los Positas Rd. Corner of State & De la Vina sts. 3055 De la Vina St
(93105). 34 rooms; 2 stories; exterior corridors. Friendly atmosphere. Adjacent to city
park. Cable TV, free movies; refrigerators. No A/C. Heated pool. No pets. Senior discount.
Reservation deposit required. AE, DS, MC, VI.   Ⓓ

The Olive House   Bed & Breakfast   ♦♦
(805) 962-4902   *Rates Subject to Change*

Mon-Thurs 5/15-10/15 1P 100.00 -155.00	2P/1B 105.00 -155.00	2P/2B ...
Mon-Thurs 10/16-5/14 1P 70.00 -124.00	2P/1B 84.00 -124.00	2P/2B ...

1 mi e of US 101; northbound exit Arrellaga St; southbound exit Mission St. 1604 Olive
St, ¼ blk n of Arrellaga St (93101). 6 rooms; 2 stories; interior corridors. 1904 California
Craftsman house located in a residential area. Smoke-free premises. Combination
shower and tub baths. No TVs; no A/C; no phones. No pets. 2-night minimum stay weekends. Reservation deposit required; 7-day refund notice. MC, VI.   Ⓓ ⊘

Pacifica Suites <img_1 alt="AAA" />
(805) 683-6722; FAX (805) 683-4121

Suites Motel ◆◆◆
AAA Special Value Rates

All year [BP]   1P 120.00 -180.00   2P/1B 120.00 -180.00   2P/2B 120.00 -180.00   XP ..10

From US 101, exit Patterson Av, ½ mi s, then ½ mi w on Hollister Av. 5490 Hollister Av (93111). Formerly Quality Suites. 75 rooms; 2 stories; interior/exterior corridors; meeting rooms. 2-room suites. Situated in a grove of exotic plants & trees, adjacent to the restored Sexton House built in 1880s. Attractively decorated. Refrigerators; cable TV, free movies; coffeemakers; microwaves, refrigerators. Heated pool, whirlpool. Fee for bicycles. Services: Data ports; valet laundry. No pets. Children 17 and under stay free. Reservation deposit required. AE, CB, DI, DS, ER, JCB, MC, VI. Complimentary beverages evenings Mon-Sat. **(See ad below.)**   ⊗

The Parsonage
(805) 962-9336

Bed & Breakfast ◆◆
Rates Subject to Change

Fri-Sun
2/1-10/31 &
Fri-Sun
11/1-1/31 [BP]   1P 105.00 -185.00   2P/1B 105.00 -185.00   2P/2B ...
Mon-Thurs
11/1-4/30 [BP]   1P 76.50 -160.00   2P/2B 76.50 -160.00   2P/2B ...

1 mi e of US 101; northbound US 101 exit Arrellaga St; southbound exit Mission St. 1600 Olive St, at Arrellaga St (93101). 6 rooms. 2 stories; interior corridors. 1892 Victorian house in residential area. Smoke-free premises. Shower or combination baths. No TVs; no A/C. Complimentary beverages each evening. No pets. 2-night minimum stay weekends. Reservation deposit required; 7-day refund notice. AE, DS, MC, VI.   Ⓓ ⊗

The Sandman Inn
(805) 687-2468; FAX (805) 687-6581

Motor Inn ◆◆
AAA Special Value Rates

All year [CP]   1P 84.00 - 94.00   2P/1B 84.00 - 94.00   2P/2B 94.00 -104.00   XP ..10

3 mi nw; ¾ mi e of jct US 101. 3714 State St (93105). 110 rooms. 7 2-bedrm units. 6 kitchens & 11 efficiencies, $10 extra. Cable TV; shower or combination baths. Some A/C; refrigerators. Coin laundry. 2 pools (1 heated), whirlpool. Services: Airport transportation. No pets. Children 18 and under stay free. Credit card guarantee. AE, CB, DI, MC, VI.   Ⓓ ⊗

Sandpiper Lodge 🏛   Motel   ◆
(805) 687-5326; FAX (805) 687-2271   *Rates Subject to Change*

5/15-9/30	1P 58.00 - 68.00	2P/1B 58.00 - 68.00	2P/2B 58.00 - 68.00	XP 5
10/1-5/14	1P 48.00 - 58.00	2P/1B 48.00 - 58.00	2P/2B 48.00 - 58.00	XP 5

¾ mi e of US 101, State St exit. 3525 State St (93105). 73 rooms; 2 stories; exterior corridors. 16 2-bedroom units. 7-night minimum stay in 3 1-bedroom units. On busy commercial strip. Cable TV, free movies. Some refrigerators. No A/C. Pool (heated 5/16-9/30). No pets. Weekly & monthly rates available. Credit card guarantee. AE, DI, MC, VI. Coffee shop nearby. **(See ad below.)**   Ⓓ ⊘

Simpson House Inn 🏛   Historic Bed & Breakfast   ◆◆◆
(805) 963-7067; FAX (805) 564-4811   *Rates Guaranteed*

5/1-9/30 [BP]	1P 95.00 -275.00	2P/1B 95.00 -275.00	2P/2B ...	XP ..25
10/1-4/30 [BP]	1P 76.00 -184.0	2P/1B 74.00 -184.00	2P/2B ...	XP ..25

1½ blks e of State St. 121 E Arrellaga St (93101). 14 rooms; 2 stories; interior/exterior corridors. Some suites with whirlpool tub & fireplace. Beautifully decorated rooms in 1874 historic Victorian home or in cottage or barn suites. Located in quiet residential area. Coffeemakers; shower or combination baths. Some cable TV, VCPs; refrigerators. Bicycles. No pets. AE, DS, MC, VI. Complimentary beverages each evening.   Ⓓ ⊘

Tiffany Inn 🏛   Bed & Breakfast   ◆◆◆
(805) 963-2283   *Rates Subject to Change*

6/1-9/30 [BP]	1P ...	2P/1B 75.00 -190.00	2P/2B ...
10/1-5/31 [BP]	1P ...	2P/1B 60.00 -150.00	2P/2B ...

1323 De la Vina St (93101). 7 rooms; 3 stories. Smoke-free premises. 5 units with woodburning fireplace. 1898 Colonial Revival-style house located in residential area. Some radios; whirlpools. No A/C; no phones. No pets. 2-night minimum stay weekends. Reservation deposit required; 7-day refund notice. AE, MC, VI.   Ⓓ ⊘

The Upham 🏛   Historic Country Inn   ◆◆
(805) 962-0058; FAX (805) 962-0058   *AAA Special Value Rates*

All year [CP]	1P 100.00 -170.00	2P/1B 100.00 -170.00	2P/2B 150.00	XP ..10

From US 101 exit Mission St, 3 blks n, then 6 blks e. 1404 De la Vina St at Sola St (93101). 49 rooms; 2 stories; interior/exterior corridors; meeting rooms. A historic Victorian hotel & garden cottages established in 1871. Cable TV. No A/C. No pets. Children 12 and under stay free. Reservation deposit required; 3-day refund notice. AE, CB, DI, DS, ER, MC, VI. Restaurant; 11:30 am-2 & 6-9 pm; $9-$19; beer & wine.   Ⓓ

Vagabond Inn - State St ⒶⒶ   Motel   ♦♦
(805) 687-6444; FAX (805) 687-4432   *Rates Subject to Change*
5/16-10/15 [CP] 1P 70.00 - 75.00 2P/1B 75.00 - 80.00 2P/2B 79.00 - 84.00 XP 5
10/16-5/15 [CP] 1P 59.00 - 64.00 2P/1B 64.00 - 69.00 2P/2B 69.00 - 73.00 XP 5
1½ mi nw. 2819 State St (93105). 55 rooms; 2 stories; exterior corridors. Many patios or balconies. Cable TV, free movies; shower or combination baths. Some A/C. Fee for refrigerators. Pool (heated 5/15-10/15). Small pets only, $5 extra charge. Children 18 and under stay free. AE, CB, DI, DS, MC, VI.   Ⓓ ⊘

Restaurants

Andria's Harborside Restaurant   Seafood $11-$20   ♦♦
(805) 966-3000
At Best Western-El Patio Beachside Inn, 336 W Cabrillo Bl (93101). Nice selection of seafood, steaks, chicken & pasta. Oyster bar. Across from beach & yacht harbor. Casual attire. A/C. Children's menu; a la carte. Cocktails & lounge; entertainment. 6 am-midnight; Fri & Sat to 1 am. AE, DS, MC, VI. **(See ad below.)**   ⊘

Beachside Cafe   Seafood $11-$20   ♦
(805) 964-7881
5905 Sandspit Rd (93117). Beachfront restaurant located adjacent to Goleta Beach County Park & Pier. Casual attire. Cocktails. Reservations required. 11:30 am-4 pm & 5-10 pm; Fri to 10:30 pm; Sat 11 am-4 pm & 5-10:30 pm; Sun 11 am-4 & 5-10 pm; closed 11/25 & 12/25. AE, MC, VI.   ⊘

Cafe del Sol   American $11-$20   ♦♦
(805) 969-0448
½ blk s of US 101, exit Cabrillo Bl. 30 Los Patos Way (93103). Nice selection of seafood, chicken, steaks & Mexican specialties. Located across from Andree Clark Bird Refuge. Sunday brunch; a la carte. Casual attire. A/C. Cocktails & lounge. 11:30 am-2:30 & 5:30-10 pm; Sun 10 am-2:30 & 5:30-10 pm; closed 1/1, 11/24 & 12/25. DS, MC, VI.   ⊘

Cattlemen's Restaurant   American $11-$20   ♦
(805) 687-2828
At The Sandman Inn, 3744 State St (93105). Casual dining with a selection of beef, seafood & barbecue specialties. Western decor. Salad bar; a la carte. Sunday brunch. A/C. Cocktails & lounge. Reservations suggested. Entertainment. 11 am-2:30 & 5-10 pm; Sat 5-10 pm; Sun 10 am-2 & 5-10 pm; closed 1/1 & 12/25. AE, MC, VI.   ⊘

Chad's   American $11-$20   ◆◆
(805) 568-1876

1 blk w of State St, ½ blk n of Cota St. 625 Chapala St (93101). Regional American cuisine served in a charming house built in 1876. A la carte. Smoke-free premises. No A/C. Casual attire. Cocktails. 11:30 am-2:30 pm & 5:30-10 pm; Fri & Sat to 10:30 pm; Sun from 10 am; closed 12/25. AE, MC, VI.   ⊘

The Chart House   Steakhouse $21-$30   ◆◆
(805) 966-2112

1 blk s of State St, across from beach. 101 E Cabrillo Bl (93101). Nice selection of steaks, prime rib, rack of lamb & fresh seafood; a la carte. Casual attire. Cocktails & lounge. 5:30-10 pm; Fri & Sat 5 -11 pm; Sun 5-10 pm. AE, CB, DI, DS, MC, VI.   ⊘

Citronelle Restaurant   French   Over $30   ◆◆◆
(805) 963-0111

In Santa Barbara Inn, 901 Cabrillo Bl (93103). Interesting selection of French & California cuisine. Fine dining with panoramic ocean view. Casual attire. Sunday brunch; a la carte. A/C. Cocktails & lounge. Fee for valet parking. 7-10 am, noon-2:30 & 6-9:30 pm; Fri to 10 pm; Sat to 10:30 pm; Sun 7-10 am, 11:30-2:30 & 6-9:30 pm. Reservations suggested. AE, DI, DS, MC, VI.   ⊘

Downey's   American $21-$30   ◆◆◆
(805) 966-5006

Downtown Santa Barbara. 1305 State St (93101). Small restaurant serving excellently prepared & presented cuisine. Casual attire. Menu changes daily; a la carte. Smoke-free premises. Beer & wine only. Reservations suggested. 11:30 am-1:45 & 5:30-9 pm; Fri to 9:30 pm; Sat 5:30-9:30 pm; Sun 5:30-9 pm; closed Mon, 1/1 & 12/25. Reservations advised. AE, MC, VI.

La Marina   Continental   Over $30   ◆◆◆
(805) 969-2261

In Four Season's Biltmore, 1260 Channel Dr (93108). Fine dining in beautifully appointed dining rooms. Semi-formal attire. Children's menu; a la carte; Sunday brunch 10 am-2 pm. Reservations suggested. 6-10 pm; Sat to 11 pm.   ⊘

Maxi's   Continental $21-$30   ◆◆◆
(805) 564-4333

In Fess Parker's Red Lion Resort, 633 E Cabrillo Bl (93103). Elegant decor. Casual attire. Sunday brunch; a la carte. Cocktails & lounge. 10 am-2 pm. 6-10 pm; closed Mon & Tue. Reservations suggested. Valet parking. AE, DI, DS, ER, MC, VI.   ⊘

Original Enterprise Fish Company   Seafood $11-$20   ♦♦
(805) 962-3313

1 blk s of US 101, 225 State St (93101). Large selection of mesquite-broiled seafood.
Casual dining. Nautical decor. No A/C. Casual attire. Children's menu; a la carte. Beer &
wine only. Reservations suggested. 11:30 am-10 pm; Fri & Sat to 11 pm; Sun 11:30 am-
10 pm; closed 11/24 & 12/25. AE, MC, VI.   ⊗

The Palace Cafe   American $21-$30   ♦♦
(805) 966-3133

Downtown area. 3 blks nw of US 101. ½ blk e of State St, 8 E Cota St (93101). Interesting
selection of Cajun, Creole & Caribbean cuisine. Casual dining in a lively atmosphere.
Casual attire. A la carte. Beer & wine only. 5:30-10 pm; Fri & Sat to 11 pm. AE, MC, VI.
⊗

Ristorante Piatti   Italian $21-$30   ♦♦
(805) 969-7520

1 mi n of US 101, exit San Ysidro Rd; in Montecito, 516 San Ysidro Rd at E Valley Rd
(93108). Selection of pasta, pizza, seafood & veal. Indoor & outdoor patio dining. Casual
attire. A la carte. Cocktails & lounge. Reservations suggested. 11:30 am 10 pm, Fri & Sat
to 11 pm; closed 1/1, 11/24 & 12/25. AE, MC, VI.   ⊗

Wine Cask Restaurant   American $21-$30   ♦♦♦
(805) 966-9463

Downtown Santa Barbara, 813 Anacapa St (93101). California cuisine served in an attractive dining room or an outdoor courtyard. Extensive wine list. Smoke-free premises.
Located in El Paseo area. Casual attire. A la carte. Beer & wine only. Reservations suggested. 11:30 am-2:30 & 5:30-9 pm; Fri to 10 pm; Sat 5:30-10 pm; Sun 5:30-9 pm; closed
7/4, 11/24 & 12/25. AE, MC, VI.   ⊗

Santa Ynez Valley

BALLARD

Lodging

The Ballard Inn   Bed & Breakfast   ♦♦♦♦
(805) 688-7770; FAX (805) 688-9560   *Rates Subject to Change*
All year [BP]   1P 160.00 -195.00   2P/1B 160.00 -195.00   2P/2B ...

3½ mi ne of Solvang via Alamo Pintado Rd. 2436 Baseline Av (93463). 15 rooms; 2
stories; interior/exterior corridors; smoke-free premises. A charming inn with individually decorated rooms, 7 with fireplaces. Shower or combination baths. No phones; no
TVs. Telephone jacks and cable TV hookups in all rooms. Rental bicycles. No pets.
Reservation deposit required; 7-day refund notice. AE, MC, VI. Afternoon tea & beverages.   ⒟ ⊗

Restaurant

The Ballard Store Restaurant   Continental $11-$20   ◆◆◆
(805) 688-5319
2449 Baseline Av (93463). Fine dining in a French country atmosphere. International cuisine. Extensive selection of California wines. Casual attire. Children's menu; early bird specials; also prix fixe menu, $17.95. Gourmet picnic boxes available with advance arrangements. Cocktails. Reservations suggested. Open 5:30-9:30 pm; Sun 10:30 am-2 & 5-8:30 pm; closed Mon, Tue, 12/24 and 12/25. AE, MC, VI.

BUELLTON

Lodging

Best Western Pea Soup Andersen's Inn ⊛   Motel   ◆◆◆
(805) 688-3216; FAX (805) 688-9767   *AAA Special Value Rates*
10/1-4/30 [CP]   1P 40.00 - 60.00   2P/1B 40.00 - 70.00   2P/2B 40.00 - 70.00   XP ..10
5/1-9/30 [CP]   1P 50.00 - 70.00   2P/1B 50.00 - 80.00   2P/2B 50.00 - 80.00   XP ..10
On SR 246; 1 blk w of jct US 101. 51 E Hwy 246 (Box 197, 93427). 97 rooms; 2 stories; exterior corridors; meeting rooms. Cable TV; some microwaves, refrigerators. Putting green; heated pool, whirlpool; playground. No pets. AE, DI, DS, ER, MC, VI. Restaurant nearby.   Ⓓ ⊘

Econo Lodge ⊛   Motel   ◆◆
(805) 688-0022; FAX (805) 688-7448   *Rates Subject to Change*
All year   1P 29.95 - 49.95   2P/1B 39.95 - 55.50   2P/2B 39.95   XP ..10
Adjacent to US 10; southbound first Buellton exit; northbound Frontage Rd exit, then 1 blk w over the frwy. 630 Avenue of Flags (93427). 60 rooms; 2-3 stories; interior/exterior corridors. 16 efficiencies, $59.95-$68.95 for 2 persons. Cable TV, free movies. Coin laundry. Small pets only. Senior discount. Weekly & monthly rates. Reservation deposit required in summer. AE, DS, MC, VI.   Ⓓ Ⓢ ⊘

Holiday Inn-Solvang/Buellton ⊛   Motor Inn   ◆◆◆
(805) 688-1000; FAX (805) 688-0380   *Rates Subject to Change*
All year   1P 90.00 -100.00   2P/1B 97.00 -110.00   2P/2B 87.00 -107.00   XP ..10
Adjacent to US 101, exit SR 246, ¼ mi n. 555 McMurray Rd (93427). 149 rooms; 4 stories; interior corridors; meeting rooms. 7 suites with whirlpool tub. Cable TV, free & pay movies, bars, coffeemakers; fee for refrigerators; whirlpools. Coin laundry. Heated pool, saunas, steamroom, whirlpool; racquetball court, tennis court; fee for massage; tanning bed; game room. No pets. Children 19 and under stay free. Senior discount. AE, CB, DI, DS, ER, JCB, MC, VI. Restaurant & coffee shop; 7 am-10 pm; $8-$13.   Ⓓ Ⓢ ⊘

Ramada Inn at the Windmill Ⓐ   Motel   ◆◆◆
(805) 688-8448; FAX (805) 686-1338   *Rates Subject to Change*

Fri-Sat 9/22-5/23	1P	86.00	2P/1B	92.00	2P/2B	92.00	XP	6
Sun-Thurs 9/22-5/23	1P	44.00 - 54.00	2P/1B	50.00 - 60.00	2P/2B	50.00 - 60.00	XP	6
Fri-Sat 5/24-9/21	1P	88.00	2P/1B	94.00	2P/2B	94.00	XP	6
Sun-Thurs 5/24-9/21	1P	56.00 - 62.00	2P/1B	66.00 - 72.00	2P/2B	66.00 - 72.00	XP	6

Adjacent to US 101. 114 E SR 246 (93427). 110 rooms; 2 stories; exterior corridors; meeting rooms. Cable TV, free movies; some refrigerators. Coin laundry. Heated pool, whirlpool. No pets. Children 18 and under stay free. Senior discount. Monthly rates. AE, CB, DI, DS, JCB, MC, VI. Cocktail lounge.   Ⓓ ⊘

Restaurants

A J Spurs Ⓐ   American $11-$20   ◆◆
(805) 686-1655

On SR 246, ¼ mi e of US 101. 350 E SR 246 (93427). Casual, western-style family dining featuring steaks, ribs, barbecue chicken & seafood. Children's menu; early-bird specials. Extra plate fee $6.95. Cocktails & lounge. Reservations suggested. Open 4-9:30 pm; Sat & Sun 2-9:30 pm; closed 1/1, 11/24, 12/24 & 12/25. AE, MC, VI.   ⊘

Federico's   Mexican $11-$20   ◆◆
(805) 688-0606

At Holiday Inn Solvang/Buellton. 585 McMurray Rd (93427). Large dining area, attractively decorated. Children's menu; senior menu; early-bird specials. Cocktails & lounge. Open 11:30 am-10 pm; Sun 10:30 am-9 pm. AE, CB, DI, DS, JCB, MC, VI.   ⊘

The Hitching Post II   Steakhouse $11-$20   ◆◆
(805) 688-0676

On SR 246, ½ mi e from jct US 101. 406 E SR 246 (93427). Well known for its steak & barbecue specialties. Children's menu; early-bird specials. Cocktails & lounge. Reservations suggested. Open 5-10 pm; Sun 4-9 pm; closed major holidays. AE, MC, VI.   ⊘

LOS OLIVAS

Lodging

Los Olivos Grand Hotel Ⓐ   Country Inn   ◆◆◆◆
(805) 688-7788; FAX (805) 688-1942   *AAA Special Value Rates*
Fri-Sat   1P 210.00 -325.00   2P/1B 210.00 -325.00   2P/2B 230.00
Sun-Thurs   1P 160.00 -300.00   2P/1B 160.00 -300.00   2P/2B 180.00
½ mi s of SR 154. 2860 Grand Av (PO Box 526, 93441). 21 rooms; 2 stories; interior/exterior corridors; meeting rooms. Charming country inn atmosphere in the center of town. Spacious, beautifully decorated rooms with gas fireplaces. Cable TV; refrigerators; some VCPs, whirlpools. Heated pool, whirlpool. Services: Valet laundry. No pets. Credit card guarantee. AE, DI, DS, MC, VI. Restaurant, see *Remington's Restaurant.*   Ⓓ Ⓢ ⊘

Restaurants

Mattei's Tavern   American $11-$20   ◆
(805) 688-4820
On SR 154 (93441). Dining in a historic stagecoach stop. Nice selection of steaks, prime rib, seafood & other entrees. Casual dress. Cocktails & lounge. Reservations suggested. Open noon-3 pm & 5:30-9 pm; Sat-Sun 4:30-9 pm; closed 12/25. MC, VI.   ⊘

Remington's Restaurant   Continental $11-$20   ◆◆◆
(805) 688-7788
In Los Olivos Grand Hotel. 2860 Grand Av (93441). Casual dress. Children's menu. Cocktails. Open 7 am-3 & 5:30-9 pm; Sat & Sun 8 am-3 & 5:30-10 pm. Cocktails. AE, CB, DI, DS, MC, VI.   ⊘

SOLVANG

Lodging

Best Western King Frederik Motel Ⓐ   Motel   ◆◆◆
(805) 688-5515; FAX (805) 688-2067   *Rates Subject to Change*
All year   1P 53.00 - 68.00   2P/1B 57.00 - 68.00   2P/2B 68.00   XP 6
On SR 246.1617 Copenhagen Dr (93463). 45 rooms; 2 stories; exterior corridors. Few smaller rooms. Cable TV; shower or combination baths. Heated pool, whirlpool. No pets. Children 12 and under stay free. AE, DI, DS, MC, VI.   Ⓓ

Best Western Kronborg Inn ⓐⓐ   Motel   ◆◆◆
(805) 688-2383; FAX (805) 688-1821   *Rates Subject to Change*
6/16-9/15
& Fri-Sat
9/16-6/15 [CP]   1P 65.00 - 75.00   2P/1B 65.00 - 75.00   2P/2B 70.00 - 80.00   XP ..10
Sun-Thurs
9/16-6/15 [CP]   1P 50.00 - 60.00   2P/1B 50.00 - 60.00   2P/2B 55.00 - 65.00   XP ..10
5 blks w on SR 246. 1440 Mission Dr (93463). Formerly Kronberg Inn. 39 rooms; 2
stories; exterior corridors. Attractive country decor. Cable TV, free movies; coffeemakers,
refrigerators. Some whirlpools. Heated pool, whirlpool. Children 12 and under stay free.
Senior discount. Reservation deposit required. AE, CB, DI, DS, MC, VI.   Ⓓ ⊘

Chimney Sweep Inn ⓐⓐ   Motel   ◆◆◆
(805) 688-2111; FAX (805) 688-8826   *Rates Subject to Change*
All year [CP]   1P 65.00 - 85.00   2P/1B 65.00 - 85.00   2P/2B 80.00 -100.00   XP ..10
1 blk s of SR 246. 1554 Copenhagen Dr (93463). 28 rooms; 2 stories; interior/exterior corridors. 8 split-level loft rooms, $89-$129; 6 cottage units with fireplace, some with private
outdoor whirlpool, $165-$245. Located in Tivoli Square. Beautifully landscaped garden
area. Cable TV; coffeemakers; shower or combination baths. Some refrigerators. Whirlpool. No pets. Children 12 and under stay free. Senior discount. Weekly rates available.
Reservation deposit required. AE, DS, MC, VI. **(See ad below.)**   Ⓓ ⊘

146

Danish Country Inn ⒶⒶⒶ   Motel   ♦♦♦
(805) 688-2018; FAX (805) 688-1156   *Rates Guaranteed*

Fri-Sat [BP]	1P 77.00	2P/1B 77.00	2P/2B 77.00	XP ..10
Sun-Thurs [BP]	1P 62.00	2P/1B 62.00	2P/2B 62.00	XP ..10

3 blks w on SR 246. 1455 Mission Dr (93463). 82 rooms; 3 stories; interior corridors; meeting rooms. 6 split-level loft rooms, $115-$150 for 2 persons. Spacious rooms. Cable TV; refrigerators. Rental VCPs. Heated pool, whirlpool. No pets. Children 12 and under stay free. Reservation deposit required. AE, DI, DS, JCB, MC, VI. Complimentary beverages each evening. **(See ad below.)** Ⓓ Ⓢ ⊘

Hamlet Motel ⒶⒶ   Motel   ♦♦
(805) 688-4413; FAX (805) 686-1301   *Rates Subject to Change*

Fri-Sat	1P ...	2P/1B 60.00 - 85.00	2P/2B 65.00 - 95.00	XP ..10
Sun-Thurs	1P 35.00 - 45.00	2P/1B 40.00 - 60.00	2P/2B 45.00 - 65.00	XP ..10

1 blk w on SR 246. 1532 Mission Dr (93463). 14 rooms; 2 stories; exterior corridors. 1 2-bedroom unit. Cable TV; shower or combination baths. Some refrigerators. No A/C. No pets. Reservation deposit required. AE, DI, DS, MC, VI. Restaurant nearby. Ⓓ ⊘

Petersen Village Inn ⒶⒶⒶ   Motel   ♦♦♦♦
(805) 688-3121; FAX (805) 688-5732   *Rates Subject to Change*

All year [CP]	1P 105.00 -170.00	2P/1B 105.00 -170.00	2P/2B ...	XP ..10

On SR 246. 1576 Mission Dr (93463). 40 rooms; 2 stories; interior/exterior corridors; meeting rooms. 1 smaller unit. Charming, old-world ambiance with spacious, beautifully decorated rooms. Cable TV; shower or combination baths. No pets. Reservation deposit required; 3-day refund notice. Package plans, golf. AE, MC, VI. Complimentary beverages each evening. Restaurant nearby. **(See ad below and on back cover.)** Ⓓ Ⓢ ⊘

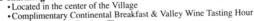

Quality Inn of Solvang ⒶⒶ   Motel   ◆◆◆
(805) 688-3210; FAX (805) 688-0026   *Rates Subject to Change*

Fri-Sat				
6/1-9/30 [CP] 1P ...	2P/1B 85.00	2P/2B 85.00	XP 5
Fri-Sat 10/1-5/31				
& Sun-Thurs				
6/1-9/30 [CP] 1P ...	2P/1B 65.00	2P/2B 65.00	XP 5
Sun-Thurs				
10/1-5/31 [CP] 1P ...	2P/1B 50.00	2P/2B 55.00	XP 5

3 blks w on SR 246. 1450 Mission Dr (93463). Formerly Dannebrog Inn. 75 rooms; 2
stories; exterior corridors. 3 rooms with whirlpool, $95-$185. Cable TV, free movies; coffeemakers; shower or combination baths. Some refrigerators; whirlpools. Large area
with indoor heated pool, video games, pinball machines & air hockey games. Recreation
program. No pets. Children stay free. Senior discount. AE, DI, DS, MC, VI.   Ⓓ ⊘

The Royal Copenhagen Motel ⒶⒶ   Motel   ◆◆◆
(805) 688-5561   *Rates Subject to Change*

All year   1P 60.00 - 80.00 2P/1B 65.00 - 80.00 2P/2B 60.00 - 80.00 XP 6

On SR 246. 1579 Mission Dr (93463). 48 rooms; 2 stories; interior/exterior corridors. 4
split-level loft rooms, $95. Exterior of buildings are replica of Danish village. Large
rooms. Cable TV, free movies; shower baths. Heated pool. No pets. Reservation deposit
required. AE, DS, MC, VI. **(See ad below.)**   Ⓓ ⊘

Solvang Royal Scandinavian Inn 🏧   Hotel   ♦♦♦
(805) 688-8000; FAX (805) 688-0761   *Rates Subject to Change*

6/1-9/30	1P ...		2P/1B 95.00 -135.00	2P/2B 95.00 -135.00	XP ..10
3/1-5/31 & 10/1-11/30	1P ...		2P/1B 85.00 -125.00	2P/2B 85.00 -125.00	XP ..10
12/1-2/28	1P ...		2P/1B 75.00 -115.00	2P/2B 75.00 -115.00	XP ..10

2 blks s of SR 246. 400 Alisal Rd (PO Box 30, 93463). Check in 4 pm. 133 units; 3 stories; interior corridors; meeting rooms. Large rooms, some with balcony or patio. Attractive pool area with view of Santa Ynez Mountains. Cable TV. Fee for movies; refrigerators. Heated pool, whirlpool. Services: Valet laundry. No pets. Children 18 and under stay free. Senior discount. Weekly & monthly rates available. Reservation deposit required; 3-day refund notice. Package plans, golf. AE, CB, DI, DS, ER, JCB, MC, VI. Restaurant; 7 am-10 pm; $9-$16; cocktails; entertainment. **(See ad below.)** 🄳 🅂 ⊘

Svendsgaard's Danish Lodge 🏧   Motel   ♦♦♦
(805) 688-3277; FAX (805) 688-3997   *Rates Subject to Change*

6/16-9/17 & Fri-Sat 9/18-6/15 [CP]	1P 57.00 - 88.00	2P/1B 57.00 - 88.00	2P/2B 69.00 - 90.00	XP 6
Sun-Thurs 9/18-6/15 [CP]	1P 44.00 - 75.00	2P/1B 44.00 - 75.00	2P/2B 49.00 - 75.00	XP 6

On SR 246 at Alisal Rd. 1711 Mission Dr (93463). 48 rooms; 3 stories; interior/exterior corridors. 3 2-bedroom units. 4 kitchen units, $5 extra. Many rooms with fireplace. Cable TV; refrigerators; shower or combination baths. Some radios. Pool, whirlpool. No pets. Weekly & monthly rates available. Reservation deposit required. AE, CB, DI, DS, JCB, MC, VI. Member, Independent Motels of America. **(See ad below.)** 🄳 ⊘

Three Crowns Inn ⓐⓐ Motel ♦♦
(805) 688-4702   *Rates Subject to Change*

Fri-Sat	1P 50.00 - 75.00	2P/1B 50.00 - 75.00	2P/2B 60.00 - 80.00	XP 5	
Sun-Thurs	1P 40.00	2P/1B 40.00 - 45.00	2P/2B 50.00	XP 5	

1½ blks w of SR 246. 1518 Mission Dr (93463). 27 rooms. 2 2-bedroom units. Cable TV. No pets. Reservation deposit required. AE, MC, VI. Restaurant nearby. Ⓓ ⊘

Viking Motel ⓐⓐ Motel ♦
(805) 688-1337   *Rates Subject to Change*

Sat	1P 52.00 - 78.00	2P/1B 52.00 - 78.00	2P/2B 58.00 - 85.00	XP 6	
Sun-Fri	1P 30.00 - 54.00	2P/1B 34.00 - 54.00	2P/2B 38.00 - 60.00	XP 6	

2 blks w on SR 246. 1506 Mission Dr (93463). 12 rooms; exterior corridors. Located in center of town. Modest rooms. Cable TV, free movies; shower or combination baths. Some refrigerators. Pets, $5 extra charge. Senior discount. Reservation deposit required. AE, DI, DS, MC, VI. Ⓓ ⊘

Restaurants

Bit O' Denmark Restaurant ⓐⓐ   American $11-$20 ♦
(805) 688-5426

½ blk s of SR 246, 473 Alisal Rd (93463). Nice selection of Danish & American entrees. Smorgasbord lunch & dinner. Casual attire. Children's menu. Beer & wine only. 8 am-9 pm; Fri & Sat to 9:30 pm; closed 12/25. AE, CB, DI, MC, VI. ⊘

The Danish Inn Restaurant   Ethnic $11-$20 ♦♦
(805) 688-4813

1 blk w on SR 246. 1547 Mission Dr (93463). Attractive restaurant featuring Scandinavian & continental cuisine. Smorgasbord lunch & dinner. Located in center of town. Casual attire. Cocktails & lounge. Reservations suggested. 11:30 am-10 pm; Sat & Sun 9 am-10 pm. AE, DI, DS, MC, VI. ⊘

Massimi Ristorante   Italian $11-$20 ♦♦♦
(805) 688-0027

On SR 246 in Petersen Village Square. 1588 Mission Dr (93463). A small, charming restaurant with indoor and outdoor dining. Smoke-free premises. Casual attire. A la carte. Reservations suggested. Beer & wine only. 5:30-9:30 pm; closed Mon & major holidays. AE, MC, VI. ⊘

Lompoc Valley

LOMPOC

Lodging

Embassy Suites Hotel   Suites Motor Inn   ◆◆◆
(805) 735-8311; FAX (805) 735-8459   *Rates Subject to Change*

All year [BP]   1P 71.00   2P/1B 81.00   2P/2B ...   XP ..10

1¼ mi n on SR 1. 1117 N H St (93436). 156 rooms; 3-story; exterior corridor; meeting rooms. 1 2-bedroom apt, $125. Refrigerators and microwaves. 2-room suites surrounding outdoor pool & garden area. Free and pay movies; shower and combination baths. Some cable TV. Heated pool, whirlpool. Coin laundry. Complimentary evening beverages. No pets. Children 12 and under stay free; senior discount. Reservation deposit required; 14-day refund notice. AE, CB, DI, DS, JCB, MC, VI. Restaurant nearby.   Ⓓ Ⓢ ⊘

Inn of Lompoc ⒶⒶⒶ   Motel   ◆◆◆
(805) 735-7744; FAX (805) 736-0421   *Rates Subject to Change*

All year [CP]   1P 51.00   2P/1B 57.00   2P/2B 57.00   XP 6

1¼ mi n. on SR 1. 1122 N H St (93436). 90 rooms; 2 stories; interior/exterior corridors; meeting rooms. Downtown location. Cable TV, free movies; coffeemakers, refrigerators; shower or combination baths. Fee for microwaves. Coin laundry. Heated indoor pool; whirlpool. Pets, $25 fee and $6 daily deposit. Children 12 and under stay free; senior discount. Weekly & monthly rates available. AE, CB, DI, DS, ER, MC, VI. Restaurant nearby.   Ⓓ ⊘

Porto Finale Inn ⒶⒶⒶ   Motel   ◆◆◆
(805) 735-7731; FAX (805) 736-8925   *Rates Subject to Change*

2/1-3/31 &			
10/1-1/31[EP]	1P 30.00	2P/1B 35.00	2P/2B 38.00 - 44.00
4/1-9/30 [EP]	1P 35.00 - 42.00	2P/1B 40.00 - 42.00	2P/2B 45.00 - 49.00

1 mi e on SR 1 & SR 246. 940 E Ocean Av (93436). 83 rooms; 2 stories; exterior corridors. Well appointed rooms; nicely landscaped. Cable TV; refrigerators. Fee for microwaves. Coin laundry. Heated pool; whirlpool. Pets, $10 extra charge. Weekly rates available. Reservation deposit required. AE, DI, DS, MC, VI. **(See ad below.)**   Ⓓ ⅃ ⊘

Quality Inn & Executive Suites ⒶⒶⒶ   Motel   ♦♦♦
(805) 735-8555; FAX (805) 735-8566   *AAA Special Value Rates*

| All year [CP] | 1P 54.00 | 2P/1B 54.00 | 2P/2B 59.00 | XP ....5 |

1¾ mi n on SR 1. 1621 North H St. (93436) 221 rooms; 3 stories; interior corridors; meeting rooms. Standard rooms & larger rooms with efficiency. 93 executive suites with efficiency, breakfast included, $75. Package plans. Downtown area. Cable TV; free and pay movies; coffeemakers. Some microwaves, refrigerators. Coin laundry. Heated pool, whirlpool. Complimentary evening beverages. Pets, $18 extra charge. Children 18 and under stay free. Weekly & monthly rates available. Reservation deposit required. AE, CB, DI, DS, ER, JCB, MC, VI. Restaurant nearby.   Ⓓ Ⓢ ⊘

Redwood Inn ⒶⒶⒶ   Motel   ♦
(805) 735-3737; FAX (805) 735-3510.   *Rates Subject to Change*

| All year | 1P 40.00 - 45.00 | 2P/1B 40.00 - 45.00 | 2P/2B 40.00 - 45.00 | XP ....2 |

1¼ mi n on SR 1. 1200 North H St (93436). 60 rooms; 2 stories; interior/exterior corridors. Downtown location. Cable TV, free movies; refrigerators; shower or combination baths; no A/C. Fee for microwaves. Coin laundry. Sauna. Pets, $10 deposit. Weekly & monthly rates available. AE, DI, DS, MC, VI. Restaurant adjacent.   Ⓓ ⊘

Tally Ho Motor Inn ⒶⒶⒶ   Motel   ♦♦
(805) 735-6444; FAX (805) 735-5558   *AAA Special Value Rates*

| All year | 1P 29.00 - 40.00 | 2P/1B 29.00 - 40.00 | 2P/2B 40.00 |

1 mi e on SR 1 & SR 246. 1020 E Ocean Av (93436). 53 rooms; 2 stories; exterior corridors. Few smaller economy rooms. 4 2-room units with efficiency, $55. Cable TV. Some refrigerators, microwaves, coffeemakers. Coin laundry. Sauna, indoor whirlpool. Pets, $10 extra charge. Senior discount. Monthly & weekly rates available. Reservation deposit required. AE, DI, DS, MC, VI.   Ⓓ ⊘

Santa Maria Valley

SANTA MARIA

Lodging

Best Western Big America ⒶⒶⒶ   Motor Inn   ♦♦♦
(805) 922-5200; FAX (805) 922-9865   *AAA Special Value Rates*

| All year [CP] | 1P 55.00 - 90.00 | 2P/1B 55.00 - 90.00 | 2P/2B 60.00 - 90.00 | XP ....7 |

On SR 135, ½ mi sw of jct US 101; Broadway exit. 1725 N Broadway (93454). 104 rooms; 2 stories; exterior corridors; meeting rooms. Attractively furnished rooms & 1-bedroom suites. Cable TV, free movies; refrigerators. Heated pool, whirlpool. Pets. Children 18 and under stay free. Credit card guarantee. AE, CB, DI, DS, MC, VI. Restaurant; 6 am-9 pm; $6-$13; cocktails.   Ⓓ ⊘

Howard Johnson Lodge
Motel ♦♦

(805) 922-5891; FAX (805) 928-9222   *Rates Subject to Change*

1/1-4/10 [EP]	1P 39.00 - 49.00	2P/1B 44.00 - 54.00	2P/2B 44.00 - 49.00	XP 8
4/11-6/15 & 9/5-12/31 [EP]	1P 44.00 - 54.00	2P/1B 49.00 - 59.00	2P/2B 49.00 - 54.00	XP 8
6/16-9/4 [EP]	1P 49.00 - 59.00	2P/1B 54.00 - 64.00	2P/2B 54.00 - 59.00	XP 8

1 blk e of 101, Main St exit. 210 S Nicholson Av (93454). 62 rooms; 2 stories; interior corridors. A/C; cable TV, free movies. Coin laundry. Heated pool, wading pool, whirlpool. Pets. Children 16 and under stay free. Senior discount. AE, DI, DS, MC, VI. Restaurant nearby. Ⓓ ⊘

Hunter's Inn Ⓐ
Motel ♦♦

(805) 922-2123; FAX (805) 925-1523   *Rates Subject to Change*

All year	1P 49.00 - 89.00	2P/1B 55.00 - 89.00	2P/2B 58.00 - 95.00	XP 6

1¼ mi s on Stowell Rd from US 101. 1514 S Broadway (93454). 70 rooms; 2 stories; exterior corridors. 5 2-bedroom units. Cable TV, free movies. No A/C. Some microwaves, refrigerators. Heated pool, whirlpool. Small pets only, $5 extra charge. Senior discount. Weekly & monthly rates available. Reservation deposit required. AE, CB, DI, DS, ER, JCB, MC, VI. Coffee shop nearby. Ⓓ ⊘

Ramada Suites Ⓐ
Suites Motor Inn ♦♦♦

(805) 928-6000; FAX (805) 928-0356   *AAA Special Value Rates*

Fri-Sat	1P 65.00 -150.00	2P/1B 65.00 -150.00	2P/2B 65.00 -150.00	XP ..10
Sun-Thurs	1P 55.00 - 96.00	2P/1B 55.00 - 96.00	2P/2B 55.00 - 96.00	XP ..10

2 mi n adjacent to US 101; Broadway exit. 2050 N Preisker Ln (93454). 210 rooms; 4 stories; interior corridors; meeting rooms. 4 2-bedroom units. Spacious, comfortably furnished suites with efficiencies. Cable TV, free & pay movies; refrigerators. Coin laundry. Heated pool, whirlpool. Pets, $20 extra charge. Children 12 and under stay free. Credit card guarantee. AE, CB, DI, DS, ER, JCB, MC, VI. Restaurant; 6-11 am & 5-10 pm; Sun 7 am-noon; $7-$18; cocktails. Ⓓ Ⓢ ⊘

Rose Garden Inn Ⓐ
Motel ♦♦

(805) 922-4505   *Rates Subject to Change*

All year	1P 49.00	2P/1B 69.00 - 79.00	2P/2B 69.00 - 79.00	XP ..10

On SR 166; 1 blk w of jct US 101, Main St exit. 1007 E Main St (93454). Formerly Western Host Motor Hotel. 81 rooms; 2 stories; exterior corridors. Cable TV, fee for movies; shower or combination baths. Some refrigerators. Heated pool, whirlpool; 2 tennis courts. Pets, $10 extra charge. Children 16 and under stay free. Senior discount. AE, CB, DI, MC, VI. Restaurant nearby. Ⓓ ⊘

Santa Maria Airport Hilton   Hotel   ◆◆◆
(805) 928-8000; FAX (805) 928-5251   *Rates Subject to Change*

All year	1P 59.00	2P/1B 59.00	2P/2B 59.00	XP ..10

From US 101, exit Betteravia Rd, 2¼ mi w, then 1¾ mi s on Skyway Dr; adjacent to airport. 3455 Skyway Dr (93455). 190 rooms; 4 stories; interior/exterior corridors; meeting rooms. Next to Santa Maria Airport. Attractive atrium lobby. Cable TV, free movies. Heated pool, whirlpool. No pets. AE, DI, DS, MC, VI. Dining room; 6 am-9 pm; Fri & Sat to 10 pm; $10-$26; cocktails.   D S ⊘

Santa Maria Inn Ⓐ   Historic Hotel   ◆◆◆
(805) 928-7777; FAX (805) 928-5690   *Rates Guaranteed*

All year	1P 69.00 - 79.00	2P/1B 69.00 - 79.00	2P/2B 69.00 - 79.00	XP ..10

½ mi s on SR 135 & US 101 business rt. 801 S Broadway (93454). 166 rooms; 2-6 stories; interior corridors; meeting rooms. Old English country motif. Small, charming rooms in the original restored building; very spacious, nicely decorated rooms in new tower section. Refrigerators; cable TV; refrigerators. Some A/C. Heated pool, sauna, whirlpool. Services: Airport transportation. No pets. Children 12 and under stay free. Senior discount. AE, CB, DI, DS, MC, VI. Dining room; 6:30 am-9 pm; Fri & Sat to 10 pm. Wine Bar & Cellar; $11-$21; cocktails. Also see *Santa Maria Inn Restaurant.* **(See ad below.)**   D S ⊘

Restaurants

Central City Broiler   American $11-$20   ◆◆
(805) 922-3700

¾ mi w of US 101, exit Donovan Rd. 1520 N Broadway (93454). Selection of barbecue, steaks, chicken, seafood & prime rib. Early American decor. Children's menu. Cocktails & lounge. 11:30 am-2 & 5-9 pm; Fri to 10 pm; Sat 5-10 pm; Sun 5-9 pm; closed 1/1, 11/24, 12/24 & 12/25. AE, MC, VI.   ⊘

Santa Maria Inn Restaurant Ⓐ   American $11-$20   ◆◆◆
(805) 928-7777

In Santa Maria Inn. 801 S Broadway (93454). Selection of prime rib, steaks, seafood, chicken & continental entrees. Very attractive dining room, Sunday brunch. Early bird specials. 11 am-9 pm; Fri & Sat to 10 pm. Cocktails & lounge. Entertainment. Reservations suggested. AE, DI, DS, JCB, MC, VI.   ⊘

Ventura County

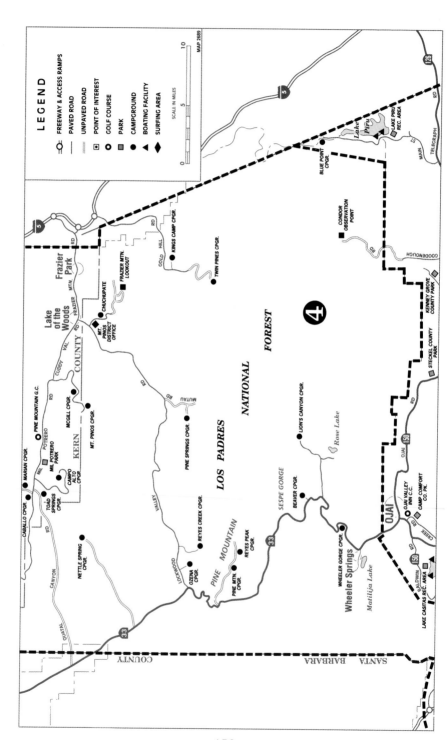

LEGEND

- Freeway & Access Ramps
- Paved Road
- Unpaved Road
- Point of Interest
- Golf Course
- Park
- Campground
- Boating Facility
- Surfing Area

SCALE IN MILES
0   5   10

MAP 2689

4

LOS PADRES NATIONAL FOREST

Frazier Park
Lake of the Woods
KERN COUNTY

Pine Mountain G.C.
Marian Cpgr.
Caballo Cpgr.
Toad Springs Cpgr.
Campo Alto Cpgr.
McGill Cpgr.
Mt. Pinos Cpgr.
Potrero
Mil Potrero Park
Nettle Spring Cpgr.
Pine Springs Cpgr.
Chuchupate
Mt. Pinos District Office
Frazier Mtn. Lookout
Kings Camp Cpgr.
Twin Pines Cpgr.
Gold Hill Rd.
Frazier Mtn. Rd.
Cuddy Val. Rd.
Mutau Rd.
Reyes Creek Cpgr.
Ozena Cpgr.
Reyes Peak Cpgr.
Pine Mtn. Cpgr.
Lockwood Valley Rd.
PINE MOUNTAIN
Sespe Gorge
Beaver Cpgr.
Lion's Canyon Cpgr.
Rose Lake
Condor Observation Point
Goodenough Rd.
Blue Point Cpgr.
Lake Piru
Lake Piru Rec. Area
Main St.
Telegraph Rd.
Kenney Grove County Park
Steckel County Park
Ojai Rd.
Ojai Valley Inn C.C.
Camp Comfort Co. Pk.
OJAI
Wheeler Springs
Wheeler Gorge Cpgr.
Matilija Lake
Creek Rd.
Baldwin Rd.
Lake Casitas Rec. Area

SANTA BARBARA COUNTY

156

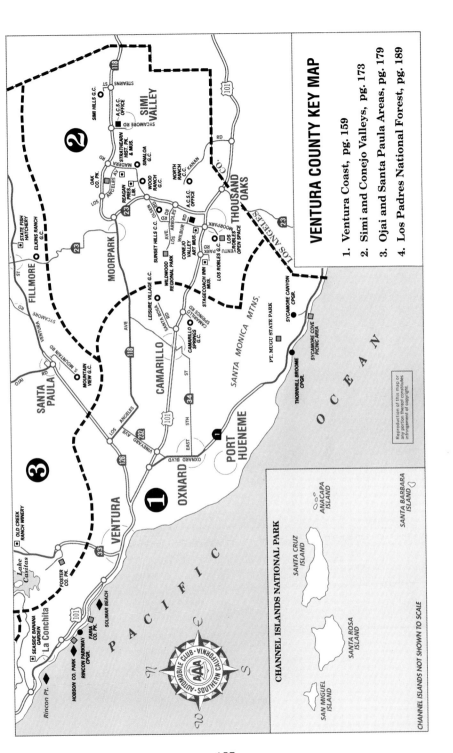

VENTURA COUNTY KEY MAP

1. Ventura Coast, pg. 159
2. Simi and Conejo Valleys, pg. 173
3. Ojai and Santa Paula Areas, pg. 179
4. Los Padres National Forest, pg. 189

Reproduction of this map or any portion thereof constitutes infringement of copyright.

CHANNEL ISLANDS NATIONAL PARK

CHANNEL ISLANDS NOT SHOWN TO SCALE

Once a year Ventura's coastline is enhanced by the County Fair.

Ventura Coast

Backed by seemingly endless ranges of hills, and facing the Santa Barbara Channel to the south, Ventura County's coastal plain supports communities, farmland, orchards, naval bases and light industry. Here are the towns of Camarillo, Port Hueneme and Ventura. Offshore lies the Channel Islands National Park.

The area enjoys a mild climate and soil that is good for growing fruits and vegetables, and it has also proven an excellent locale for a U.S. Navy construction center and air station that bracket Port Hueneme. Southeast of Port Hueneme, Point Mugu State Park embraces sandy beaches and the rugged Santa Monica Mountains.

The agricultural, military and light industry bases for this region's economy are bolstered by the oil industry, both on and offshore, and by tourism, especially with regard to boating.

The city of Ventura is the birthplace of the county and site of the historically important Mission San Buenaventura. With a symphony orchestra and archaeological, art and history museums, the city reflects the county's culture. Additionally, the city—attractive and important in its own right—is the gateway to the inland Ojai and Santa Paula valleys, Lake Casitas and Los Padres National Forest.

Within the following information, grid coordinates refer to the Automobile Club of Southern California's *Ventura County* map, unless otherwise noted.

CAMARILLO

Although it is about eight miles from the coast, Camarillo has been placed in this book's coastal section because it lies on the Oxnard Plain, an area with a mild coastal climate comfortable for people and conducive to agriculture. Camarillo is a city of approximately 55,800 people who enjoy living within an area of planned residential and light industrial growth.

Originally called Pleasant Valley, Camarillo began as part of the Rancho Calleguas in the 1890s, and was named for the Juan Camarillo family, owners of the ranch. The townsite was laid out in 1910, with much of the land, houses and stores located around the Southern Pacific train depot. As elsewhere in the

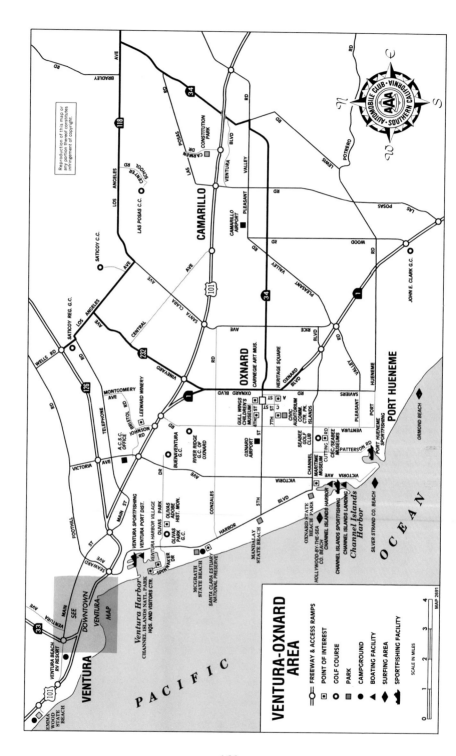

160

county, most of the economy depended upon ranching and farming. All was not work, however, as Juan Camarillo's descendants upheld the tradition of hosting fiestas and rodeos for the townspeople.

Throughout the first half of the 20th century Camarillo remained a small farming community, but the 1950s and '60s brought the freeway and though a good portion of the land is still devoted to crops, many farmers took the opportunity to sell their land to developers.

CONCERTS IN THE PARK
Constitution Park, Camarillo and Carmen drives (ACSC Simi & Conejo Valleys map, D-7). (805) 987-7847. From blue grass groups to armed forces' concert bands—everyone is sure to find music they like in this summertime outdoor series of live performances. Audience members need to bring a blanket to sit on, and picnicking is welcome. Concerts take place every other Saturday at 7 p.m., beginning the first part of June and running through Labor Day weekend, weather permitting. Admission is free.

CHANNEL ISLANDS AVIATION
at Camarillo Airport, 305 Durley Ave. (ACSC Simi & Conejo Valleys map, F-5). (805) 987-1301. Scenic flights go along the Ventura coast, to the Channel Islands, over the Ojai Valley or south to Malibu. Passengers may decide upon the route and the time spent. Scenic rides are given daily, weather and visibility permitting, between 8 a.m. and 5 p.m.; closed Christmas. The basic fare is $30 per person. Reservations are suggested.

Day trips to Santa Rosa Island are also available. Planes depart at 9 a.m., flying the Channel Islands chain to Santa Rosa, where passengers are met by a park ranger for a tour of the island. The fare is $85 per person; lunch is not provided. Reservations are necessary.

CHANNEL ISLANDS NATIONAL PARK

Less than 15 miles off the Santa Barbara and Ventura coastline, along the Santa Barbara Channel, lie the Channel Islands. Within this group of eight islands, five constitute Channel Islands National Park: Anacapa, San Miguel, Santa Barbara, Santa Cruz and Santa Rosa. The ocean for six nautical miles around these islands is designated Channel Islands National Marine Sanctuary. Of the flora and fauna that have evolved in this isolated environment, most have made unique adaptations to the winds and surf. Plant life on the islands includes delicate pink mallow and bright yellow coreopsis, and perched on the rocky cliffs are cormorants and brown pelicans. Within the sea's kelp forests are hundreds of marine species, while along the shore seals and sea lions often haul out. Archeological remains attest to the American Indians who once made their home here.

Because the islands and surrounding water support such a fragile balance of nature, strict regulations govern visitors' activities. There are no refreshment stands on the islands; the limited number of visitors who are

161

allowed must take their own food and water. Primitive camping is permitted on all the islands but Santa Cruz, and guided hikes are conducted by rangers on San Miguel and Santa Rosa islands. Camping and hiking must be arranged in advance through park headquarters; call (805) 658-5730. Private boats going to the islands must have landing permits; call (805) 964-7839.

Transportation to the islands is limited to private boats and chartered craft. Trips are offered by the following establishment; write or telephone for schedules, prices and reservations. (It is advisable to make reservations at least two weeks in advance.)

Island Packers Company, *1867 Spinnaker Drive, Ventura 93001; (805) 642-1393.*

Channel Islands National Park Visitor Center *1901 Spinnaker Drive, Ventura (C-6). (805) 658-5730.* Within this harbor-side structure are exhibits that graphically describe the park, including stuffed and mounted mammals and birds, and an indoor tidepool. Books and pamphlets about this and other national parks are available, and there is a video and a movie about the islands. On an outdoor deck are large, detailed models of the park's islands. A stairway and elevator lead up to the observation tower that affords a 360° view of the harbor and, on a clear day, the islands. Special live programs are offered on Saturday and Sunday. The center is open daily 8 a.m. to 5:30 p.m. Memorial Day through Labor Day;

Norma E. Palmer

Animals and artifacts found on the Channel Islands are displayed in the park's Visitor Center.

Monday through Friday 8:30 a.m. to 4:30 p.m., Saturday and Sunday 8 a.m. to 5 p.m. the rest of the year; closed Thanksgiving and Christmas.

LA CONCHITA

With a population around 200, La Conchita is among the smallest towns in Ventura County. La Conchita lies on the coast, on the north side of US 101, about 10 miles north of Ventura. The tiny community's claim to fame is the Seaside Banana Garden, at the west end of Santa Barbara Avenue.

SEASIDE BANANA GARDEN
La Conchita exit, off US 101. 6823 Santa Barbara Avenue (J-2). (805) 643-4061. This plantation of banana trees is situated on a narrow shelf of land between the ocean and 300-foot-high bluffs; the resultant blanket of relatively warm air that covers the trees comes close to approximating tropical temperatures. Fifty varieties of bananas are grown here, and much of the unusual and tasty fruit is for sale on the premises. Among the exotic bananas are the ice cream banana, lady finger, Hawaiian apple (Brazilian) and the Polynesian Haa-Haa. The fruit ripens at various times throughout the year, but the pickings are somewhat sparse in January and February. Also for sale are other types of fruit, as well as honey, dates and tropical plants. The banana garden's sales hut is open daily from 9 a.m. to 5 p.m.; closed major holidays.

Norma E. Palmer

Bananas in their natural state delight visitors to Seaside Banana Garden.

OXNARD

In 1898 a sugar beet processing factory owned by the Oxnard brothers—Henry, Robert, Benjamin and James—and the homes of the factory workers were the beginnings of any serious growth of the town which became Oxnard. The railroad came to Oxnard in that same year, and soon other businesses, homes, churches and schools were established, leading to incorporation of the city in 1903.

The sugar beet factory has passed into history, but Oxnard continued to grow and prosper, and is now the largest of Ventura County towns, with a population of nearly 147,000. In addition to residential areas from the ocean to the foothills, Oxnard has rich agricultural land, well-designed business parks, and a coastline offering sandy beaches and full-service marinas.

Oxnard has not forgotten its history, as can be clearly seen by a visit to Heritage Square. Another of the city's cultural advantages is the Ventura County Symphony, with an annual performance schedule that runs from October through the first week in May. Concerts are given in the Oxnard Civic Auditorium on Hobson Way in the Community Center Park. For ticket and schedule information call (805) 643-8646.

CARNEGIE ART MUSEUM *424 South C Street (K-11). (805) 385-8157.* Art works are displayed in an imposing, two-story structure that was built as a library in 1906. The museum's permanent collection focuses on 20th century California painters. Changing exhibits include oil paintings, sketches, photographs and sculpture—ranging from the sublime to the hilarious. The museum is open Thursday through Saturday from 10 a.m. to 5 p.m. and Sunday from 1 to 5 p.m.; closed New Year's Day, Thanksgiving, Christmas and periodically between exhibits. Admission is $2 for adults, $1 for ages 5-12 and seniors.

HERITAGE SQUARE *715 South A Street (K-11). (805) 483-7960.* Constructed in the late 1800s and early 1900s, the church, water tower, pump house and eleven homes here reflect such architectural styles as Queen Anne, Italianate and

Norma E. Palmer

Heritage Square preserves a number of Oxnard's imposing Victorian-era structures.

Craftsman. The buildings were moved from various parts of the Oxnard area to a single block, carefully restored and enhanced by landscaping and walkways. These charming houses are now occupied by offices and shops. The square is open during daylight hours; guided tours are offered on Saturday at 11 a.m. and 2 p.m. or by appointment; call for details. Admission is free.

SANTA CLARA ESTUARY NATURAL PRESERVE *McGrath State Beach (D-9). (805) 654-4744.* This preserve protects two endangered bird species, and fresh- and salt-water plants. A ½-mile self-guided trail winds among some of the preserve's trees and plants and leads to an estuary where the fresh water of the Santa Clara River meets the salt water of the ocean, and great flocks of shore birds gather. Trail guides are available at the state beach entrance station. The trail is open daily from 8 a.m. to sunset.

VENTURA COUNTY GULL WINGS CHILDREN'S MUSEUM *418 West Fourth Street (K-11). (805) 483-3005.* Children will find plenty to do here, for a variety of hands-on exhibits and activities include puppets and a stage, costumes and uniforms for acting out adult occupations, a make-believe campground with a tent and "fishing pond," a medical room with cutaway anatomical models and medical equipment, apparatus for making giant bubbles, and a rock and mineral display that includes fossil remains. The museum is open Wednesday through Friday and Sunday from 1 to 5 p.m.; Saturday

from 10 a.m. to 5 p.m. Admission is $3 for adults, $2 for ages 2-12.

VENTURA COUNTY MARITIME MUSEUM *2731 South Victoria Avenue, just past Channel Islands Boulevard (G-13). (805) 984-6260.* This museum harbors a collection of ship models reflecting maritime history from ancient times to the present and made from material that ranges from bone to wood to metal. The museum walls are graced by paintings of seagoing vessels. The museum is open Thursday through Monday 11 a.m. to 5 p.m.; closed New Year's Day, Thanksgiving and Christmas. Admission is $2 for adults; over age 65, $1 on Monday only; ages 5-12, $1.

POINT MUGU STATE PARK

Located between the Pacific Coast Highway (SR 1) and Potrero Valley Road, Point Mugu State Park is a place of dramatic contrasts: rugged mountains and sandy beaches; ferns growing by inland springs and chaparral-covered hillsides. Within the park's 15,000 acres are a five-mile shoreline just right for swimming, fishing or strolling. The backcountry offers hiking, camping and horseback riding (see *Recreation*).

Point Mugu's wildlife includes deer and rabbits, foxes and coyotes, and marine life such as seals and sea lions. In the early autumn hundreds of migrating monarch butterflies cluster here within sheltered groves of trees. For information about the park call (800) 533-7275.

PORT HUENEME

A land grant of 44,883 acres called *Rancho el Rio de Santa Clara o la Colonia* (Ranch of the River of Santa Clara or the colony) was awarded in 1840 to eight Mexican soldiers. The land included the western edge of the Oxnard Plain, with a point of land reaching into the Pacific. Twenty-four years later over 32,000 acres of the rancho were acquired by a Pennsylvania speculator, who in turn sold the land to a group of farmers and ranchers.

The town was plotted in 1869 and took its name from the Chumash settlement, *Weneme* or *Wenemu*, which had once occupied that area. Within two years the town included warehouses and a deepwater wharf, thus making Port Hueneme (wy-NEE-mee) the focal point for the transportation of grain and livestock. The town continued to grow through the remainder of the 19th century, but eventually was overshadowed by neighboring Oxnard.

In 1941 the U.S. Navy took advantage of the only deep-water port between Los Angeles and San Francisco to build a construction battalion (Seabee) training and shipping base at Port Hueneme. The center is the site of a museum to which civilian visitors are welcomed.

About four miles south of the Seabee base, the Navy launched a missile from Pt. Mugu in 1946 and went on to build facilities for the development and testing of many more missiles. From these beginnings grew the Naval Air Weapons Station. The base is used for research, testing, and engineering for air warfare's weapons systems and all their technical ramifications. Visitors, except on official business, are not permitted on the weapons station.

The military presence aside, Port Hueneme, with a population of more than 20,000, is an area of farmland and residential neighborhoods, and the site of a number of beaches and sportfishing landings (see *Recreation*).

U.S. NAVAL CONSTRUCTION BATTALION CENTER *off Cutting Road just west of Ventura Road (J-14).* First built in the early days of World War II, this is the Pacific center for the Navy Seabees, skilled construction experts. Seabees have actively fought in military engagements from World War II through Desert Storm and built camps, roads, airstrips and bridges in these war zones. CBC serves as home port, training, and logistical support for Seabees serving around the world. Visitors are allowed on base to visit the Seabee Museum (see below) or as members of group tours. For tour information call (805) 982-2059.

CEC/Seabee Museum *(805) 982-5163.* Models of equipment and battle scenes, weapons, uniforms, and arts and crafts by and about the Civil Engineer Corps and the Navy Seabees are housed here. Obtain a visitor pass at the Ventura Gate; those under age 16 must be accompanied by an adult. The museum is open Monday through Friday 8 a.m. to 4:30 p.m.; open Saturday at 9 a.m. and Sunday at 12:30; closed holidays; phone to confirm hours. Admission is free.

Norma E. Palmer

Completed in 1809, Mission San Buenaventura marked the beginning of the community of Ventura.

VENTURA

Following the secularization of Mission San Buenaventura's land in 1834, Spanish and Mexican settlers built adobe homes near the mission and took their places as tradespeople and government workers and officials. In the 1860s American and European settlers began coming into the area, and by the 1870s, because of economics and government regulations, most of the ranch lands had passed into American hands. Added to these were "Yankee" merchants and oil speculators, so that by the time the railroad arrived in 1887 San Buenaventura—now called Ventura—had become a thriving town of two-and three-story frame houses, stores with plate glass windows, mills and brickyards, school and churches.

Today Ventura, with a population of about 94,000, is considered a major agricultural center and oil producer, with the added advantage of miles of beaches and a warm, sunny climate, averaging 74 degrees year round. Ventura Harbor shelters a number of marinas and is the gateway to Channel Islands National Park. The city's ties to its past are beautifully displayed in the Albinger Archaeological Museum, the County Art and History Museum and the Olivas Adobe.

Like Santa Barbara, the city of Ventura boasts a Moreton Bay fig

167

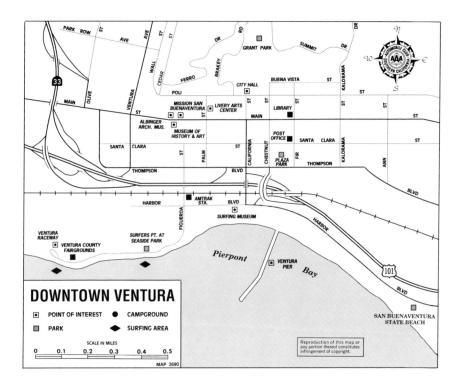

tree. It stands at the northwest corner of Plaza Park at Chestnut and Santa Clara streets. The tree is 73½ feet high, with a branch spread of 139 feet. Beneath that tree, and throughout the park on the first Sunday of each month (except January) from 10 a.m. to 4 p.m., a celebration of creativity is held—First Sunday in the Park. California arts and crafts people are represented by paintings, jewelry, needlework, handmade clothing and other handcrafted wares; food booths are also set up. Call (805) 658-4742.

ALBINGER ARCHAEOLOGICAL MUSEUM *113 East Main Street (A-3). (805) 648-5823.* Artifacts spanning 3,500 years are displayed here; all were excavated from a single site next to Mission San Buenaventura. Evidence of an early Indian culture dating from 1600 B.C. and the later Chumash Indians dating from A.D. 1500 is exhibited, along with objects dating from the mission's founding to the early 1900s. The original mission foundation and an earthen oven lie outside in the dig area. Two audiovisual programs are presented to visitors on request. The museum is open Wednesday through Sunday 10 a.m. to 4 p.m. Memorial Day weekend through Labor Day, Wednesday to Friday 10 a.m. to 2 p.m., Saturday through Sunday 10 a.m. to 4 p.m. the rest of the year; closed January 1, Easter, Thanksgiving and Christmas. Admission is free.

168

C STREET SURFING MUSEUM

342 South California Street, in the plaza on the east side of Holiday Inn (A-4). (805) 643-2742. This small museum contains surfboards—both historically significant and modern. Additionally there are photographs, paintings, sketches and memorabilia pertaining to surfing. The museum is open Saturday and Sunday 10 a.m. to 4 p.m. Donations are appreciated.

MISSION SAN BUENAVENTURA

225 East Main Street; entrance is through a gift shop just east of the mission (A-3). (805) 648-4496. Founded in 1782 and completed in 1809, the present mission includes a restored church and a small museum. Within the museum are Chumash artifacts and vestments, books and other items from the mission's early days. The courtyard is centered by a tiled fountain and contains an antique olive press. The mission church still serves an active congregation and is open to visitors Monday through Saturday 10 a.m. to 5 p.m., Sunday 10 a.m. to 4 p.m.; closed major holidays. Admission $1; under age 16, 50¢.

OLIVAS ADOBE HISTORICAL PARK

4200 Olivas Park Drive (E-7). (805) 644-4346. A two-story adobe home was built in the Monterey style in 1847 by Raymundo Olivas, and its displays of period furnishings and handicrafts help to make early California history come alive. An exhibit building contains artifacts from the adobe and rancho eras in Ventura County. The grounds include a small adobe, an adobe pit, rose and herb gardens. The grounds are open Tuesday through Friday 10 a.m. to 4 p.m.;

Norma E. Palmer

Through these wrought-iron gates lies the 1847 adobe structure that was once home of the Raymundo Olivas family.

the house and exhibit building are open Saturday and Sunday 10 a.m. to 4 p.m.; self-guided tours are available. Both house and grounds are closed major holidays. Admission is free.

THE LIVERY ARTS CENTER

North Palm Street just north of Main Street (A-3). Colorful murals mark the place where a handful of whimsical shops and outdoor eating places are centered around a plaza. The Plaza Players, a community theatrical group, perform here throughout the year in a 135-seat indoor theater. Presentations range from children's theater to adult drama to Broadway musicals. Performances are given

169

Norma E. Palmer

From the city hall, a Spanish padre continues to oversee life in San Buenaventura.

Wednesday, Friday and Saturday at 8 p.m. Tickets are priced from $7 to $10. Since the theater is dark between each six-week run of a production, it is best to call ahead; phone (805) 643-9460.

SAN BUENAVENTURA CITY HALL *501 Poli Street, north end of California Street (B-3). (805) 654-7850.* This imposing city landmark was built in 1913 and served originally as the county courthouse. Set on a hillside and beautifully landscaped, the building is noted for its terra cotta exterior, copper-covered dome, marble foyer, rooms and hallways with paneled walls and coffered ceilings. A statue of Junipero Serra stands in its own small plaza south of the city hall across the street. The building is open Monday through Friday 9 a.m. to 5 p.m. Tours are available for a fee upon request; call (805) 658-4756.

VENTURA COUNTY MUSEUM OF HISTORY & ART *100 East Main Street (A-4). (805) 653-0323.* Native American, Spanish and pioneer influences in Ventura County are all reflected in the exhibits in this attractive museum. In addition to historical artifacts, space is devoted to visual art. The museum includes displays of agricultural equipment, the George Stuart Historical Figures, changing exhibits and a research library. The museum is open Tuesday through Sunday 10 a.m. to 5 p.m.; closed January 1, Thanksgiving and Christmas. Admission is $2 for adults; ages 6 through 12 are free when accompanied by an adult; free to all on the second Tuesday of each month.

VENTURA HARBOR VILLAGE *1559 Spinnaker Drive, about one mile west of Harbor Boulevard (D-7). (805) 644-0169.* This shopping and entertainment center is situated beside a marina and offers specialty shops, restaurants, a carousel and a community theater.

Theatre-by-the-Sea. This is a 65-seat, arena-style venue that features comedies, drama, musicals and children's theater. Adult prices range from $8 to $15; children's performances are $4 to $5. The theater also presents an audience-participation murder mystery, with dinner included, at a cost of $28 per person. Call (805) 655-7790 for information and reservations.

VENTURA PIER *just east of the south end of California Street; parking area through entrance to San Buenaventura State Beach off Harbor Boulevard (B-4).* The first pier at this location was completed in 1872 and served as a harbor for steamships. Today this 1958-foot-long pier, reputedly the longest wooden pier in California, boasts a sturdy Douglas fir deck, bait shop, snack bar and restrooms. This is a good place to enjoy ocean and city views while fishing or strolling. There are benches along the way, and plaques on the railings explain the area's marine life and the pier's history.

VENTURA RACEWAY *at Ventura Fairgrounds, 10 West Harbor Boulevard (A-4). (805) 656-1122.* This seaside, ⅛-mile dirt oval racetrack hosts street stock cars, ¾ midgets, motorcycles and just about everything else that comes under the categories of open-wheel cars, stock, off-road vehicles and motocross. Races are held most Fridays and Saturdays April through November; call for exact dates. Gates open at 6 p.m. and racing starts at 8 p.m. on Fridays; open at 5 p.m., with racing beginning 7 p.m. on Saturdays. Admission prices range from $8-$12 for adults; under age 12, free.

FARMERS MARKETS

Ventura County's coastal area is rich in agricultural land that produces a variety of fruits, nuts and vegetables. This produce is available at weekly farmers markets . The markets sometimes include plants, crafts, prepared food and entertainment. Call the numbers shown for details.

Camarillo

2220 Ventura Boulevard on Saturdays from 8:30 a.m. to noon. (805) 482-0089.

Oxnard

Corner of B and Seventh streets on Thursdays from 10 a.m. to 1 p.m. (805) 483-7960.

Ventura

Corner of Santa Clara and California streets on Saturdays from 8:30 a.m. to noon. (805) 529-6266.

Montgomery Wards' parking lot, Main Street and Mills Road, on Wednesdays from 10 a.m. to 1 p.m. (805) 529-6266.

WINERY

Leeward Winery *2784 Johnson Drive, near southeast corner of Capri Avenue and Johnson Drive (J-6), Ventura. (805) 656-5054.* This small winery purchases grapes from California vineyards to produce Cabernet Sauvignon, Chardonnay, Pinot Noir and Merlot. Tours and tasting are offered daily from 10 a.m. to 4 p.m.; closed Thanksgiving and Christmas.

Norma E. Palmer

A whole-access interpretive trail in Thousand Oaks offers dappled sunlight through great oak trees.

Simi and Conejo Valleys

The Conejo and Simi valleys lie on plateaus approximately 800 feet in elevation, and in any direction there is a view of rolling hills or mountain peaks. The largest communities here, Thousand Oaks in the Conejo Valley and the city of Simi Valley, are centers of residence and commerce that nevertheless retain something of a feeling of country living, in marked contrast to the urban sprawl just across the Los Angeles County border. This area is also home to a private four-year school, California Lutheran University.

From the mid-1800s to the early 1900s, ranching and agriculture were an important economic factor in this area, and horse ranches and orchards continue to border residential neighborhoods. In the 1920s and '30s movie-making came to the valleys; the Santa Monica Mountains were irresistible backgrounds, and a lake was named Sherwood following the filming of *Robin Hood*. The Simi Hills have provided a believable locale for dozens of television and feature-film Westerns.

Within the following information, grid coordinates refer to the Automobile Club of Southern California's *Simi & Conejo Valleys* map, unless otherwise noted.

SIMI VALLEY

In 1795 Rancho Simi became the first land grant in present Ventura County and, with its more than 113,000 acres, one of California's largest. Following the usual scenario, the land was ultimately acquired by American settlers. In 1888 a colony called Simiopolis was established as a health resort that included an imposing hotel. After three years, the colony died out, and only a few farm families remained in the area. They established a school, built stores and shortened the town's name to Simi. ("Simi" is apparently derived from the name of the original Chumash village that stood here: *Shimiyi* or *Shimii*.)

Simi began to grow as the Southern Pacific Railroad tunneled through the Santa Susana Mountains on the way to Los Angeles from 1900 to 1904. Farmers, attracted to a land in which fruit and walnut orchards prospered, were aided by the presence of a packing house near the railroad in the vicinity of what is now the town of Simi Valley.

173

The valley remained a small farming community until the real estate boom of the early 20th century brought more settlers to the area. The proliferation of the automobile and the construction of the Simi/San Fernando Valley Freeway (SR 118) in the 1970s brought even more people into the area. Simi Valley, population over 100,800, has grown as a town in its own right and as a bedroom community for people working in Los Angeles or the San Fernando Valley.

RONALD REAGAN PRESIDENTIAL LIBRARY *40 Presidential Drive (E-9). (805) 522-8444.* This significant library and museum is housed in a Spanish Mission-style structure built around a courtyard. The complex is set upon a hilltop that affords a view of the surrounding countryside, including the Simi Hills. Included in the library's collection are photographs and memorabilia of President Reagan's life, gifts of state received during his administration, a full-size replica of the Oval Office and a large section of the Berlin Wall. The library is open Monday through Saturday 10 a.m. to 5 p.m., Sunday noon to 5 p.m; closed New Year's Day, Thanksgiving and Christmas. Admission is $4 for adults; over age 62, $2; age 15 and under, free.

STRATHEARN HISTORICAL PARK AND MUSEUM *137 Strathearn Place (D-10). (805) 526-6453.* Today's park was originally part of a Mexican land

Norma E. Palmer

Strathearn Historical Park and Museum attracts visitors interested in the early history of Simi Valley.

grant given to Santiago Pico in 1795, then purchased by Jose de la Guerra in 1842. The Robert P. Strathearn family acquired a portion of the land and built a two-story house there in 1892-93, incorporating two rooms of the original 1840s adobe.

A docent-led tour includes the Strathearn house and its period furnishings, as well as structures which have been relocated to the site. These include a Simi Colony house, the original Simi Library and two barns. A visitor center, through photos, maps, paintings and artifacts, evokes Simi Valley's history from the 1800s to the mid-1900s. A film that is shown before the tour includes information on Chumash culture, Spanish rancho days and turn-of-the-century American farm life. Tours are given Saturday and Sunday from 1 to 4 p.m.; one tour is given on Wednesday at 1 p.m.; closed during rainy weather, New Year's Day, Mother's Day and Christmas.

THOUSAND OAKS

Thousand Oaks, with a population of approximately 104,000, was once an extensive land grant called *Rancho El Conejo* (*conejo* is Spanish for rabbit). When the three families which had come to own the land in the 1840s began selling off acreage to other ranchers, they in turn began farming and raising cattle and horses. Ranching and agriculture thrived for decades, and in the 1920s and '30s movie-making became an added industry in the Conejo Valley. Tourists were attracted to a large menagerie of

animals used for motion pictures, and as businesses grew to serve the visitors, the town of Thousand Oaks began to develop. It remained a very small town, however, until the construction of the US 101 freeway in the 1950s, followed by a master plan which led to incorporation in 1964.

Today Thousand Oaks is a pleasant and attractive community of wide streets, well-kept houses and carefully tended parks and business areas. Parenthetically, it is doubtful that anyone has ever counted the oak trees in Thousand Oaks; the name was determined by the winner of a contest sponsored by land developers in the 1920s.

In the western portion of Thousand Oaks lies Newbury Park, named for the Newbury family, one of the three families originally holding title to Rancho El Conejo. Today Newbury Park, in addition to being a pleasantly sited bedroom community, boasts what was originally the imposing two-story Grand Hotel. Constructed in 1876, the structure was rebuilt following a move and a disastrous fire. Now it is the Stagecoach Inn Museum, an important repository of Conejo Valley history and memorabilia.

CONEJO VALLEY ART MUSEUM
193 North Moorpark Road, in the Janss Mall (K-6). (805) 373-0054.
Here is a small museum with a great range of art works presented in various exhibits throughout the year. Among the museum's exhibitions at one time or another have been oil paintings, prehistoric pottery, quilts, photographs, sketches and print making. On the premises is a shop

featuring folk art, jewelry and books. The museum is open Wednesday through Sunday noon to 5 p.m., closed major holidays and periodically between exhibits.

OAK CREEK CANYON WHOLE ACCESS INTERPRETIVE TRAIL

Green Meadow Drive, ½ mile north of Moorpark Road (K-6). (805) 495-6471. Part of the Los Robles Open Space, this ¼-mile trail follows a portion of Oak Creek Canyon and is designed for those with special mobility and communication challenges. A wide, specially surfaced trail winds past oak and sycamore trees, following a sturdy wooden fence, with a bridle path on the opposite side of the fence. Along the way are blind-guide cables, Braille interpretive posts and picnic tables.

STAGECOACH INN MUSEUM *51 South Ventu Park Road in Newbury Park (K-4). (805) 498-9441.* This structure first opened in 1876 as a stopping place for travelers journeying between Los Angeles and Santa Barbara. The reconstructed Monterey-style building houses changing exhibits, Victorian furnishings and artifacts from Conejo Valley's early days. A restored carriage house, pioneer house and adobe with displays of Chumash artifacts are open on Sunday only. The museum is open Wednesday through Sunday 1 to 4 p.m.; closed holidays. Donations.

WILDWOOD REGIONAL PARK

Parking area at Avenida Los Arboles and Big Sky Drive (G-5). (805) 495-6471. At the northwest edge of carefully planned and tended residential neighborhoods are over a thousand acres of wild and open space called Wildwood Regional Park. Within the park is a wide range of plant and animal life, unusual geologic forms and archaeological sites. Among the vegetation are spring wildflower displays and, all year, oak, chaparral and sage. Wildlife includes mule deer, ground squirrels, rabbits and coyotes. Within the bird community are hummingbirds, kestrels, scrub jays and meadowlarks. Running through the park from east to west is a dramatic volcanic outcropping named Mountclef Ridge. The north fork of the Arroyo Conejo flows through one of the park's two canyons, and following a rainy season, waterfalls are evident. Artifacts such as stone tools, shell beads and arrowheads have been found here. Believed to date back many thousands of years, they indicate seasonal and permanent Native American settlements.

The park is not open to motor vehicles except for park department vehicles.

From the parking area at Avenida Los Arboles and Big Sky Drive, people can hike, bicycle or horseback ride on designated trails. The gate into the park is locked at 8 p.m. from May 1 through September 15; it is locked at 5 p.m. the rest of the year.

Primitive camping is allowed twice a year by reservation only; a fee is charged. From February through May free naturalist-guided hikes are given on Saturdays from 9 to 11 a.m. Call (805) 494-8301 for information on camping and hiking. Admission to the park is free.

FARMERS MARKET

The Simi and Conejo valley's agricultural area is particularly rich in citrus fruit, avocados and nuts. This and other produce is available in season at a farmers market held weekly. The market sometimes includes crafts and entertainment.

Thousand Oaks

In the Janss Mall at Moorpark Road and Hillcrest Drive on Thursdays from 4 to 7 p.m. (805) 529-6266.

This 1890 building in Santa Paula now houses the UNOCAL Oil Museum.

Ojai And Santa Paula Areas

With the founding in 1874 of the town of Nordhoff (later to be called Ojai), people began coming to the Ojai Valley for the mild, invigorating climate, sightseeing among the hills and valleys or establishing farms and orchards.

When the railroad began running from Ventura in 1898, even more people ventured into the valley, including wealthy Easterners such as millionaire John D. Rockefeller Sr., Charles Pratt (secretary of Standard Oil) and glass manufacturer Edward D. Libbey. It was Libbey who ultimately had a great influence on the distinctive architecture of the town of Ojai.

In the meantime, the fledgling citrus industry in the Santa Paula and Fillmore area was given a boost in 1887 when a branch of the Southern Pacific Railroad reached the area and began providing transportation for the growers' oranges and lemons. A second important industry had made a spectacular comeback in the 1880s—oil. By 1886 one company was producing 6000 barrels a day, and in 1890 this and two other companies met in Santa Paula to incorporate as the Union Oil Company.

Within the following information, grid coordinates refer to the Automobile Club of Southern California's *Ojai Valley Area* map, unless otherwise noted.

FILLMORE

Named for a Southern Pacific Railroad Official, J.P. Fillmore, the town was laid out in 1887 by the Sespe Land and Water Company and grew up around the railroad depot. Only 150 residents occupied the town by 1900, and the remaining land was divided into parcels on which ranchers built homes and planted citrus orchards. In the early 1860s oil had been discovered around Fillmore and Santa Paula, but the biggest boom came to Fillmore after 1915. Soon many of the citrus orchards were subdivided and houses built for the oil workers and others who began pouring into the area. The town continued to expand, as citrus orchards, walnut and apricot groves kept pace with the oil industry.

Surrounded by orchards, vegetable farms and oil fields, and with a population near 13,000, Fillmore today is a pleasant town of tree-shaded streets. Many houses, business structures and churches remain from the late 1800s, and visitors to the

Norma E. Palmer

*Built at the turn of the 20th century, this church
is one of Fillmore's landmark buildings.*

LAKE CASITAS RECREATION AREA

Lake Casitas is set in a valley surrounded by rolling hills and graced with oak, fir and sycamore trees, while the Santa Ynez Mountains serve as dramatic background. The main entrance to the recreation area is off SR 150, approximately three miles west of its junction with SR 33.

Lake Casitas is actually a reservoir which provides water for the daily use of more than 50,000 Ventura County residents, and recreation for residents and visitors. The lake has a 35-mile-long, irregularly shaped shoreline from which fishermen haul in trout, bass, crappie, catfish and red-ear sunfish. At the north end of the lake are more than 700 picnicking and camping sites (see *Recreation*). In March and September Lake Casitas is the site of the Ojai Renaissance Festival (see *Annual Events*).

town are welcome to view these buildings, using a free guide available from the Chamber of Commerce at 567 Sespe Avenue; telephone (805) 524-0351.

FILLMORE FISH HATCHERY
One mile east of Fillmore off I-126 (J-8, ACSC Ventura County map). (805) 524-0962. Over a million rainbow trout are on view here. Raised from eggs to catchable size, the fish are then transported in specially equipped trucks to California lakes and streams. A nickel in a machine buys a handful of special food for these finny friends. California Department of Fish and Game personnel are on hand to answer questions. The hatchery is open daily 7 am. to 3:30 pm; closed major holidays. Admission is free.

From mid-April through mid-September a small store is open at the lake, and a snack bar is open all year. There is also a bait and tackle shop, and fish cleaning areas are available. Because the lake is a domestic drinking water supply, water skiing and swimming are not allowed. Fees are charged for day use and for camping. For information about the lake's recreational activities, call (805) 649-2233.

OJAI

A gentleman named Charles Nordhoff wrote a book in the 1870s called *California for Health, Pleasure and Residence* and consequently in 1874 had a California town named for him. In 1917, however, Nordhoff (the town) became Ojai, thanks to the even greater influence of the area's original inhabitants—*ojai* is derived from the Chumash word *Awhai*, meaning "moon."

Founded in 1874, the town soon began to assume the role of vacation destination, particularly for Edward D. Libbey, glass manufacturing millionaire. Eventually, under his direction, architect Richard Requa designed the arched arcade fronting two blocks of the downtown shops.

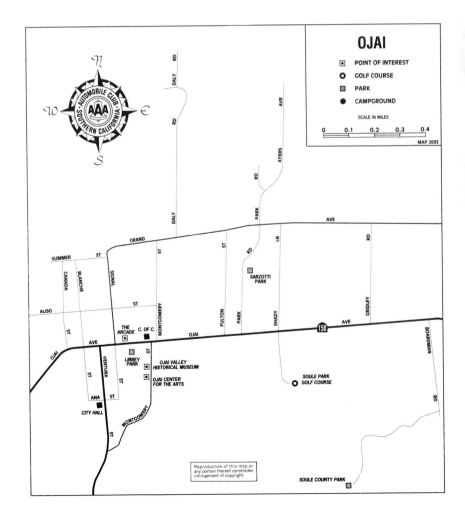

The arcade remains today, as does Libbey Park just south of the arcade and Requa's Spanish-style tower that rises above Ojai's post office.

With a population of approximately 7600 and boasting only three traffic signals, Ojai sits in an especially beautiful valley, sheltered by rugged mountains and gentle hills, and bordered with horse ranches and citrus orchards. Perhaps best known for its artists, musicians and philosophers, Ojai shows off its artists and their works every Sunday from 9 a.m. to 5 p.m. at the corner of Blanche Street and Ojai Avenue. Many of the artists open their studios to visitors; contact the Ojai Chamber of Commerce, 338 East Ojai Avenue, telephone (805)

646-8126, for details. April is the month for the decades-old Ojai Festival, when classical music is presented outdoors in Libbey Park. The Ojai Valley Tennis Tournament, held annually since 1899, is another April event (see *Annual Events*).

Map coordinates in the following descriptions refer to the *Ojai Valley Area* map unless noted otherwise.

THE ARCADE *North side of Ojai Avenue between Signal and Montgomery streets (C-7)*. This Mission Revival-style shopping arcade, built in 1917, has shops that offer such tempting merchandise as hand-crafted jewelry, sculpted figures and vessels, "wearable art," clothing

Norma E. Palmer

Built in the early 1900s, an arcade and post office are Ojai landmarks.

182

and objects from Central America and Mexico, and American Indian jewelry and clothing. There's even an English tea room. A medium-sized, traditional department store is also located here. An air of relaxed independence prevails among the store owners, so most stores open about 10 a.m., and a few close at 4 p.m., more at 5 p.m., with some staying open until 6 p.m. on weekends.

THE OJAI CENTER FOR THE ARTS *113 Montgomery Street (C-7). (805) 646-0117.* Displayed here are the works of California artists: paintings, sketches and sculpture that in a diversity of media capture a diversity of people and moods. Since these are changing exhibits, and the gallery is closed during changeovers, visitors are advised to call ahead. A vital cultural asset to Ojai, the center also offers fine arts classes, workshops and seminars.

Upstairs, a 100-seat community theater presents live performances of musical comedy and drama on weekends throughout the year. The art gallery is open Tuesday through Sunday noon to 4 p.m. Call for theater performance schedules. Admission to the art gallery is free. Tickets for theater performances range from $5 to $10 each.

THE OJAI TROLLEY COMPANY
A bus that's made to look like an old fashioned trolley car, inside and out, takes passengers all over Ojai for just 25¢. Running along Ojai Avenue from Maricopa Highway and Rancho Drive on the west to Gridley Road on the east, the trolley also takes in Grand Avenue. Stops are clearly marked with trolley signs. A central boarding point is in front of the Chamber of Commerce office on the north side of Ojai Avenue near Montgomery Street. The trolley does not run on major holidays.

OJAI VALLEY HISTORICAL MUSEUM *109 Montgomery Street (C-7). (805) 646-2290.* In what was once a fire station, the local historical society has assembled attractive displays of the natural and human history of the Ojai Valley. Among the exhibits are flora, fauna, shells and rocks found in the area; a representative array of Chumash artifacts; and tools, furniture, household items and photographs that reflect the early settlement of Nordhoff/Ojai. The museum is open Wednesday through Monday. Donations are appreciated.

OUTDOOR ART EXHIBIT *corner of Blanche Street and Ojai Avenue (C-7). (805) 646-6433.* Over many years, this exhibit has become a weekly Ojai tradition. Ventura County artists in painting, sketching, sculpting and other art forms display and sell their works. The art works are on display each Sunday from 9 a.m. to 5 p.m. Admission is free.

SANTA PAULA

Santa Paula, with hundreds of acres already devoted to fruit trees, was established as a townsite in the Santa Clara River Valley in 1875. Orchards, particularly lemon and orange, continue to prosper, and the oil industry has kept pace with the citrus industry. During the 1880s three oil com-

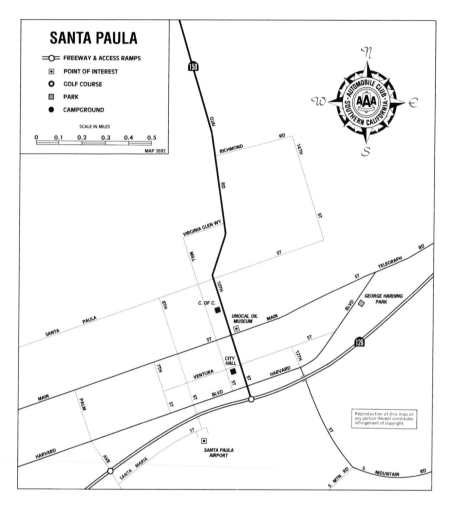

panies, Hardison and Stewart, Sespe Oil, and Torrey Cañon Oil, made significant strikes in Ventura County. In October 1890, in the Santa Paula building now housing the UNOCAL Oil Museum, the principal stockholders of these companies signed incorporation papers to become the Union Oil Company. Three years later a group of businessmen and growers formed the Limoneira Company in Santa Paula, a partnership that eventually became one of the largest lemon producers in the world.

Santa Paula was incorporated in 1902, and today its population of nearly 26,000 enjoys a small town ambience, along with such modern amenities as shopping centers and a general aviation airport. Visitors can enjoy good examples of Victorian architecture throughout the town and in the countryside. One of the finest examples is the 1894 Faulkner House at 4292 Telegraph Road, just west of Briggs Road. While this beautifully restored three-story mansion is not open to the public, it can be seen from the road. The bright red barn on the grounds houses the Ayers Pumpkin Patch; pumpkins are sold to the public in October, and Christmas trees are offered for sale from the day after Thanksgiving until December 22.

A brochure outlining scenic areas and historic buildings is available free of charge from the Santa Paula Chamber of Commerce, in the train depot at 10th and Santa Barbara streets; telephone (805) 525-5561.

Along SR 126 east of Santa Paula there are views of citrus groves and ranches, with hills and mountains as a backdrop. Roadside stands offer such local produce as avocados, strawberries, lemons, grapefruit and oranges. A little over four miles east of Santa Paula on the south side of SR 126 stands Santa Clara School, a genuine "Little Red Schoolhouse," built in 1896. With its belltower and white Colonial Revival trim, this historical landmark is still in use as an elementary school, and is the county's only one-room schoolhouse.

Map coordinates in the followng descriptions refer to the *Ojai Valley Area* map unless noted otherwise.

Norma E. Palmer

Completed in 1894, this mansion near Santa Paula was the culmination of George Washington Faulkner's dream of "a beautiful home."

Norma E. Palmer

The nearly century-old Little Red Schoolhouse is still in use.

SANTA PAULA AIRPORT *entrance off Santa Maria Street, just east of 8th Street (D-4). (805) 933-1155.* This well-maintained general aviation airport was founded in 1930, and today is probably best known for its extensive collection of privately owned antique, classic, home-built and modern small planes. The antique and classic aircraft are on public display the first Sunday of each month from 10 a.m. to 3 p.m. Admission is free.

Santa Paula Flight Center—Scenic Rides *at Santa Paula Airport (D-4). (805) 525-3561.* For an exhilarating high-in-the-sky view of the Santa Clara River Valley, these scenic flights take you over farmland, houses,

orchards, hills and canyons to the Ventura coast and back. The aircraft is a Cessna 172, which has room for three passengers. Scenic rides are given daily, weather and visibility permitting, between 8 a.m. and 5 p.m.; closed Christmas. The basic flight lasts 20 minutes and costs $40; additional time for flying up or down the coast or to view the Channel Islands is available for an additional $1 per minute. Reservations are suggested.

UNOCAL OIL MUSEUM *1001 East Main Street (D-3). (805) 933-0076.* The 1890 landmark building in which the Union Oil Company was founded is today devoted to showing the history and science of oil exploration in California, through memorabilia, photographs, murals and interactive videos. One room in the museum houses changing exhibits on various subjects, from Santa Paula's airport to works by local artists. Visitors may take a guided tour of the building's second floor where the oil company's 19th-century offices and an apartment have been recreated, including original woodwork, ten fireplaces with original tiles, and journals and ledgers dating back to the late 1800s.

In a separate building stands an impressive 100-year-old steam-powered Cable-Tool drilling rig. A pleasant outdoor area with wooden benches adjoins the museum, just right for resting and picnicking. The museum is open Wednesday through Sunday from 10 a.m. to 4 p.m.; closed major holidays. Donations are appreciated.

FARMERS MARKET

Ventura County's inland agricultural area is particularly rich in citrus fruit, avocados and nuts. This and other produce is available in season at a farmers market held weekly. The market sometimes include potted plants, crafts, prepared food and entertainment. Call the number shown for details.

Ojai

In a parking area between Signal, Aliso, Montgomery and Matilija streets on Sunday from 10 a.m. to 2 p.m. In addition to fresh fruits and vegetables, there are herbs, flowers, baked goods and fresh seafood. (805) 646-4444.

WINERY

Old Creek Ranch Winery *1½ miles south of Oak View at the end of Old Creek Road (J-3, ACSC Ventura County map). (805) 649-4132.* Grapes from the Santa Maria Valley and Ventura County are used in six varietal wines produced here. Open for tasting Friday through Sunday from 10 a.m. to 4:30 p.m.; tours by appointment.

Norma E. Palmer

One of the many produce markets that beckon motorists along SR 126.

Near SR 33 in Los Padres National Forest, a waterfall feeds a branch of Matilija Creek.

Los Padres National Forest

As with Santa Barbara County, a major portion of Ventura County's backcountry lies within Los Padres National Forest, including the rugged mountains and deep valleys. On Ventura County's northern border with Kern County stands Mount Pinos, its peak rising to 8831 feet.

Within Ventura County two well-maintained, paved roads venture into a large portion of the national forest: SR 33 and Lockwood Valley Road that leads west off SR 33. Cuddy Valley and Frazier Mountain roads in Kern County go west and east off Lockwood Valley Road.

Both paved and unpaved roads lead to picnic areas and campgrounds within the forest. A word of warning: Following a season of heavy rain, creekbeds which cross highways may contain deep water, making crossing difficult. Signs along Lockwood Valley Road warn, "Next 17 miles, road may be impassable due to rain or snow."

Following are a few of the possible sightseeing trips in Los Padres, starting from Ojai. Map coordinates in the descriptions refer to ACSC's *Ventura County* map.

SR 33 northwest of Ojai goes past residential areas, then ranches and orchards and winds through a valley at the foot of Nordhoff Ridge. About

5½ miles from Ojai lies Wheeler Springs (G-3), a tiny mountain settlement, with a campground nearby. Through Wheeler Gorge (G-4), mountain peaks rise on all sides, and in the spring wild flowers and flowering bushes splash color along the roadside. If the winter has been wet enough, a waterfall near the highway splashes down into Matilija Creek.

About seven miles north of Wheeler Springs is the road to Rose Lake and Lion's Head Campground (G-5). The road is paved, but bumpy in spots. There are rugged hills on either side of the road, where manzanita is visible, and wildflowers bloom in season. Rose Lake, small and picturesque, serves as a home or stopover for waterfowl. Not far from the lake are a work camp, gun club and ranch.

Turning back north to Lion's Head Campground affords a view of Piedra Blanca (G-5)—a large rock formation with layers of white rock standing in sharp contrast to the dark green and brown of the soil and stone which

Norma E. Palmer

Rose Lake provides a calm oasis in Los Padres National Forest.

surround it. Back on SR 33 going northward, the road winds through scenic Sespe Gorge (F-4) at the foot of Pine Mountain (F-3), where Reyes Peak rises to 7510 feet.

East on Lockwood Valley Road (E-3) from SR 33 brings varied terrain: Placid farmland, hills of red soil, wind- and water-sculpted mountainsides, forested land, plains covered with scrub and sage, cattle ranches.

Lake of the Woods, in Kern County (C-7), is at the northern terminus of Lockwood Valley Road. Cuddy Valley Road (C-6) goes west about five miles to the road leading south to campgrounds and Mt. Pinos Ski Center. Approximately five miles west of that intersection is Pine Mountain (C-5), a golf course and campgrounds. To the east of Lakewood Valley Road, Frazier Mountain Road (C-7) leads through the small town of Frazier

Park (C-7) to the I-5 Freeway (C-8) in Los Angeles County. This portion of the national forest may receive two to three feet of snow in winter, with eight feet often recorded at Mt. Pinos. When visiting the area in winter, it is always best to bring tire chains.

LAKE PIRU RECREATION AREA

This four-mile-long lake, formed by the Santa Felicia Dam, takes its name from the Chumash word for the reeds that once grew on the site. In addition to its recreational uses, Lake Piru provides water for industrial and domestic consumers in Ventura County.

Although administered by the United Water Conservation District in Santa Paula, the northern portion of Lake

Piru lies within Los Padres National Forest. Approximately 7½ miles east of Fillmore off SR 126, the six-mile Piru Canyon Road leads north to Lake Piru through the small town of Piru. The recreation area offers boating, camping, fishing, swimming and waterskiing. For more information on these activities, see *Recreation*.

SESPE CONDOR SANCTUARY

Although endangered California condors were not, at press time, living in Los Padres National Forest, there are plans to reintroduce these largest of North American land birds back into this area during 1994 or 1995.

Sightseeing, camping and picnicking are all popular activities within Los Padres National Forest. Hiking, fishing and horseback riding can also be enjoyed. Information about these and other recreational activities are in *Recreation*.

Los Padres National Forest has two district offices in this portion of the forest. Ojai Ranger District (H-4), 1190 East Ojai Avenue, Ojai 93023, is open Monday through Friday from 8 a.m. to 4:30 p.m.; phone (805) 646-4348. Mt. Pinos Ranger District (C-7), 34580 Lockwood Valley Road, Frazier Park 93225, is open Monday through Saturday from 8 a.m. to 4:30 p.m.; phone (805) 245-3731; mailing address: HC-1, Box 400, Frazier Park 93225. The ranger stations have descriptive literature about the forest, its flora and fauna, and regulations governing camping, hiking, biking, etc.

The lake in Rancho Simi Community Park offers good fishing.

Recreation

Weather and terrain combine in Ventura County to make outdoor recreation an ideal way to spend one's time. Among the possibilities are camping that varies from seaside to mountainside; hiking on paths that lead through city parks or up mountain trails; or fishing that's rewarding from an ocean-going vessel or from a boat on a lake.

Maps and grid coordinates within the following information refer to maps produced by the Automobile Club of Southern California.

BEACHCOMBING

Faria and Hobson county parks can be good areas for rockhounding, with pebbles worn smooth by tumbling in the tides or larger rocks marked by wind and water erosion. Shells and driftwood are very much in evidence after winter storms along Point Mugu State Park.

BICYCLING

Bicycling is both enjoyable and challenging through Ventura County's relatively flat valleys, gently rolling hills and rugged mountains. Many communities within the county have marked routes to accommodate cyclists, and most state highways are wide enough for motor vehicles and bicycles.

Class I bikeways represent a separate right-of-way for bicycles, often fenced and found along the beach and flood control channels. Access may be limited to designated points. Class II bikeways are restricted rights-of-way for bicycles, most often designated by a line and signs on the road. Motor vehicles are permitted to use the bike lane to make turns and to park. Class III bikeways are travel lanes shared by bicycles and motor vehicles, designated by signs only. This type of bikeway does not provide cyclists with increased privileges, but does inform motorists of the cycling route. Additionally, there are unsigned state routes where bicycles are permitted. A difficulty rating of "A" indicates that the ride is level throughout. "B" denotes a partially or moderately hilly route, not too strenuous for the average cyclist.

Following is a brief sampling of bike paths in Ventura County. To obtain a comprehensive map of designated bike paths, with a list of local bicycle clubs, contact Ventura County

Transportation Commission, 950 County Square Drive, Suite 205, Ventura 93003; phone (805) 642-1591.

Ventura Coast

Ventura Harbor Area Length, approximately 3 miles; Class I; Difficulty Rating B.

The northwest end of this bikeway starts at the Ventura River Group Camp near the intersection of US 101 and SR 33 (*Ventura County* map, L-3). It continues to the Ventura County Fairgrounds and winds along the beach, past the Ventura Pier to San Buenaventura State Beach.

Ventura to Port Hueneme Length, approximately 5 miles; Class II; Difficulty Rating A.

This bikeway runs from Harbor Boulevard and Olivas Park Drive, (city of Ventura, *Ventura County* map, D-7) passes McGrath State Beach and Mandalay State Beach before entering seaside residential areas and ending at Channel Islands Harbor.

RENTALS

Surrey Cycle & Bicycle Rentals *819 East Thompson Boulevard; (805) 653-0449.* This establishment rents mountain bikes, beach cruisers, surrey cycles (quad bikes) and roller skates. Open Monday through Friday 10 a.m. to 5 p.m., Saturday 10 a.m. to 4 p.m.; closed major holidays.

Simi and Conejo Valleys

Simi Valley Length, approximately 3½ miles; Class I; Difficulty Rating A.

A good introduction to Simi Valley is afforded by this ride through the city. Beginning at Madera Road near Easy Street (*Simi & Conejo Valleys* map, D-10), the route follows the Arroyo Simi waterway, skirts Rancho-Simi Community Park and just east of Sycamore Drive goes north to Los Angeles Avenue or south to Hollister Street.

Thousand Oaks Length, approximately 7 miles; Class II; Difficulty Rating B.

This ride begins at the intersection of Potrero Road and Westlake Boulevard (*Simi & Conejo Valleys* map, M-7). Westlake Boulevard leads to Kanan Road, through foothills and valleys that shelter upscale homes and country clubs. (This journey can be combined with a challenging, uphill bike ride from the coast on SR 23 that ends at the intersection of Potrero Road and Westlake Boulevard.)

RENTALS

Michael's Bicycles *2253 Michael Drive, Newbury Park; (805) 498-6633.* Michael's rents mountain bikes, tandems, racing and BMX bikes and trailers. Open Monday through Friday 9 a.m. to 7 p.m., Saturday 9 a.m. to 6 p.m., Sunday 10 a.m. to 5 p.m.; closed New Year's Day, Thanksgiving and Christmas.

Newbury Park Bicycle Shop *1536-A Newbury Road, Newbury Park; (805) 498-7714.* This shop rents mountain bikes and tandems. Open Monday through Friday 9 a.m. to 7 p.m., Saturday 9 a.m. to 6 p.m., Sunday 11 a.m. to 5 p.m.; closed New Year's Day, Easter Sunday, Thanksgiving and Christmas.

Ojai and Santa Paula Areas

Fillmore to Moorpark Length, approximately 9 miles; not classified, not rated.

Taking SR 23 south from Fillmore (Fillmore on *Ojai Valley Area* map, D-3) gives motorists and bicyclists a good view of Oak Ridge and Big Mountain, as well as the Santa Clara Valley, with its creek beds, orange groves, stands of eucalyptus and the Santa Clara River. About three miles south of Fillmore the highway begins a steep and twisting climb through the mountains, with a summit at 1100 feet. In Moorpark, SR 23 connects with Los Angeles Avenue (*Simi and Conejo Valleys* map, C-6), and bicycling west from there permits a good view of distant hills and mountains.

Ojai Valley Trail, Length, approximately 9 miles; Class I; Difficulty Rating B.

This trail, shared by hikers and equestrians, begins at Soule Park, just east of downtown Ojai on Ojai Avenue (Ojai Area on *Ojai Valley Area* map, C-8). It ends nine miles south at Foster Park, just off SR 33; there are a number of places along the trail where one can enter or exit. The trail is a wide, fenced path that offers pleasant vistas of mountains, oak groves, orchards, fields and a golf course. Trail maps are available at the Ojai Chamber of Commerce, 338 East Ojai Avenue.

Santa Paula Length, approximately 2 miles; Class II; Difficulty Rating A.

This ride offers a good look at Santa Paula and some of its Victorian houses. Beginning at the intersection of SR-150 and Santa Paula Street (Santa Paula on *Ojai Valley Area* map, D-3), bicyclists can continue west to Peck Road, south to Telegraph Road, then turn west to the countryside. Another pleasant ride is Santa Paula Street west to Palm Avenue, then south to Santa Maria Street and east to the airport.

RENTALS

Bicycle Doctor and Rentals *212 Fox Street, Ojai; (805) 646-7554.*

This establishment rents only beach cruisers. Open Tuesday through Sunday 9 a.m. to 5 p.m.; closed major holidays.

Bicycles and Collectables *108 Canada Street, Ojai; (805) 646-7736.*

This shop rents only mountain bicycles. Open Monday and Tuesday and Thursday through Saturday 10 a.m. to 6 p.m.; closed Thanksgiving and December 24 through January 1.

Los Padres National Forest

Within the forest are many mountain biking trails. These are usually shared with hikers and equestrians; complete information is available at Los Padres National Forest offices. The Ojai Ranger District is at 1190 East Ojai Avenue, Ojai; phone (805) 646-4348. Mt. Pinos Ranger District is at 34580 Lockwood Valley Road, Frazier Park; phone (805) 245-3731. A book entitled *Mountain Biking the Coast Range* is available in the national forest's Ojai District office.

BOATING AND WATERSKIING

There are numerous boating opportunities in Ventura County, and the

Marina at Ventura Harbor

following listings indicate where boats can be launched or moored. Entries also give each establishment's location and phone number, with information on rental equipment, fuel, boat repairs and other facilities and services available nearby.

There are no good areas for ocean waterskiing in the waters off Ventura County. Waterskiing is permitted at Lake Piru, six miles northeast of Piru (about eight miles east of Fillmore) off Piru Canyon Road (*Ventura County* map, H-9). Hours for waterskiing are 8:30 a.m. to one hour before sunset.

Ventura Coast

Map coordinates refer to the Ventura city side of the *Ventura County* map.

Ventura Port District *1603 Anchors Way Drive, off Harbor Boulevard, Ventura (C-6). (805) 642-8538.* Open daily all year. Facilities: paved ramp (free), slips, dry storage, boat fuel,

engine and hull repairs, marine waste station. Rentals: pedal boats, fishing tackle. Miscellaneous: marine hardware, bait, groceries, ice, snack bar, restaurant, picnic area.

Channel Islands Harbor Public Launch Ramp *¼ mile south of Channel Islands Boulevard on Victoria Avenue, Oxnard (G-13). (805) 385-8693.* Open daily all year. Facilities: paved ramp (free); parking fee. Rentals: none. Miscellaneous: bait, groceries, restaurant, picnic area.

Channel Islands Landing *3821 South Victoria Avenue, Oxnard (G-14). (805) 985-6059.* Open daily all year. Facilities: eyebolt and sling hoist, temporary mooring, slips, dry storage. Rentals: sailboats. Misc: bait, groceries, ice, snack bar, restaurant, picnic area.

Ojai and Santa Paula Areas

Map coordinates refer to the county side of the *Ventura County* map.

LAKE CASITAS

Casitas Boat Rentals *Santa Ana Road, Lake Casitas (J-3). (805) 649-2043.* Open daily all year. Facilities: slips, dry storage, boat fuel, engine repairs. Rentals: rowboats, motorboats (4 to 10 hp), pedal boats, fishing tackle. Miscellaneous: bait, ice, snack bar, picnic area.

Lake Casitas Recreation Area *Santa Ana Road, Lake Casitas (J-3). (805) 649-2233.* Open daily all year. Facilities: paved ramp (fee). Rentals: none. Miscellaneous: groceries, ice, tent and RV sites.

LAKE PIRU

Lake Piru Marina *on west shore on Piru Canyon Road (G-11). (805) 521-1231.* Open daily all year. Facilities: temporary mooring, slips, dry storage, boat fuel. Rentals: motorboats (8 hp), fishing tackle, water skis. Miscellaneous: bait, groceries, ice, snack bar, picnic area.

Lake Piru Recreation Area *on west shore on Piru Canyon Road (H-11). (805) 521-1500.* Open daily all year. Facilities: paved ramp (free), temporary mooring, slips, dry storage, boat fuel. Rentals: motorboats (6 hp), fishing tackle, water skis. Miscellaneous: bait, groceries, ice, restaurant, tent and RV sites, picnic area.

CAMPING

Camping can be an enjoyable experience, given the terrain in Ventura County that varies from seaside to mountainside. Within the following campground listings, fees shown are for one night's camping, usually for two people plus a recreational vehicle. Electricity, water and sewer hookups are indicated by the letters E, W and S. Where showers are indicated, there may be a nominal fee. The private campgrounds listed have been inspected by an Automobile Club representative and meet current AAA quality standards. The ⓐ symbol preceding a listing identifies that establishment as a AAA Official Appointment; it means that the campground has expressed a particular interest in serving AAA members. All rates are subject to change. For a detailed listing of additional public and private campgrounds, see the Auto Club's *Central and Southern California Camping* map.

RESERVATIONS

In making campground reservations, be aware that in addition to the camping fee, reservation and cancellation fees are usually charged. Policies vary regarding reservation and cancellation notices, reservation hours and accepted forms of payment.

Reservations for state park campsites must be made through **MISTIX** as follows: Charge reservations by phone with American Express, DiscoverCard, MasterCard or VISA by calling (800) 444-7275. The TTD/TTY number for hearing or speech impaired is (800) 274-7275.

Reservations for Wheeler Gorge campground in Los Padres National Forest must be made with **National Forest Reservation Center** as follows: Charge reservations by phone with DiscoverCard, MasterCard or VISA by calling (800) 280-2267. The TTD/TTY number for hearing- or speech-impaired is (800) 879-4496.

For other campgrounds, reservations sometimes can be made with the campground directly or, in some cases, reservations are not accepted. Automobile Club members can make reservations through any Club office-for private campgrounds that accept reservations. In many cases reservations are accepted only during a campground's peak season. If this is the case, campsites are available on a first-come, first-served basis during the remainder of their open period.

Ventura Coast

Map coordinates refer to the county side of the *Ventura County* map.

PRIVATE

Ventura Beach RV Resort *Ventura, 800 W. Main St., adjacent to US 101, northbound exit California St., right turn to Main St., left on Main St. 1 mi. (K-3). (805) 643-9137.* 144 RV spaces, 21 tent or RV spaces, 168 EW, 144 S, flush toilets, hot showers, disposal station, swimming pool, putting green, recreation room for adults only; walkway to beach; coin laundry, groceries and propane within 5 miles. Open all year. $16-$26.95 for 4 persons; $3 per night for each additional person. Fee for pets.

STATE

Reservations can be made through MISTIX for these state park campgrounds and are required during the busy summer months. Camping fees are $16 per night from April 1 through October 30 and $14 the rest of the year, unless otherwise noted. A fee of $1 per night is charged for pets. Dogs are not allowed on the beaches.

Emma Wood State Beach *3 mi. N.W. of Ventura off US 101 on Pacific Coast Hwy. (K-3). (805) 899-1400.* 61 tent or RV spaces, 40-ft. RV max. length, non-piped water, fire rings; swimming and fishing within 1 mi.; propane, groceries, laundromat within 5 mi. Basic camping fee is $12.

McGrath State Beach *3½ mi. S. of Ventura off US 101 via Harbor Blvd. (L-4). (805) 654-4744.* 174 tent or RV spaces, 34-ft. RV max. length, piped water, flush toilets, showers, fire rings, tables; swimming and fishing within 1 mi.; propane, groceries, laundromat within 5 mi.

Point Mugu State Park *15 mi. S.E. of Oxnard off SR 1 (N-6). (818) 880-0350.* There are two campgrounds within the park.

Sycamore Canyon 57 tent or RV spaces, 31-ft. RV max. length, sanitary disposal station, piped water, flush toilets, showers, fire rings, tables; swimming and fishing within 1 mi.; groceries within 5 mi.

Thornhill Broome Beach 75 tent or RV spaces, 31-ft. RV max. length, piped water, chemical toilets, fire rings, tables; swimming and fishing within 1 mi.; groceries within 5 mi. Basic camping fee is $7-$9.

Simi and Conejo Valleys

COUNTY

Oak County Park *4 mi. E. of Moorpark off SR 118 (Simi and Conejo Valleys map, B-9). (805) 654-3951.* $12 basic camping fee. 15 tent sites, 41 tent or RV spaces, 16E, sanitary disposal station, piped water, flush toilets, fire rings, tables; playground; propane, groceries, laundromat within 5 mi.

Ojai and Santa Paula Areas

Map coordinates refer to the county side of the *Ventura County* map.

COUNTY

Camp Comfort *2 mi. S.W. of Ojai on Creek Rd. (J-4). (805) 654-3951.* 43 tent or RV spaces, 34-ft. RV max. length, 16E, piped water, flush toilets, showers, fire rings, tables; playground; swimming within 1 mi., fishing within 5 mi.; propane, groceries, laundromat within 5 mi. $11 basic camping fee.

Faria County Park *7 mi. N.W. of Ventura off US 101 on Pacific Coast Hwy. (K-2). (805) 654-3951.* 42 tent or RV spaces, piped water, flush toilets, showers, fire rings, tables; playground within ½ mi.; swimming and fishing within 1 mi.; propane groceries, laundromat within 5 mi. $16 basic camping fee.

Foster Park *2 mi. S.W. of Casitas Springs off SR 33 on Casitas Vista Rd. (K-3). (805) 654-3951.* 30 tent or RV spaces, piped water, flush toilets, fire rings, tables; playground; fishing within 5 mi.; propane, groceries, laundromat within 5 mi. $11 basic camping fee.

Hobson Park *9 mi. N.W. of Ventura off US 101 on Pacific Coast Hwy. (K-1). (805) 654-3951.* 31 tent or RV spaces, 34-ft. RV max. length, piped water, flush toilets, showers, fire rings, tables; playground within ½ mi.; swimming and fishing within 1

mi.; propane, groceries, laundromat within 5 mi. $16 basic camping fee.

Kenney Grove *3 mi. N.W. of Fillmore via Old Telegraph Rd. on Oak Ave. (J-7). (805) 654-3951.* 33 tent or RV spaces, 20E, piped water, flush toilets, showers, fire rings, tables; playground; fishing within 5 mi.; propane, groceries, laundromat within 5 mi. $10 basic camping fee.

Rincon Parkway *6 mi. N. of Ventura off US 101 on Pacific Coast Hwy. (K-2). (805) 654-3951.* 112 RV spaces, no water, chemical toilets; swimming and fishing within 1 mi.; propane, groceries, laundromat within 5 mi. $11 basic camping fee.

Steckel County Park *4 mi. N. of Santa Paula off SR 150. (J-6). (805) 654-3951.* 75 tent or RV spaces, 50E, piped water, flush toilets, fire rings and barbecues, tables; playground.; fishing within 5 mi.; propane, groceries, laundromat within 5 mi. $12 basic camping fee.

SPECIAL DISTRICTS

Lake Casitas Recreation Area *5 mi. S.W. of Ojai off SR 150 (J-3). (805) 649-2233.* 750 tent or RV spaces, 141 EW, sanitary disposal station, piped water, flush toilets, showers, barbecues or fire rings, tables; playground; fishing; propane, groceries, laundromat within 5 mi. $12 basic camping fee.

Lake Piru Recreation Area *5 mi. N. of Piru on W. shore of Lake Piru (H-9). (805) 521-1500.* 247 tent or RV spaces, 106E, sanitary disposal station, piped water, flush toilets, showers, barbecues or fire rings, tables; playground; swimming and fishing within 1 mi.; propane, groceries, laundromat within 5 mi. $12 basic camping fee.

Mil Potrero Park *11 mi. W. of Lake of the Woods via Cuddy Valley Rd. (C-5). (805) 763-4246.* 10 tent spaces, 33 tent or RV spaces, 28-ft. RV max. length, piped water, flush toilets, showers, barbecues or fire rings, tables; playground; propane, groceries, laundromat within 5 mi. $12 basic camping fee.

Los Padres National Forest

U.S. FOREST SERVICE

There are many campgrounds within the Ventura County portion of Los Padres National Forest. Unless noted, these campgrounds are open all year and can be reached by car, usually from SR 33, Lockwood Valley Road or I-5. In some cases the road to the campground may be gravel or graded dirt, and special care should be taken, especially in inclement weather.

Although these campsites do not have electric, water or sewer hookups, many are equipped with piped water. No campground has flush toilets; they are either pit or chemical toilets. Each site has a table and fire pit. There are no showers, and sanitary disposal stations are not available. Fees for one night vary, depending upon facilities, and reservations are not accepted, with the exception of Wheeler Gorge campground through National Forest Reservation Center (see page 197). Pets are allowed at no extra charge but must be kept on a leash or physically controlled at all times.

Changes in campground information may occur, depending upon road and weather conditions and campground maintenance. Fishing is seasonal. For further information, contact Los Padres National Forest Headquarters at 6144 Calle Real, Goleta 93117; (805) 683-6711.

Beaver *17 mi. N.W. of Ojai off SR 33 (G-4).* El. 3000 ft. 12 tent or RV spaces, 23-ft. RV max., length; fishing within 5 mi. No fee.

Blue Point *15½ mi. N. of Piru via Piru Rd. (G-9).* El. 1000 ft. 43 tent or RV spaces, 16-ft. RV max. length, piped water; swimming and fishing within 1 mi. $7.

Caballo *15½ mi. W. of Lake of the Woods (B-4).* El. 5800 ft. 5 tent or RV spaces, 16-ft. RV max. length. No fee.

Campo Alto *24½ mi. W. of Lake of the Woods (C-4).* El. 8200 ft. 17 tent or RV spaces, 22-ft. RV max. length. No fee.

Chuchupate *3½ mi. S. of Lake of the Woods off Lockwood Valley Rd. (D-6).* El. 6200 ft. 30 tent or RV spaces, 16-ft. RV max. length, piped water. $5.

Kings Camp *13 mi. SW of Gorman off I-5 via Hungry Valley Rd. (E-8).* El. 4200 ft. 4 tent or RV spaces, 16-ft. RV max. length. No fee.

Lion's Canyon *21½ mi. N.E. of Ojai off SR 33. (G-5).* El. 3000 ft. 30 tent or RV spaces, 16-ft. RV max. length, piped water; swimming and fishing within 5 mi. $7.

Marian *16½ mi. W. of Lake of the Woods. (B-4).* El. 6600 ft. 5 tent or RV spaces, 16-ft. RV max. length. No fee.

McGill *10½ mi. W. of Lake of the Woods on Mt. Pinos Rd. (C-5).* El.

7400 ft. 73 tent or RV spaces, 16-ft. RV max. length, piped water. $6.

Mt. Pinos *12½ mi. W. of Lake of the Woods on Mt. Pinos Rd. (C-5).* El. 7800 ft. 19 tent or RV spaces, 16-ft. RV max. length, piped water. $6.

Nettle Spring *34 mi. S.E. of New Cuyama off SR 33 via Apache Canyon Rd. (C-3).* El. 4400 ft. 9 tent sites, 9 tent or RV spaces, 22-ft. RV max. length, piped water. No fee.

Ozena *25 mi. S.W. of Lake of the Woods via Lockwood Valley Rd. (E-3).* El. 3600 ft. 12 tent or RV spaces, 22-ft. RV max. length, piped water; propane and groceries within 5 mi. $8.

Pine Mountain *35 mi. N. of Ojai off SR 33 on Reyes Peak Rd. (F-3).* El. 6700 ft. 6 tent spaces. No fee.

Pine Springs *14 mi. S.W. of Lake of the Woods off Lockwood Valley Rd. (E-5).* El. 5800 ft. 10 tent or RV spaces, 22-ft. RV max. length. No fee.

Reyes Creek *25 mi. S.W. of Lake of the Woods off Lockwood Valley Rd. (E-3).* El. 4000 ft. 23 tent spaces, 6 tent or RV spaces, 22-ft. RV max. length, piped water, fishing within 1 mi. $5.

Reyes Peak *36 mi. N. of Ojai off SR 33 on Reyes Peak Rd. (F-3).* El. 6800 ft. 6 tent spaces. No fee.

Rose Valley Falls *21 mi. N.E. of Ojai off SR 33 (G-4).* El. 3400 ft. 9 tent or RV spaces, 16-ft. RV max. length, piped water; swimming and fishing within 1 mi. $7.

Toad Spring *15½ mi. W. of Lake of the Woods (C-4).* El. 5700 ft. 4 tent spaces, 3 tent or RV spaces, 16-ft. RV max. length. No fee.

Twin Pines *20½ mi. S.W. of Gorman off I-5 (E-7).* El. 6600 ft. 5 tent spaces. No fee.

Wheeler Gorge *9 mi. N.W. of Ojai on SR 33 (G-4).* El. 2000 ft. 73 tent or RV spaces, 16-ft. RV max. length, piped water; swimming and fishing within 1 mi. $9. National Forest Reservation Center.

FISHING

A California State Fishing License is required for anyone over age 16 fishing in either fresh water or the ocean; a license is not required, however, for fishing from a public saltwater pier.

Freshwater Fishing

Simi and Conejo Valleys

Rancho Simi Community Park *1765 Royal Avenue (D-12, Simi Valley, Simi and Conejo Valleys map).* 805-584-4400. Children under age 15 and seniors over 55 will enjoy dropping their lines in the park's lagoon during the summer, when it is stocked with channel catfish, bluegill, large-mouth bass and crappie. (A fishing license is not required.)

Ojai and Santa Paula Areas

Lake Casitas *off SR 150, approximately three miles west of its junction with SR 33 (J-3, Ventura County map). (805) 649-2233.* Trout, bass, crappie, channel catfish and red-ear sunfish. $5 day-use fee.

Los Padres National Forest

Sespe Creek from Lion's Canyon Campground to Cherry Canyon provides good fishing for rainbow trout. The creek is stocked from February through May, and there are roadside access points along SR 33.

Lake Piru *6 miles north of SR 126 on Piru Canyon Road (H-9,* Ventura County *map).* Rainbow and brown trout, black bass, catfish, bluegill, sunfish and crappie. $5 day-use fee.

Ocean Fishing

Norma E. Palmer

Halibut, barracuda, calico bass and mackerel are among the fish that pier fishermen can hope to pull in. Deep-sea fishing can yield white seabass, bonito,

Ventura Pier

sculpin and sheephead. April through October are usually the best fishing months in this area.

Ventura Pier, in the city of Ventura, is just east of the foot of California Street. It is lit for night fishing and includes fish-cleaning stations in its amenities. Port Hueneme Pier, at Port Hueneme Beach Park, is also lit for night fishing and offers fish-cleaning stations.

SPORTFISHING CHARTERS

Map coordinates refer to the Ventura/Oxnard/Port Hueneme side of the ACSC *Ventura County* map.

Channel Islands Sportfishing *at Channel Islands Harbor, 4151 South Victoria Avenue, Oxnard (G-13). (805) 985-8511.* Charters are available year round for ¾-day and all-day trips.

Port Hueneme Sportfishing *301 West Hueneme Road, Port Hueneme (H-16). (805) 488-1000.* This establishment offers ¾-day and all-day charters year round.

Ventura Sportfishing Landing *at Ventura Harbor, 1516 Anchors Way, Ventura (C-6). (805) 650-1255, 644-7363.* This company offers ¾-day and all-day charters year round.

GOLFING

Golfing is a year-round sport in Ventura County. Following is information on public, semi-private and private courses,

202

listed by area and community. Each golf course listing includes name, location, mailing address, phone number and facilities, plus yardage, par and slope and USGA ratings (all from men's white tees). Unless otherwise stated, each course is open daily all year. The abbreviation N/A means the information was not available. Package plan indicates a special rate combining hotel or resort rooms and golfing fees. Greens fees are given for weekday and weekend play during peak season. Many courses have senior citizen rates. Military golf courses show greens fees that apply to civilian guests of military personnel.

The listings have been made as complete as possible; a few courses, however, have been intentionally omitted at the request of the owners.

All semi-private and private courses have restrictions on public play ranging from members and guests only to liberal reciprocal agreements with members of other courses. It is impossible to list all of the restrictions for each course, so please telephone the course directly if in doubt. Reservations are advised at most courses; some country clubs require reservations months in advance.

Each golf course listing gives general street directions from the nearest freeway. For detailed directions refer to Automobile Club of Southern California street maps.

Ventura Coast

Map coordinates refer to the *Ventura County* map unless noted otherwise.

CAMARILLO

Camarillo Springs Golf Course
(Public)
(805) 484-1075
South of US 101 at 791 Camarillo Springs Rd, 93012 (F-12 on Camarillo map on Simi and Conejo Valleys map).

The course is 18 holes; 5931 yards; par 72; 108 slope; 67.9 rating. Rates: $20 weekdays, $40 weekends (mandatory golf cart included). Clubhouse, golf shop, professional, power and hand carts, rental clubs, lighted driving range; restaurant, coffee shop, cocktails.

Las Posas Country Club (Private)
(805) 482-4518
3 mi n of US 101 via Las Posas Rd at 955 Fairway Dr, 93010 (B-6 on Camarillo map on Simi and Conejo Valleys map). Closed Mon, Jan 1 and Dec 25.

The course is 18 holes; 6211 yards; par 71; 124 slope; 70.1 rating. Rates: $60 weekdays and weekends. Clubhouse, locker room, golf shop, professional, power carts, driving range; tennis, swimming; restaurant, snack bar, cocktails.

Spanish Hills Golf and Country Club (Private)
(805) 388-5000
3 mi n of US 101 via Central Av, W Ponderosa Rd and Avenida de Aprisa at 999 Crestview Av, 93010 (C-4 on Camarillo map on Simi and Conejo Valleys map). Closed Mon.

The course is 18 holes; 6310 yards; par 71; N/A rating. Rates: N/A. Clubhouse, locker room, golf shop, professional, power carts, driving range; tennis, swimming; restaurant, coffee shop, snack bar, cocktails.

OXNARD

River Ridge Golf Club (Public)
(805) 983-4653
*1 mi s of US 101 off South Bank Dr
and Ventura Rd at 2401 W Vineyard
Av, 93030 (L-4).* Closed Dec 25.
Package plan.

The course is 18 holes; 6111 yards;
par 72; 109 slope; 68.7 rating. Rates:
$17 weekdays, $22 weekends. Clubhouse, golf shop, professional, power
and hand carts, rental clubs, lighted
driving range; snack bar, beer, wine.

POINT MUGU

Point Mugu Golf Course
(Semi-private)
(805) 989-7109
*5 mi se of Oxnard off SR 1 at Naval Air
Station; Naval Air Weapons Station,
Bldg 153, 93042-5000 (N-5).*

The course is 9 holes; 2943 yards; par
35; 102 slope (18 holes); 66.8 rating
(18 holes). Rates: $7 (9 holes), $9 (18
holes) weekdays; $9 (9 holes), $12 (18
holes) weekends. Clubhouse, locker
room, golf shop, professional, power
and hand carts, rental clubs, driving
range; coffee shop, snack bar, cocktails.

PORT HUENEME

SeaBee Golf Club of Port Hueneme
(Private)
(805) 982-2620
*2 mi w of SR 1 on Channel Islands Bl;
c/o Special Services, Code 19, NCBC
93043 (M-4).* Closed Dec 25.

The course is 18 holes; 5945 yards;
par 71; 107 slope; 67.4 rating. Rates:
$13 weekdays, $16 weekends.
Clubhouse, golf shop, professional,
power and hand carts, rental clubs,
driving range; tennis; restaurant,
snack bar, cocktails.

SATICOY

Saticoy Regional Golf Course
(Public)
(805) 647-6678
*6 mi e of Ventura off SR 126 at 1025 S
Wells Rd, 93004 (L-5).*

The course is 9 holes; 2781 yards; par
34; 116 slope (18 holes); 69.1 rating
(18 holes). Rates: $9 (9 holes), $11 (18
holes) weekdays; $11 (9 holes), $13
(18 holes) weekends. Golf shop, professional, power and hand carts,
rental clubs, lighted driving range;
beer, wine.

Saticoy Country Club (Private)
(805) 485-5216
*3 mi n of US 101 via Santa Clara Av at
4450 N Clubhouse Dr, 93010 (L-5).*
Closed Mon, Jan 1 and Dec 25.

The course is 18 holes; 6407 yards;
par 72; 128 slope; 71 rating. Rates:
N/A. Clubhouse, locker room, golf
shop, professional, power carts,
driving range; swimming.

VENTURA

Buenaventura Golf Course (Public)
(805) 642-2231, 485-3050
*1 mi s of US 101 off Victoria Av at
5882 Olivas Park Dr, 93003-7673 (L-4).*

The course is 18 holes; 6146 yards;
par 72; 116 slope; 69.2 rating. Rates:
$15 weekdays, $19 weekends.
Clubhouse, locker room, golf shop,
professional, power and hand carts,
rental clubs; coffee shop, snack bar,
cocktails.

Olivas Park Golf Course (Public)
(805) 642-4303
*1½ mi w of US 101 off Victoria Av at
3750 Olivas Park Dr, 93003 (L-4).*

The course is 18 holes; 6353 yards;
par 72; 121 slope; 69.5 rating. Rates:

$15 weekdays, $20 weekends. Clubhouse, golf shop, professional, power and hand carts, rental clubs, lighted driving range; restaurant, coffee shop, snack bar, cocktails.

Simi and Conejo Valleys

Map coordinates refer to the *Simi and Conejo Valleys* map unless noted otherwise.

SIMI VALLEY

Simi Hills Golf Course (Public)
(805) 522-0803
¼ mi n of SR 118 off Stearns St at 5031 Alamo St, 93063 (B-16).

The course is 18 holes; 6500 yards; par 71; 110 slope; 68.7 rating. Rates: $13 weekdays, $20 weekends. Clubhouse, golf shop, professional power and hand carts, rental clubs, lighted driving range; restaurant, snack bar, beer, wine.

Sinaloa Golf Course (Public)
(805) 581-2662
2 mi s of SR 118 at 980 Madera Rd, 93065 (E-10). Closed Dec 25.

The course is 9 holes; 1003 yards; par 27; N/A slope; N/A rating. Rates: $4 weekdays, $5 weekends. Clubhouse, golf shop, professional, hand carts, rental clubs.

Wood Ranch Golf Club (Private)
(805) 522-7262
2½ mi e of SR 23 off Olsen Rd at 301 Wood Ranch Pkwy, 93065 (E-9). Closed Mon, Jan 1 and Dec 25.

The course is 18 holes; 6126 yards; par 72; 135 slope; 70.3 rating. Rates: $50 weekdays, $75 weekends. Clubhouse, locker room, golf shop, professional, power carts, rental

clubs, driving range; restaurant, snack bar, cocktails.

THOUSAND OAKS

Los Robles Golf Course (Public)
(805)495-6421
South of US 101 at 299 S Moorpark Rd, 91361.

The course is 18 holes; 5868 yards; par 70; 110 slope; 67 rating. Rates: $15 weekdays, $20 weekends. Golf shop, professional, power and hand carts, rental clubs, driving range; snack bar.

North Ranch Country Club
(Private)
(818) 889-3531
2½ mi n of US 101 off Westlake Bl at 4761 Valley Spring Dr, 91362 (K-5). Closed Mon.

The Lakes course is 9 holes; 3262 yards; par 36; N/A rating. The Oaks course is 9 holes; 3148 yards; par 36; N/A rating. The Valley course is 9 holes; 3090 yards; par 36; N/A rating. Rates: $40 (18 holes) weekdays, $60 (18 holes) weekends. Clubhouse, locker room, golf shop, professional, power carts, rental clubs, driving range; tennis; restaurant, coffee shop, snack bar, cocktails.

Sunset Hills Country Club (Private)
(805) 495-6484
4 mi n of US 101 via SR 23 and Olsen Rd at 4155 Erbes Rd N, 91360 (F-7). Closed Jan 1 and Dec 25.

The course is 18 holes; 5804 yards; par 71; 107 slope; 67.4 rating. Rates: $35 weekdays, $45 weekends. Clubhouse, locker room, golf shop, professional, power carts; tennis, swimming; restaurant, coffee shop, snack bar, cocktails.

Ojai and Santa Paula Areas

Map coordinates refer to *Ojai Valley Area* map unless noted otherwise.

FILLMORE

Elkins Ranch Golf Course (Public)
(805) 524-1121, 524-1440
2 mi s off SR 23 at 1386 Chambersburg Rd; PO Box 695, 93016 (F-7). Closed Dec 25.

The course is 18 holes; 6010 yards; par 71; 110 slope; 68.5 rating. Rates: $20 weekdays, $25 weekends. Golf shop, professional, power and hand carts, rental clubs, driving range; snack bar, cocktails.

OJAI

Ojai Valley Inn and Country Club (Public)
(805) 646-5511
1 mi w off SR 33 on Country Club Rd, 93023 (C-6). Package plan.

The course is 18 holes; 5892 yards; par 70; 117 slope; 68.9 rating. Rates: $86 weekdays and weekends. Clubhouse, locker room, golf shop, professional, power carts, rental clubs, driving range; tennis, swimming; restaurant, coffee shop, snack bar, cocktails.

Soule Park Golf Course (Public)
(805) 646-5633
½ mi e at 1033 E Ojai Av (SR 150); PO Box 758, 93023 (C-8). Closed Dec 25.

The course is 18 holes; 6350 yards; par 72; 107 slope; 69.1 rating. Rates: $18 weekdays, $22 weekends. Clubhouse, locker room, golf shop, professional, power and hand carts, rental clubs, driving range; restaurant, coffee shop, snack bar, cocktails.

SANTA PAULA

Mountain View Golf Course (Semi-private)
(805) 525-1571
½ mi s of SR 126 at 16799 S Mountain Rd, 93060 (C-5).

The course is 18 holes; 5335 yards; par 69; 113 slope; 69.4 rating. Rates: $12 weekdays, $14 weekends. Clubhouse, golf shop, professional, power and hand carts, rental clubs, lighted golf course; snack bar, cocktails.

Los Padres National Forest

Map coordinate refers to *Ventura County* map.

FRAZIER PARK

Pine Mountain Club Golf Course (Private)
(805) 242-3734
18 mi w of I-5 via Frazier Mountian and Cuddy Valley rds at 2524 Beechwood Wy, 93222 (C-5). Closed by snow and Dec 25.

The course is 9 holes; 1791 yards; par 30; N/A slope; N/A rating. Rates: $5 weekdays, $9 weekends. Clubhouse, golf shop, professional, power and hand carts, rental clubs, driving range; tennis, swimming; snack bar, cocktails. **Note:** This golf course is not connected with and is not administered by the National Forest.

HIKING

Hikers can enjoy Ventura County's numerous foothills and canyons. The trails listed here are just a sampling of those that afford moderate to challenging hikes. The Los Padres chapter of the Sierra Club (covering Santa Barbara and Ventura counties) sponsors group hikes planned for differing abilities and can provide further hiking information; call (805) 966-6622.

Simi and Conejo Valleys

Los Robles Trail System *begins at 482 Greenmeadow Drive near the Oak Creek Canyon Whole Access Interpretive Trail (K-6 on* Simi and Conejo Valleys *map). (805) 495-6471.* Five trails that vary in difficulty from easy to moderate to strenuous have their trailhead here. Distances covered range from ⅓ mile to 4½ miles.

Wildwood Regional Park *Parking area at Avenida Los Arboles and Big Sky Drive (G-5 on* Simi and Conejo Valleys *map). (805) 495-6471.* An extensive trail system runs through the park, with varying distances and degrees of difficulty. (See Wildwood Regional Park under seperate listing for *Thousand Oaks*.)

Ojai and Santa Paula Area

Ojai Valley Trail *begins at Soule Park in Ojai (C-8, Ojai Area on* Ojai Valley Area *map).* The 9-mile trail stretches south from Soule Park to Foster Park, with pathways for walkers, bicyclists and horseback riders. The trail is open from dawn to dusk.

Los Padres National Forest

Map coordinates refer to the *Ventura County* map unless noted otherwise.

Cozy Dell Trail *begins about 8 miles north of Ojai east off SR 33 behind Friends Ranch Packing House (H-3).*

This is an easy to moderate 1⅗-mile hike that ties into Foothill Trail and Cozy Dell Road. From this junction, a loop follows the Foothill Trail and continues along the road from Stewart Canyon. This is a scenic hike that includes large, shady oak trees.

Howard Creek Trail *begins off Rose Valley Road, about ½ mile east of SR 33; trail is on the right, going south (G-4).* This is a moderately difficult 3-mile hike to Nordhoff Ridge where, on a clear day, there are good views of the coastline and the Ojai Valley.

Gene Marshall-Piedra Blanca National Recreation Trail *begins on the left-hand trail across the steam bed at Lion Campground (G-5).* Turn right at junction after ½ mile. Hiking another 2⁷⁄₁₀ miles brings you through the impressive white rocks and to Piedra Blanca Campground. Twin Fork Campground is ½ mile farther, with water most of the year. At the end of a steep 3-mile climb is Pine Mountain Lodge Campground, nestled in conifers. From there the Piedra Blanca Trail continues northwest to Haddock and Reyes Creek campgrounds. An eastbound trail leads to Fishbowls or Cedar Creek campgrounds in the Mt. Pinos Ranger District.

Potrero John Trail *begins about 7½ miles north of Wheeler Springs east off SR 33 (F-4).* This easy 1⅗-mile hike follows a canyon bottom and has running water most of the year. It ends at Potrero John Campground, but can be explored beyond that.

For those interested in more extensive hiking and backpacking, contact Los Padres National Forest headquarters at 6144 Calle Real, Goleta 93117,

(805) 683-6711; Ojai Ranger District at 1190 East Ojai Avenue, Ojai, (805) 646-4348; or Mt. Pinos Ranger District at 34580 Lockwood Valley Road, Frazier Park, (805) 245-3731. Fire permits are issued on an annual basis and are required for backcountry camping during fire season.

HORSEBACK RIDING

There are good trails for horseback riding throughout Ventura County, including parts of Los Padres National Forest. People who wish to ride must bring their own horses, since there are no stables in the county which rent horses.

In the Ojai Valley, equestrians are welcome on the Ojai Valley Trail. Many of the hiking trails in Los Padres National Forest, particularly in the Mt. Pinos Ranger District, are also suitable for horses. (See Ojai and Santa Paula Areas and Los Padres National Forest under *Hiking*.)

PICNICKING

All of the parks listed offer picnic tables; other amenities are noted.

Ventura Coast

CAMARILLO

Map coordinates refer to the Camarillo side of the *Simi and Conejo Valleys* map, unless otherwise indicated.

Adolfo Park *Adolfo Road and Canoga Drive (D-9)*. Barbecues, playground.

Arneill Ranch Park *Sweetwater Avenue and Truman Street (D-8)*. Barbecues, jogging track, playground, volleyball area.

Camarillo Grove County Park *2 miles east of Camarillo, off US 101 (M-7)*. Barbecues, equestrian trails, horseshoe pits, playground, softball field.

Charter Oak Park *Charter Oak and Amber drives (C-9)*. Barbecues, basketball court, jogging track, playground, volleyball area.

Community Center Park *Carmen Drive and Burnley Street (D-8)*. Barbecues, horseshoe pits, jogging track, playground.

Crestview Park *Earl Joseph Drive and Bradford Avenue (D-6)*. Barbecues, playground, volleyball area.

Dizdar Park *Glenn and Chapel drives (E-8)*. Barbcues, playground.

Dos Caminos Park *Belota Road and Ponderosa Drive (C-10)*. Barbecues, playground.

Encanto Park *Avenida Encanto and Madre Selva Court (E-12)*. Barbecues, playground, volleyball area.

Foothill Park *Cranbrook Street and Lathan Avenue (C-7)*. Barbecues, playground, volleyball area.

Freedom Park *Pleasant Valley Road and Freedom Park Drive (F-5)*. Barbecues, playground, horseshoe pits, softball field, volleyball area.

Heritage Park *Via Latina and San Onofre Drive (C-12)*. Barbecues, playground.

Laurelwood Park *Dexter Street and Ascot Place (D-8)*. Barbecues, playground.

Mission Oaks Park *Mission Oaks Boulevard between Oak Canyon Road and Butterfield Street (D-12)*. Barbecues, playground, softball field, tennis courts, volleyball area.

Pleasant Valley Park *Ponderosa Drive and Brookhaven Avenue (D-9)*. Barbecues, horseshoe pits, playground, softball field, swiming pool, tennis courts, volleyball area.

Valle Lindo Park *Coe Street and Harris Avenue (D-7)*. Barbecues, playground, tennis courts, volleyball area.

Woodside Park *Flora Vista Avenue and Ridge View Street (F-10)*. Barbecues, basketball court, jogging track, playground, volleyball area.

OXNARD

Map coordinates refer to the Ventura/Oxnard/Port Hueneme side of the *Ventura County* map.

Carty Park *Zion Avenue and G Street (K-14)*. Playground, tennis courts.

College Estates Park *Gary and Boston drives (L-14)*. Basketball court, jogging path, playground, tennis courts, volleyball area.

Colonia Memorial Park *2 blocks south of Camino de la Raza on Juanita Street (L-10)*. Basketball court, playground, swimming and wading pool, volleyball area.

Community Center Park *2 blocks east of Ventura Road on 7th street (J-11)*. Basketball court, playground, tennis courts, volleyball area, wading pool.

Del Sol Park *Camino de la Raza and Rose Avenue (M-10)*. Basketball court, playground, soccer field, volleyball area.

Johnson Creek Park *3 blocks east of Saviers Road on Yucca Street at Cloyne Street (L-14)*. Playground, soccer field.

Lathrop Memorial Park *2 blocks east of Saviers Road on Gisler Avenue at East Hemlock Street (L-13)*. Basketball court, playground, wading pool, volleyball area.

Lemonwood Park *Mateo Place and Farragut Drive (M-13)*. Basketball court, playground, tennis courts, volleyball area .

Marina West Park *3 blocks south of Wooley Road on Novato Drive at Hill Street (H-12)*. Playground, soccer field, tennis courts.

Orchard Park *Geranium Place and Edelweiss Avenue (K-9)*. Playground, tennis courts, volleyball area.

Peninsula Park *south end of Peninsula Road off Channel Islands Boulevard (F-14)*. Playground, tennis courts.

Pleasant Valley Park *5 blocks east of Saviers Road on Dollie Street at Justin Way and Rubens Place (L-15)*. Basketball court, playground, soccer field, tennis courts, volleyball area.

Rudolph Beck Park *1 block west of Saviers Road on Laurel Street at C Sreet (K-13)*. Basketball court, playground, tennis courts.

Sea Air Park *6 blocks west of Ventura Road on 9th Street at Novato Drive (H-11)*. Basketball court, jogging path, playground, tennis courts.

Seaview Park *2 blocks west of Patterson Road on Oarfish Lane (H-11)*. Basketball court, jogging path, playground, tennis courts, volleyball area.

Sierra Linda Park *3 blocks east of Ventura Road on Holly Avenue at Lantana Street (J-8)*. Jogging path, playground, tennis courts, volleyball area.

Southwinds Park *2 blocks west of Saviers Road on Clara Street (K-15)*. Basketball court, playground, shuffleboard, tennis courts, volleyball area.

Thompson Park *2 blocks south of Camino de la Raza on Gibraltar Street at San Luis Street (M-10)*. Basketball court, playground, volleyball area.

Via Marina Park *3 blocks south of Wooley Road on Offshore Street at Keel Way (H-12)*. Basketball court, playground, soccer field, tennis courts, volleyball area.

Wilson Park *2 blocks west of Oxnard Avenue on Palm Drive at C Street (K-10)*. Jogging path, playground, shuffleboard, tennis courts.

PORT HUENEME

Bolker Park *1 block north of Channel Islands Boulevard on Bolker Drive at Cindy Place (H-13)*. Playground.

Bubbling Springs Park *4 blocks east of Ventura Road on Bard Road at Park Avenue (J-14)*. Playground.

Moranda Park *1 block south of Port Hueneme Road at south end of Moranda Parkway (J-16)*. Basketball court, playground, tennis courts, volleyball area.

Port Hueneme Beach Park *south end of Ventura Road at Surfside Drive (J-16)*. Fire rings, fishing pier, playground, ocean swimming.

VENTURA

Map coordinates refer to the Ventura/Oxnard/Port Hueneme side of the *Ventura County* map.

Arroyo Verde Park *at Day and Foothill roads (G-2)*. Barbecues, basketball court, horseshoe pits, playground.

Barranca Vista Park *Ralston Street, east of Johnson Drive (J-5)*. Barbecues, basketball court, horseshoe pits, playground.

Camino Real Park *Dean Drive and Varsity Street (F-5)*. Barbecues, baseball fields, basketball courts, playgrounds, soccer space, softball fields, tennis courts, volleyball area.

Chumash Park *Petit Avenue at Waco Street (K-4)*. Barbecues, basketball court, playground.

Hobart Park *Telegraph Road at Petit and Cambria avenues (K-3)*. Barbecues, playground.

Junipero Serra Park *Neath Street and Swansea Avenue (L-5)*. Playground.

Marina Park *south end of Pierpont Boulevard (C-6)*. Barbecues, boat dock, fishing, volleyball area.

Marion Cannon Park *Saratoga Avenue between Ralston and Shenandoah streets (G-5)*. Barbecues, basketball courts, playground.

Ocean Avenue Park *west end of Ocean Avenue (C-4)*. Barbecues, basketball courts, playground.

Plaza Park *Santa Clara and Chestnut streets (B-4)*. Playground.

Surfers' Point *at Seaside Park Figueroa Street at the Promenade (A-4)*.

Simi and Conejo Valleys

Map coordinates refer to the *Simi and Conejo Valleys* map.

SIMI VALLEY

Atherwood Park *2271 Alamo Street (C-13)*. Volleyball area.

Mayfair Park *2550 Caldwell Street (C-12)*. Basketball court, handball backboard, softball diamond.

Oak County Park *901 Quisma Drive (B-9)*. Barbecues, playground, horseshoe pits, volleyball area.

Rancho Simi Community Park *1765 Royal Avenue (D-12)*. Basketball courts, horseshoe pits, lagoon, playgrounds, shuffleboard courts, softball diamonds, swimming pool, tennis courts.

Rancho Tapo Community Park *3700 Avenida Simi (B-14)*. Barbecues, basketball courts, horseshoe pits, jogging course, playgrounds, softball diamond.

Santa Susana Park *6503 Katherine Road (D-18)*. Baseball diamond, basketball court, rock-climbing area, train depot, volleyball area.

Sycamore Park *1692 Sycamore Drive (E-13)*. Barbecues, swimming pool, volleyball area, wading pool.

Tapo Canyon County Park *2 miles north of Simi Valley at 4651 Tapo Canyon Road (A-15)*. Equestrian trails, playground.

THOUSAND OAKS

Banyan Park *3605 Erinlea Avenue in Newbury Park (L-2)*. Barbecues, playground.

Beyer Park *280 Conejo School Road (K-8)*. Barbecues, basketball courts, handball backboards, playground, softball field, volleyball area.

Borchard Park *190 Reino Road in Newbury Park (K-2)*. Barbecues, basketball court, bocci courts, horseshoe pits, playground, soccer field, softball fields, tennis courts.

Canada Park *1619 Calle Zocalo (F-8)*. Barbecues, basketball court, playground, tetherball courts.

Conejo Creek Park *Janss Road and El Monte Drive (H-7)*. Barbecues, basketball court, fitness/jogging trail, horseshoe pit, playground, shuffleboard court, volleyball area.

Cypress Park *459 Havenside Avenue in Newbury Park (K-1)*. Barbecues, playground, softball field.

Estella Park *300 Erbes Road (K-8)*. Barbecues, playground, tennis court.

Hickory Park *3877 South Camphor Circle (L-1)*. Barbecues, basketball court, playground.

Thousand Oaks' Conejo Creek Park

Lynn Oaks Park *350 Capitan Street in Newbury Park (K-5).* Basketball court, jogging path, playground, volleyball area.

Oakbrook Neighborhood Park *2787 Erbes Road (G-8).* Barbecues, playground.

Old Meadows Park *1600 Marview Drive (H-8).* Barbecues, playground.

El Parque De las Paz *100 Oakview Drive (K-8).* Barbecues, basketball court, horseshoe pits, playground.

Spring Meadow Park *3283 Spring Meadow Avenue (G-6).* Barbecues, basketball court, croquet court, fitness trail, playground.

Stagecoach Inn Park *51 South Ventu Park Road in Newbury Park (K-4).* Barbecues, basketball court, horseshoe pits, playground.

Suburbia Park *2600 Tennyson Street (G-5).* Barbecues, playground.

Sunset Hills Park *3350 Monte Carlo Drive (G-8).* Barbecues, basketball court, playground.

Thousand Oaks Community Park *2625 North Moorpark Road (G-6).* Basketball court, fitness trail, playground, softball fields, volleyball area.

Waverly Park *1300 Avenida de las Flores (H-7).* Barbecues, playground, softball field.

Wendy Park *813 American Oaks Avenue in Newbury Park (L-2).* Barbecues, basketball court, playground.

Wildwood Neighborhood Park *6850 Avenida de los Arboles (G-5).* Barbecues, playground.

Wildwood Regional Park *550 West Avenida de los Arboles (F-4)*. Barbecues, hiking and nature trails, nature center (see Wildwood Regional Park under separate listing for *Thousand Oaks.*).

Ojai and Santa Paula Areas

Map coordinates refer to the ACSC *Ojai Valley Area* map, unless otherwise indicated.

Camp Comfort County Park *Creek Road, two miles south of Ojai (E-6)*. Barbecues, horseshoe pits, playground, softball field.

Charles M. Teague Park *Harvard Boulevard and Steckel Drive, Santa Paula (B-4)*. Barbecues, basketball court, playground, soccer field, softball field.

Ebell Park *Main and 7th streets, Santa Paula (C-3)*.

George Harding Park *1330 East Harvard Boulevard, Santa Paula (E-3)*. Barbecues, playground, soccer field, softball field.

Kenney Grove Park *823 North Oak Avenue two miles northwest of Fillmore (B-1)*. Barbecues, horseshoe pits, playground, softball field.

Lake Casitas *5 miles southwest of Ojai, off SR 150 (J-3, Ventura County map)*. Barbecues, boating, fishing, playgrounds. Day-use fee. (See Lake Casistas under separate listing for *Ojai and Santa Paula Areas.*)

Foster County Park *1 mile south of Casitas Springs, off SR 33 (M-1)*. Barbecues, equestrian path, horse-shoe pits, playground, softball field, volleyball area.

Las Piedras Park *Saticoy and 13th streets, Santa Paula (D-3)*. Barbecues, playground, soccer field, softball field.

Libby Park *Downtown Ojai on Ojai Avenue (C-7)*. Tennis courts.

Mill Park *Ojai Road and Bedford Street, Santa Paula (D-2)*. Barbecues, basketball court, horseshoe pits, playground.

Sarzotti Park *east of downtown Ojai on Park Road (B-8)*. Ball field, barbecues, playground,

Soule Park *east of downtown Ojai on Ojai Avenue (C-8)*. Baseball field, tennis courts, volleyball area.

Steckel County Park *four miles north of Santa Paula off SR 150 (J-6, Ventura County map)*. Barbecues, horseshoe pits, playground, softball field, volleyball area.

Veterans Memorial Park *Ventura and 10th streets, Santa Paula (D-3)*. Horseshoe pits, playground.

SKIN AND SCUBA DIVING

The best diving areas off Ventura County's coastline are the reefs and kelp beds that enrich the waters of the channel islands, including Catalina. Chartered dive boats go to these areas, inhabited by game fish, lobster and abalone. A valid California sportfishing license is required to spearfish in the waters off the mainland and the islands.

RENTALS

Rental equipment, air refills and information on water conditions are available at the establishments listed below. Many shops also offer chartered scuba diving trips; call for details.

Aqua Ventures *2172 Pickwick Drive, Camarillo (D-8,* Simi and Conejo Valleys *map). (805) 647-8344, 484-1594.* Open Monday through Friday 10 a.m. to 6:30 p.m., Saturday 9 a.m. to 6:30 a.m., Sunday 4:30 to 7 p.m.

Aquatics *695 West Channel Islands Boulevard, Port Hueneme (G-13,* Ventura County *map). (805) 984-3483.* Open Monday through Friday noon to 7 p.m., Saturday 9 a.m. to 6 p.m.

Channel Islands Scuba *4255-4 East Main Street, Ventura (F-5,* Ventura County *map). (805) 644-3483.* Open Monday through Saturday 9 a.m. to 7 p.m., Sunday 10 a.m. to 4 p.m.

Gold Coast Scuba *2464 East Main Street, Ventura (D-4,* Ventura County *map). (805) 652-0321.* Open 10 a.m. to 6 p.m. daily. For charters call Chieftain Charters at this address, telephone (805) 652-2166.

SURFING

Surfing in the Ventura Coast area is possible off a number of beaches. At Rincon Point the surfing is poor in summer, but excellent in winter, with surf at four to ten feet. At Solimar Beach, there is a fair winter surf, three to five feet. San Buenaventura State Beach offers surfing for novice and intermediate, with a good winter surf at four to eight feet. A three-to-eight-foot winter surf can be experienced at

Hollywood and Silver Strand County beaches. At the Los Angeles/Ventura county line off SR 1, one mile west of Leo Carrillo State Beach, there is good year-round surf at two to three feet.

SWIMMING

Ocean swimming in Ventura County is good at San Buenaventura State Beach (B-4), with lifeguards on duty in summer. At Channel Islands Beach Park, near Victoria Avenue and Pelican Way (G-14), there is good swimming in small, lifeguarded areas. Port Hueneme Beach Park (J-16) offers swimming; lifeguards are there during the summer.

Public Swimming Pools

Ventura Coast

Pleasant Valley Park *Ponderosa Drive and Brookhaven Avenue,* Camarillo *on* Simi and Conejo Valleys *map (D-9). (805) 482-1996.* Open for recreational swimming daily in summer 1 to 3 p.m.; weekends only in winter 1:30 to 4 p.m. Fees are $2.75 adults, $1.50 ages 6 to 17; there is a 25% surcharge for people from outside the district.

Colonia Memorial Park *2 blocks south of Camino de la Raza on Juanita Street,* Oxnard *on* Ventura County *map (L-10).* Open for recreational swimming in summer. Call (805) 385-7992 for detailed information.

Simi and Conejo Valleys

Map coordinates refer to the ACSC *Simi and Conejo Valleys* map.

Detailed information on the following swimming pools was not available at press time; call (805) 495-4674 for information on rates and schedules.

Newbury Park High School *456 Reino Road, Newbury Park (J-2).* The pool is open for recreational swimming during the summer months.

Thousand Oaks High School *2323 North Moorpark Road, Thousand Oaks (H-6).* The pool is open for recreational swimming during the summer months.

Ojai and Santa Paula Areas

Map coordinates refer to the *Ojai Valley* map.

Nordhoff Community Pool *Nordhoff High School, 1401 Maricopa Highway, Ojai (C-5, Ojai Area). (805) 646-1872.* Open for recreational swimming daily in summer 12:30 to 5 p.m. Fees are $1 per person.

Santa Paula Union High School *404 North 6th Street, Santa Paula (C-3, Santa Paula).* Open for recreational swimming in summer; call (805) 933-4226 for information on rates and schedules.

TENNIS

The following tennis courts, except for those on school campuses, are open all year. Permits or fees are generally not required for public use. School tennis courts are usually open daily during the summer, but only on weekends during the school year. Play at most courts is on a first-come, first-served basis when players are waiting; individuals should limit play to 30 minutes, one hour for singles and 1½ hours for doubles.

Ventura Coast

Map coordinates refer to the *Ventura County* map.

CAMARILLO

Mission Oaks Park *Mission Oaks Boulevard between Oak Canyon Road and Butterfield Street (D-12).* Five lighted courts.

Pleasant Valley Park *Ponderosa Drive and Brookhaven Avenue (D-9).* Six lighted courts.

Valle Lindo Park *Coe Street and Harris Avenue (D-7).* Five lighted courts.

OXNARD

Carty Park *Zion Avenue and G Street (K-14).* Two lighted courts.

College Estates Park *Gary and Boston drives (L-14).* One court.

Community Center Park *2 blocks east of Ventura Road on 7th street (J-11).* Eight lighted courts; fee.

Lemonwood Park *Mateo Place and Farragut Drive (M-13).* Two courts.

Marina West Park *3 blocks south of Wooley Road on Novato Drive at Hill Street (H-12).* Two courts.

Orchard Park *Geranium Place and Edelweiss Avenue (K-9).* Two courts.

Peninsula Park *South end of Peninsula Road off Channel Islands Boulevard (F-14).* Two courts.

Pleasant Valley Park 5 blocks east of Saviers Road on Dollie Street at Justin Way and Rubens Place (L-15). Two courts.

Rudolph Beck Park 1 block west of Saviers Road on Laurel Street at C Street (K-13). Two lighted courts; fee.

Sea Air Park 6 blocks west of Ventura Road on 9th Street at Novato Drive (H-11). One court.

Seaview Park 2 blocks west of Patterson Road on Oarfish Lane (G-11, H-11). Two courts.

Sierra Linda Park 3 blocks east of Ventura Road on Holly Avenue at Lantana Street (J-8). Two courts.

Southwinds Park 2 blocks west of Saviers Road on Clara Street (K-15). Two courts.

Via Marina Park 3 blocks south of Wooley Road on Offshore Street at Keel Way (H-12). Two courts.

Wilson Park 2 blocks off Oxnard Avenue on Palm Drive at C Street (K-10). Two courts.

PORT HUENEME

Moranda Park 1 block off Port Hueneme Road at south end of Moranda Parkway (J-16). Eight courts; fee.

VENTURA

Detailed information on the following tennis courts was not available at press time. For school courts, call (805) 641-5000; for Camino Real Park, call (805) 658-8175.

Anacapa Middle School 100 South Mills Road (E-4).

Buena High School 5620 Telegraph Road (G-4).

Camino Real Park Dean Drive and Varsity Street (F-5).

De Anza Middle School 2060 Cameron Street (B-2).

Ventura College Courts 4667 Telegraph Road (F-4).

Ventura High School 2155 East Main Street (D-4).

Simi and Conejo Valleys

Map coordinates refer to the *Simi and Conejo Valleys* map.

SIMI VALLEY

Rancho Simi Community Park 1765 Royal Avenue (D-12). Eight lighted courts.

THOUSAND OAKS

Borchard Park 190 Reino Road in Newbury Park (K-2). Four lighted courts; fee.

Estella Park 300 Erbes Road (K-8). One lighted court.

Thousand Oaks Community Park 2625 North Moorpark Road (G-6). Four lighted courts; fee.

Wildflower Playfield 635 Avenida de los Arboles (G-5). Four lighted courts.

Ojai and Santa Paula Areas

Map coordinates refer to the *Ojai Valley Area* map.

OJAI

Libbey Park *Downtown Ojai on Ojai Avenue (C-7, Ojai Area).* Eight courts.

Nordhoff High School *1401 Maricopa Highway, Ojai (C-5, Ojai Area).* Four courts, open daily during the summer; after school hours and on weekends the rest of the year.

Soule Park *East of downtown Ojai on Ojai Avenue (C-8, Ojai Area).* Four lighted courts.

SANTA PAULA

Santa Paula Union High School *404 North 6th Street, Santa Paula (C-3).* Four courts (2 lighted).

Lodgings and Restaurant Listings

....

The lodging and restaurant properties listed in these pages have been inspected at least once in the past year by a trained representative of the Automobile Club of Southern California. In surprise inspections, each property was found to meet AAA's extensive and detailed requirements for approval. For a detailed explanation of lodging and restaurant property listings, please refer to page 117.

Ventura Coast

CAMARILLO

Lodging

Best Western Camarillo Inn 🆎   Motel   ♦♦♦
(805) 987-4991; FAX (805) 388-3679   *AAA Special Value Rates*

| All year [CP] | 1P 50.00 | 2P/1B 55.00 | 2P/2B 60.00 | XP ....5 |

Adjacent to US 101, ¼ mi ne, exit Los Posas Rd. 295 E Daily Dr (93010). 58 rooms; 2 stories; exterior corridors; conference facilities; meeting rooms. Free movies. Some refrigerators, whirlpools. Heated pool, whirlpool. No pets. Children 12 and under stay free. Reservation deposit required; 3-day refund notice. AE, CB, DI, DS, ER, MC, VI. Restaurant nearby.   Ⓓ ∅

Comfort Inn 🆎   Motel   ♦♦
(805) 987-4188; FAX (805) 987-3450   *AAA Special Value Rates*

| 5/1-9/15 | 1P 47.00 | 2P/1B 53.00 | 2P/2B 59.00 | XP ....6 |
| 9/16-4/30 | 1P 45.00 | 2P/1B 49.00 | 2P/2B 53.00 | XP ....6 |

Adjacent to US 101, ½ mi se; exit Central Av. 984 Ventura Bl (93010). 70 rooms; 3 stories; exterior corridors; meeting rooms. 11 suites, $65-$69. Cable TV, free movies. Some refrigerators. Small heated pool, whirlpool. Pets, $5 extra charge. Children 17 and under stay free. AE, CB, DI, DS, ER, JCB, MC, VI.   Ⓓ Ⓢ ∅

Country Inn at Camarillo ⓐ   Motel   ◆◆◆
(805) 983-7171; FAX (805) 983-1838   *Guaranteed Rates*

All year [BP]   1P 66.00   2P/1B 66.00   2P/2B 66.00   XP ..10

Adjacent to US 101, n side, ½ mi w; exit Central Av. 1405 Del Norte Rd (93010). 100 rooms; 3 stories; interior corridors. Cable TV; refrigerators. Small heated pool, whirlpool. Coin laundry. No pets. Children 12 and under stay free. AE, CB, DI, DS, MC, VI. Complimentary beverages each evening.   Ⓓ Ⓢ ⊘

Courtyard by Marriott   Motel   ◆◆◆
(805) 388-1020; FAX (805) 987-6274   *Rates Subject to Change*

Sun-Thurs   1P 58.00   2P/1B 67.00   2P/2B 67.00   XP ..10
Fri-Sat   1P 50.00   2P/1B 59.00   2P/2B 59.00   XP ..10

Adjacent n side of US 101, exit Pleasant Valley Rd/Santa Rosa Rd. 4994 Verdugo Wy (93012). 130 rooms; 2 stories; interior corridors; conference facilities; meeting rooms. Many patios or balconies. Cable TV, free & pay movies. Some microwaves, refrigerators. Heated pool, whirlpool. Coin laundry. Services: Data ports. No pets. Children 12 and under stay free. Senior discount. AE, CB, DI, DS, ER, MC, VI. Restaurant; 6:30 am-2 & 5-10 pm; cocktails.   Ⓓ Ⓢ ⊘

Days Inn ⓐ   Motel   ◆◆
(805) 482-0761   *AAA Special Value Rates*

All year [CP]   1P 45.00   2P/1B 50.00   2P/2B 55.00   XP 5

Adjacent to US 101; exit Los Posas Rd. 165 Daily Dr (93010). 82 rooms; 2 stories; exterior corridors. Adjacent to shopping plaza. Free movies; shower or combination baths. Some whirlpools. Fee for refrigerators. Heated pool. No pets. Children 13 and under stay free. Reservation deposit required; 3-day refund notice. AE, CB, DI, DS, ER, JCB, MC, VI. Restaurant nearby.   Ⓓ ⊘

Del Norte Inn ⓐ   Motel   ◆◆◆
(805) 485-3999; FAX (805) 485-1820   *Guaranteed Rates*

All year [CP]   1P 49.00   2P/1B 49.00   2P/2B 49.00   XP ..10

Adjacent to US 101, n side; exit Central Av. 4444 E Central Av (93010). 111 rooms; 3 stories; interior corridors. 24 efficiencies. Patios or balconies. Cable TV; refrigerators. Some microwaves. Small heated pool, whirlpool. Coin laundry. No pets. Children 12 and under stay free. Senior discount. AE, CB, DI, DS, MC, VI. Restaurant nearby.   Ⓓ Ⓢ ⊘

Restaurants

Giovanni's   Northern Italian $11-$20   ◆◆
(805) 484-4376

2½ mi ne of US 101, via Dawson Rd & Mission Oaks Bl, exit Dawson Rd (Mission Oaks Plaza). 5227 Mission Oaks Bl (93012). Homemade pasta, fresh fish & eastern veal. Semi-formal atmosphere. Carry-out; a la carte. 11 am-2:30 & 5-10 pm; Sat & Sun from 5 pm. Closed Mon. Cocktails and lounge. Reservations suggested. AE, MC, VI.   ⊘

Ottavio's   Italian $11-$20   ♦♦
(805) 482-3810
½ blk se of US 101; exit Carmen Dr. 1620 Ventura Bl (93010). Selection of seafood, steaks & pasta. Informal atmosphere. Buffet lunch Mon-Fri 11:30 am-1:30 pm. Children's menu; carry-out; a la carte. Minimum charge $5.50 weekends. 11 am-10 pm; Sun to 9 pm; closed 12/25. Cocktails & lounge. Reservations suggested weekends. AE, CB, DI, DS, MC, VI.   ⊘

OXNARD

Lodging

Casa Sirena Marina Resort ⏺⏺   Motor Inn   ♦♦
(805) 985-6311; FAX (805) 985-4329   *Guaranteed Rates*

All year	1P 60.00	2P/1B 60.00	2P/2B 60.00	XP ..10

½ mi w of Victoria Bl via Channel Islands Bl at Channel Islands Harbor. 3605 Peninsula Rd (93035). 275 rooms; 3 stories; interior/exterior corridors; meeting rooms. 24 2-bedroom units. Some efficiencies. Many rooms overlooking marina. Patios or balconies. Spacious, nicely landscaped grounds. Cable TV; coffeemakers, refrigerators. Fee for movies. No A/C. Heated pool, saunas, whirlpools; lighted tennis court; exercise room; putting green. Hair & tanning salon. Services: Massage (fee); rental bicycles. No pets. Children 12 and under stay free. AE, CB, DI, DS, MC, VI. Coffeeshop; 6:30 am-10 pm. *Lobster Trap Restaurant*, see separate listing.   Ⓓ ⊘

Oxnard Hilton Inn ⏺⏺   Hotel   ♦♦♦
(805) 485-9666; FAX (805) 485-2061   *Rates Subject to Change*

Mon-Thurs	1P 65.00	2P/1B 65.00	2P/2B 65.00	XP ..10
Fri-Sun	1P 59.00	2P/1B 59.00	2P/2B 59.00	XP ..10

2 blks s of US 101 exit Vineyard Av. 600 Esplanade Dr (93030). Formerly Financial Plaza Hilton. 160 rooms; 6 stories; interior corridors; meeting rooms; conference facilities. Many balconies. Near shopping plaza. Cable TV; refrigerators. Heated pool, whirlpool; lighted tennis court. Services: Child care (fee). No pets. Children 12 and under stay free. AE, CB, DI, DS, MC, VI. Restaurant; 6:30 am-10 pm; $9-$18; cocktails; entertainment.   Ⓓ Ⓢ ⊘

Radisson Suite Hotel at River Ridge ⏺⏺   Apartment Motor Inn   ♦♦♦
(805) 988-0130; FAX (805) 983-4470   *Rates Subject to Change*

All year [BP]	1P 69.00	2P/1B 69.00 - 85.00 2P/2B 69.00 - 85.00	XP ..10

1¼ mi sw of US 101, exit Vineyard Av. 2101 Vineyard Av (93030). 250 rooms; 2 stories; exterior corridors; meeting rooms; conference facilities. 60 2-bedroom units. 60 loft suites with fireplace & kitchen, $85. 120 fireplace units. Nicely landscaped grounds. Cable TV, free & pay movies; kitchens, coffeemakers, microwaves, refrigerators. Fee for VCPs. 2 heated pools, whirlpools. Fee for golf (18 holes), 5 lighted tennis courts. Coin laundry. Services: Airport transportation. No pets. Monthly rates. Children 17 and under stay free. Senior discount. AE, DI, DS, ER, JCB, MC, VI. Restaurant; 6:30 am-10 pm; $9-$17; cocktails. **(See ad on facing page.)**   Ⓓ ⊘

Restaurants

Furr's Cafeteria — American — Up to $10 — ♦♦
(805) 483-0187
1 blk e of Ventura Rd.1301 W Channel Islands Bl (93033). Cafeteria. A la carte. 11 am-9 pm; closed 12/25. AE, MC, VI. ⊗

The Greek — Greek — $11-$20 — ♦♦
(805) 981-1891
3 blks s of US 101 on the nw corner of Oxnard Bl & Vineyard Av. 2343 N Oxnard Bl (93030). Steaks, seafood, lamb, chicken, vegetarian plate, pasta & casseroles. Casual attire. Children's menu; early bird specials; a la carte; carry-out. 11 am-10 pm; Fri to 11 pm; Sat & Sun 5-11 pm. Beer and wine only. Reservations suggested Fri & Sat. AE, CB, DI, DS, MC, VI. ⊗

Lobster Trap Restaurant — Steak & Seafood — $11-$20 — ♦♦
(805) 985-6361
In Casa Sirena Marina Resort, 3605 Peninsula Rd (93035). Salads, seafood, chicken, steak & prime rib. Overlooking marina. Casual attire. Sunday brunch 10 am-2 pm. Early bird specials. 11:30 am-10 pm. Cocktails & lounge; entertainment. AE, CB, DI, DS, MC, VI. ⊗

Tugs Restaurant — Steak & Seafood — $11-$20 — ♦
(805) 985-8847
½ mi se of Channel Islands Bl, via Harbor Bl at Channel Islands Harbor. 3600 S Harbor Bl (93035). Steaks, fresh seafood, chicken & pasta. Casual atmosphere, located on the 2nd floor of Marine Emporium Bldg; view of harbor. Patio dining, weather permitting No A/C. Casual attire. 8 am-9 pm; closed 11/24 & 12/25. Cocktails. AE, MC, VI ⊗

PORT HUENEME
Lodging

Casa Via Mar Inn & Tennis Club ⓐⓐⓐ   Motel   ♦♦♦
(805) 984-6222; FAX (805) 984-9490   *Rates Subject to Change*
All year [BP]   1P 59.00 - 69.00   2P/1B 69.00 - 79.00   2P/2B 69.00 - 77.00   XP ..10
5 blks w of Ventura Rd. 377 W Channel Islands Bl (93041). 74 rooms; 2 stories; exterior corridors; meeting rooms. 31 efficiencies. Some rooms with patio or balcony. Attractive Spanish-style exterior. Refrigerators, coffeemakers; shower or combination baths. No A/C. Heated pool, whirlpool; 6 tennis courts. No pets. Children 3 and under stay free. Senior discount. Reservation deposit required. AE, CB, DI, MC, VI.   Ⓓ

Country Inn at Port Hueneme ⓐⓐⓐ   Motel   ♦♦♦
(805) 986-5353; FAX (805) 986-4399   *Guaranteed Rates*
Sun-Thurs [BP]   1P 76.00   2P/1B 76.00   2P/2B 76.00   XP ..10
Fri-Sat [BP]   1P 69.00   2P/1B 69.00   2P/2B 69.00   XP ..10
Port Hueneme & Ventura rds. 350 E Port Hueneme Rd (93041). 135 rooms; 3 stories; interior corridors; meeting rooms. 8 kitchens. Attractive exterior; nicely furnished rooms. Cable TV; bars, microwaves, refrigerators. Small heated pool, whirlpool. Coin laundry. No pets. Children 12 and under stay free. AE, CB, DI, DS, MC, VI. Complimentary beverages each evening.   Ⓓ Ⓢ ⊘

VENTURA
Lodging

Bella Maggiore Inn ⓐⓐⓐ   Hotel   ♦♦♦
(805) 652-0277   *AAA Special Value Rates*
All year [BP]   1P 75.00 -150.00   2P/1B 75.00 -150.00   2P/2B ...   XP ..10
¼ mi n of US 101, exit California St. 67 S California St (93001). 24 rooms; 3 stories; no elevator; interior corridors; meeting rooms. Renovated historic landmark built in 1926. Attractive southern European ambiance. Shower or combination baths. Some A/C; refrigerators; whirlpools. No pets. Reservation deposit required. AE, CB, DI, DS, MC, VI. Complimentary beverages and cheese each evening. Restaurant nearby.   Ⓓ ⊘

Best Western Inn of Ventura ⓐⓐⓐ   Motel   ♦♦
(805) 648-3101   *Rates Subject to Change*
4/1-9/30   1P 52.00 - 62.00   2P/1B 59.00 - 69.00   2P/2B 60.00 - 70.00   XP 5
10/1-3/31 &   1P 49.00 - 59.00   2P/1B 54.00 - 64.00   2P/2B 56.00 - 66.00   XP 5
2 blks e of California St; from US 101, northbound exit California St, southbound exit Ventura Av. 708 E Thompson Bl (93001). 75 rooms; 2 stories; exterior corridors. Cable TV, free movies; shower or combination baths. Heated pool, whirlpool. No pets. Reservation deposit required in summer. AE, CB, DI, DS, ER, MC, VI. Coffee shop nearby.   Ⓓ ⊘

Colony Harbortown Marina Resort ⓐⓑ

Motor Inn ♦♦♦

(805) 658-1212; FAX (805) 658-6347   *Rates Subject to Change*

5/1-9/30 [BP]	1P 79.00 - 99.00	2P/1B 79.00 - 99.00	2P/2B 79.00 - 99.00	XP ..10
10/1-4/30 [BP]	1P 69.00	2P/1B 69.00	2P/2B 69.00	XP ..10

From US 101, exit Seaward Ave, then 1½ mi s on Harbor Bl, at Ventura Harbor. 1050 Schooner Dr (93001). Check in 4 pm. 154 rooms; 3 stories; exterior corridors; meeting rooms; conference facilities. 4 2-bedroom units. Many rooms with marina view & balcony or patio. Cable TV, free movies; coffeemakers. Some refrigerators. No A/C. Heated pool, whirlpool; 3 lighted tennis courts. Services: Secretarial services. No pets. Children 17 and under stay free. Reservation deposit required. AE, CB, DI, DS, MC, VI. Complimentary beverages each evening. Restaurant; 6:30 am-10 pm; $12-$22; cocktails; entertainment. Ⓓ Ⓢ ⊘

Country Inn at Ventura ⓐⓑ

Motel ♦♦♦

(805) 653-1434; FAX (805) 648-7126   *Rates Guaranteed*

All year [BP]	1P 66.00	2P/1B 66.00	2P/2B 66.00	XP ..10

1 blk e of California St & 1 blk s of Thompson Bl; from US 101; northbound exit California St, southbound exit Ventura Av. 298 Chestnut St (93001). 120 rooms; 3 stories; interior corridors. Some balconies. Ocean & mountain views. Cable TV; refrigerators, microwaves. Fee for movies and VCPs. Heated pool, whirlpool. Coin laundry. No pets. Children 12 and under stay free. AE, CB, DI, DS, MC, VI. Complimentary beverages each evening. Restaurant nearby. Ⓓ Ⓢ ⊘

Doubletree Hotel at Ventura ⓐⓑ

Motor Inn ♦♦♦

(805) 643-6000; FAX (805) 643-7137   *Rates Subject to Change*

All year	1P 89.00 -119.00	2P/1B 99.00 -129.00	2P/2B 99.00 -129.00	XP ..10

Adjacent to w side of US 101, exit Seaward Av. 20558 Harbor Bl (93001). 285 rooms; 4 stories; interior corridors; meeting rooms; conference facilities. Attractively landscaped courtyard & pool area. 1 blk to San Buenaventura State Beach. Cable TV, free & pay movies. Fee for refrigerators. Heated pool, saunas, whirlpool. Services: Data ports, secretarial services. No pets. Children 18 and under stay free. Reservation deposit required. AE, CB, DI, DS, MC, VI. Restaurant; 6:30 am-10 pm; Sat & Sun from 7 am; $9-$16; cocktails. Ⓓ Ⓢ ⊘

Holiday Inn Beach Resort ⓐⓑ

Hotel ♦♦♦

(805) 648-7731; FAX (805) 653-6202   *Rates Subject to Change*

All year	1P 79.00	2P/1B 89.00	2P/2B 89.00

Adjacent to US 101; northbound exit California St, southbound exit Main St. 450 E Harbor Bl (93001). Check in 4 pm. 260 rooms; 12 stories; interior corridors; meeting rooms; conference facilities. Beachfront hotel with balconies. Cable TV, free & pay movies. Some refrigerators. Heated pool, wading pool; playground. Services: Secretarial services. No pets. Monthly rates available. Children 18 and under stay free. Senior discount. Monthly rates available. Reservation deposit required. AE, CB, DI, DS, MC, VI. Dining room; 6 am-10 pm; Fri & Sat to 11 pm; $13-$17; cocktails; entertainment. Ⓓ ⊘

Inn on the Beach ⏺   Motel   ♦♦
(805) 652-2000   *AAA Special Value Rates*

All year [CP]   1P   80.00 -130.00   2P/1B   80.00 -130.00   2P/2B 100.00 -130.00   XP 5

½ mi w of US 101; exit Seaward Av. 1175 S Seaward Av (93001). 24 rooms; 3 stories; interior corridors. At the beach; ocean view. Patios or balconies. Cable TV, free movies. Some refrigerators. No pets. Children 6 and under stay free. Reservation deposit required. AE, CB, DI, MC, VI.   Ⓓ Ⓢ ⊘

La Mer European Bed & Breakfast   Historic Bed & Breakfast   ♦♦
(805) 643-3600   *Rates Guaranteed*

All year [BP]   1P 100.00 -150.00   2P/1B 105.00 -155.00   2P/2B ...

½ mi n of US 101; northbound exit California St, southbound exit Ventura Av, 1 blk w of California St. 411 Poli St (93001). Check in 4 pm. 2-night minimum stay weekends. 5 rooms; 2 stories; interior/exterior corridors. Each room furnished in a different European motif. House built in 1890. Shower & tub baths. No A/C; no phones; no TV. No pets. Reservation deposit required; 7-day refund notice. MC, VI.   Ⓓ ⊘

La Quinta Inn   Motel   ♦♦♦
(805) 658-6200; FAX (805) 642-2840   *Rates Subject to Change*

All year [CP]   1P   48.00 - 55.00   2P/1B   53.00 - 60.00   2P/2B   53.00 - 55.00   XP 6

½ blk s of US 101; exit Victoria Av. 5818 Valentine Rd (93003). 142 rooms; 3 stories; exterior corridors; meeting rooms. Cable TV, free & pay movies. Fee for refrigerators. Heated pool, whirlpool. Small pets only. Children 18 and under stay free. AE, CB, DI, DS, MC, VI. Restaurant nearby.   Ⓓ Ⓢ ⊘

Pierpont Inn ⏺   Motor Inn   ♦♦
(805) 653-6144; FAX (805) 641-1501   *Rates Subject to Change*

All year   1P   58.00 - 79.00   2P/1B   69.00 - 79.00   2P/2B   69.00 - 79.00   XP ..10

Adjacent to US 101; northbound exit Sanjon Rd, southbound exit Seaward Av. 550 Sanjon Rd (93001). 70 rooms; 2 stories; interior/exterior corridors. 8 ocean-view suites with balcony, $110. 2 cottages, $125-$175. 14 units with fireplace. Rental bicycles. Across freeway from beach. Attractive grounds. Many rooms with ocean views and balconies. Cable TV, free movies; shower or combination baths; coffeemakers. Some refrigerators. No A/C. 2 heated pools (1 indoors). Fee for racquetball courts, 12 lighted tennis courts, exercise room. Rental bicycles. Services: Fee for massage. No pets. Children 12 and under stay free. Senior discount. Monthly rates available. AE, CB, DI, DS, MC, VI.   Ⓓ ⊘

Ramada Inn ⏺   Motor Inn   ♦♦♦
(805) 652-0141; FAX (805) 643-1432   *AAA Special Value Rates*

All year [CP]   1P   75.00   2P/1B   80.00   2P/2B   80.00   XP ..10

½ mi nw of US 101; northbound exit California St, southbound exit Ventura Av. 181 E Santa Clara St (93001). Formerly Clock Tower Inn. 49 rooms; 2 stories; interior corridors. 5 rooms with fireplace & 8 with balcony. Attractive Southwest decor. Adjacent to Mission San Buenaventura & Mission Park. Cable TV. No pets. Children 12 and under stay free. Reservation deposit required. AE, CB, DI, DS, ER, JCB, MC, VI. Restaurant; 11 am-2:30 & 5-9 pm; closed Sun; $11-$20; cocktails.   Ⓓ Ⓢ ⊘

Vagabond Inn ⓐⓐⓐ   Motor Inn   ◆◆
(805) 648-5371; FAX (805) 648-5613   *Rates Subject to Change*

4/16-9/15 [CP]   1P   50.00 - 55.00   2P/1B   55.00 - 60.00   2P/2B   60.00 - 65.00   XP 5
9/16-4/15 [CP]   1P   43.00 - 48.00   2P/1B   47.00 - 52.00   2P/2B   52.00 - 57.00   XP 5

¼ mi e on US 101 business rt; from US 101 northbound exit California St, southbound exit Ventura Av. 756 E Thompson Bl (93001). 82 rooms. 2 2-bedroom units. Cable TV, free movies; coffeemakers. Some refrigerators. Heated pool, whirlpool; playground. Small pets, $3 extra charge. Children 18 and under stay free. Reservation deposit required. AE, CB, DI, DS, MC, VI. Coffeeshop; 24 hrs; $5-$10.   Ⓓ ∅

Restaurants

The Chart House   Steak & Seafood $11-$20   ◆◆
(805) 643-3725

Adjacent to US 101; northbound exit Sanjon Rd; southbound exit Seaward Av. 567 Sanjon Rd (93001). Steak, fresh seafood, chicken & prime rib. Contemporary-style restaurant overlooking the ocean. Children's menu. Cocktails & lounge. Reservations suggested. 5:30-10 pm; Fri to 10:30 pm; Sat 5-11 pm; Sun 4-10 pm. AE, CB, DI, DS, MC, VI.   ∅

Old Vienna Restaurant ⓐⓐⓐ   German $11-$20   ◆◆
(805) 654-1214

1 mi e of Main St. 3845 Telegraph Rd (92003). Large selection, including venison, roast goose in season. Children's menu. Cocktails. Reservations suggested weekends. 11:30 am-2 & 5-9:30 pm; Mon from 5 pm; Fri to 10 pm; Sat 5-10 pm; Sun 11 am-2 & 4:30-9 pm; closed 12/25. AE, CB, DI, DS, MC, VI.   ∅

Pierpont Inn   American $11-$20   ◆◆
(805) 653-6144

In Pierpont Inn, 550 San Jon Rd (93001). Entrees include beef, chicken & seafood. Desserts made on premises. Fine ocean-view dining at inn established 1928. Children's menu; early bird specials; carryout. Cocktails & lounge; entertainment. Reservations suggested. 6:30-10:30 am,11:30 am-2 & 4:30-9 pm; Sat 6:30-10:30 am, 11:30-3 & 5:30-10 pm; Sun 8 am-3 & 5-8:30 pm. AE, CB, DI, DS, MC, VI.   ∅

Yolanda's Mexican Cafe   Mexican   Up to $10   ◆◆
(805) 643-2700

½ mi e of Seaward Av. 2753 E Main St (93003). Southwestern cuisine. Colorfully decorated restaurant. Children's menu; carryout. Cocktails & lounge. Reservations suggested. 11 am-10 pm; Fri & Sat to 11 pm; Sun 10 am-9 pm; closed 11/24 & 12/25. AE, MC, VI.   ∅

Simi and Conejo Valleys

SIMI VALLEY

Lodging

Clarion Hotel   Motor Inn   ♦♦♦
(805) 584-6300; FAX (805) 527-9969   *Rates Guaranteed*

All year   1P 70.00 - 90.00   2P/1B 80.00 -100.00   2P/2B 80.00 -100.00   XP ..10
1 mi s of SR 118; exit Madera Rd. 1775 Madera Rd (93065). 120 rooms; 2 stories; interior/exterior corridors; meeting rooms; conference facilities. 1 3-bedroom unit. 16 2-bedroom units. Many balconies. 2 mi n of the Ronald Reagan Presidential Library. Cable TV, free & pay movies; bars, coffeemakers, refrigerators. Heated pool, whirlpool. Coin laundry. No pets. Children 17 and under stay free. Senior discount. Reservation deposit required. AE, CB, DI, DS, ER, JCB, MC, VI. Complimentary beverages each evening. Restaurant; 6:30 am-1 am; $7-$12.   Ⓓ Ⓢ ⊘

Radisson-Simi Valley ⒶⒶ   Motor Inn   ♦♦♦
(805) 583-2000; FAX (805) 583-2779   *Rates Guaranteed*

All year   1P 69.00   2P/1B 69.00   2P/2B 69.00   XP ..10
Adjacent to SR 118; exit 1st St. 999 Enchanted Wy (93065). 195 rooms; 2-4 stories; interior corridors; meeting rooms; conference facilities. 6 suites with whirlpool tub, $129-$139. Cable TV, free & pay movies; coffeemakers. Some bars. Heated pool, whirlpool. Services: Data ports, secretarial services. Small pets only, $35 deposit. Children 17 and under stay free. Senior discount. AE, CB, DI, DS, ER, JCB, MC, VI. Restaurant; 6:30 am-11 pm; $9-$15; cocktails; entertainment.   Ⓓ Ⓢ ⊘

Travelodge ⒶⒶ   Motel   ♦♦
(805) 584-6006; FAX (805) 527-5629   *Rates Guaranteed*

All year [CP]   1P 62.00   2P/1B 72.00   2P/2B 76.00   XP 6
Adjacent s side SR 118, exit Erringer Rd. 2550 Erringer Rd (93065). 96 rooms; 3 stories; exterior corridors; meeting rooms. 6 1-bedroom suites with microwave & refrigerator, $120-$145. Free & pay movies; coffeemakers. Some microwaves, refrigerators, whirlpools. Heated pool, sauna, whirlpool. Coin laundry. No pets. Children 17 and under stay free. Senior discount. Reservation deposit required. AE, DI, DS, JCB, MC, VI. Restaurant nearby.   Ⓓ Ⓢ ⊘

Restaurants

Marie Callender's   American $11-$20   ♦♦
(805) 582-0552

¼ mi s of SR 118, exit Madera Rd. 20 W Cochran St (93065). Selection of entrees, salads, sandwiches, pasta. Pies made & baked on premises. Salad bar. Casual attire. Sunday brunch. Children's menu; senior's menu; carryout; a la carte. Beer & wine only. 6:30 am-10 pm; Fri to 11 pm; Sat 8 am-11 pm; Sun 8 am-10 pm; closed 12/25. AE, DS, MC, VI. ⊘

The Olive Garden   Italian $11-$20   ♦♦
(805) 526-0057
1 blk s of SR 118, exit Sycamore Dr. 2410 Sycamore Dr (93065). Casual attire. Children's menu; carryout; a la carte. Cocktails & lounge. 11 am-10 pm; Fri & Sat to 11 pm; closed 12/25. AE, CB, DI, DS, MC, VI.   ⊗

THOUSAND OAKS

Lodging

Best Western Oaks Lodge ⓐ   Motel   ♦♦
(805) 495-7011; FAX (805) 495-0647   *AAA Special Value Rates*
All year [CP]   1P 47.00 - 57.00   2P/1B 52.00 - 62.00   2P/2B 52.00 - 62.00   XP 5
1 blk n of US 101, 1 blk nw on Thousand Oaks Bl; exit Moorpark Rd. 12 Conejo Bl (91360). 76 rooms; 2 stories; exterior corridors. 6 efficiencies, $5 extra (7-night minimum stay). Adjacent to shopping plazas. Free movies; shower or combination baths. Some refrigerators. Pool, whirlpool. Coin laundry. Small pets only, $5 extra charge. Children 12 and under stay free. Weekly rates available. AE, CB, DI, DS, ER, JCB, MC, VI. Restaurant nearby.   Ⓓ ⊗

Days Inn ⓐ   Motor Inn   ♦♦
(805) 499-5910; FAX (805) 498-5783   *Rates Guaranteed*
All year   1P 48.00   2P/1B 48.00   2P/2B 48.00   XP ..10
1 blk se of US 101, exit Ventu Park Rd. 1320 Newbury Rd (91320). 124 rooms; 3 stories; exterior corridors; meeting rooms. Quiet location. Free & pay movies; coffeemakers; safes. Some refrigerators. Heated pool, whirlpool. Coin laundry. No pets. AE, CB, DI, DS, MC, VI. Restaurant; 6 am-1 & 5-9 pm; $7-$12; cocktails.   Ⓓ Ⓢ ⊗

Econo Lodge ⓐ   Motel   ♦♦
(805) 496-0102; FAX (805) 494-1295   *AAA Special Value Rates*
5/26-9/1 [CP]   1P 38.00- 44.00   2P/1B 42.00 - 48.00   2P/2B 44.00 - 54.00   XP 5
9/2-5/25 [CP]   1P 36.00 - 40.00   2P/1B 38.00 - 44.00   2P/2B 40.00 - 50.00   XP 5
3 blks ne of US 101, exit Rancho Rd. 1425 Thousand Oaks Bl (91362). 60 rooms; 2 stories; exterior corridors; meeting rooms. Located off the main street. Cable TV, free movies. Some microwaves, refrigerators. Pool. No pets. Weekly rates available. Reservation deposit required. AE, CB, DI, DS, JCB, MC, VI.   Ⓓ ⊗

Howard Johnson Hotel 🆎		Motor Inn	♦♦
(805) 497-3701; FAX (805) 497-1875		*Rates Guaranteed*	

4/1-10/31	1P 62.00	2P/1B 72.00	2P/2B 72.00	XP ..10
11/1-3/31	1P 55.00	2P/1B 65.00	2P/2B 65.00	XP ..10

Adjacent to US 101, exit Moorpark Rd, then ¼ mi w. 75 W Thousand Oaks Bl (91360). 107 rooms; 4 stories; exterior corridors; meeting rooms; conference facilities. Adjacent to shopping plaza. Free & pay movies. Some refrigerators. Heated pool, whirlpool. Coin laundry. Small pets only, $5 extra charge. Children 17 and under stay free. Senior discount. AE, CB, DI, DS, JCB, MC, VI. Restaurant; 6 am-10 pm; $7-$12; cocktails. Ⓓ ⊘

Restaurants

Black Angus	American	$11-$20	♦♦
(805) 497-0757			

Adjacent to US 101, exit Moorpark Rd, ½ mi w. 139 W Thousand Oaks Bl (91360). Beef, seafood, chicken, pasta, salads, prime rib, rack of lamb, lobster. Children's menu. Cocktails & lounge. Reservations suggested Fri & Sat. 11 am-10 pm; Fri & Sat to 11 pm; closed 12/25. AE, DI, DS, MC, VI. ⊘

Hunan Chinese Restaurant 🆎	Chinese	Up to $10	♦
(805) 291-0075			

Corner of Moorpark Rd & Janss St, s end of shopping plaza. 1352 N Moorpark Rd (91360). Authentic Hunan-style cooking. Carryout. Beer & wine only. Minimum charge, $4-$6. 11:30 am-9:30 pm; Fri & Sat to 10 pm. AE, MC, VI. ⊘

Ojai and Santa Paula Areas

FILLMORE

Lodging

Best Western La Posada Motel 🆎		Motel	♦♦
(805) 524-0440; FAX (805) 524-1463		*Rates Guaranteed*	

All year	1P 45.00 - 55.00	2P/1B 50.00 - 60.00	2P/2P 50.00 - 70.00	XP 6

½ mi w on SR 126. 827 Ventura St (93015). 49 rooms; 2 stories; exterior corridors. Orange trees in planted areas. Cable TV, free movies; shower or combination baths. Some radios, VCPs. Pool, sauna, whirlpool. No pets. Senior discount. Weekly rates available. Reservation deposit required; 7-day refund notice. AE, CB, DI, DS, MC, VI. Restaurant nearby. Ⓓ ⊘

OJAI

Lodging

Best Western Casa Ojai ⊛
Motel ♦♦

(805) 646-8175; FAX (805) 640-8247   *AAA Special Value Rates*

Fri & Sat [CP]   1P   80.00 - 90.00   2P/1B   90.00 -100.00   2P/2B   95.00 -105.00   XP 5
Sun-Thurs [CP] 1P   55.00 - 65.00   2P/1B   65.00 - 75.00   2P/2B   70.00 - 80.00   XP 5

¾ mi e on SR 150. 1302 E Ojai Av (93023). 45 rooms; 2 stories; exterior corridors. Cable TV; coffeemakers. Some refrigerators; VCPs. Heated pool, whirlpool. No pets. Children 12 and under stay free. Reservation deposit required weekends. AE, CB, DI, DS, ER, JCB, MC, VI   Ⓓ ⊘

Ojai Valley Inn & Country Club ⊛
Resort Complex ♦♦♦

(805) 646-5511; FAX (805) 646-7969   *Rates Subject to Change*

All year [BP]   1P 195.00 -260.00   2P/1B 195.00 -260.00   2P/2B 195.00 -260.00   XP ..25

1 mi w on SR 150, ¼ mi s. Country Club Rd (PO Box 1866, 93024). Check in 4 pm. 212 rooms; 2 stories; interior/exterior corridors; meeting rooms; conference facilities. 16 suites with fireplace. Charming resort on 200 acres of beautifully landscaped grounds. Cable TV; coffeemakers. Some VCPs. Fee for movies. 2 heated pools, saunas, whirlpool; playground. Putting green. Children's program, recreation program; bicycles, hiking and jogging trails. Fee for 18 holes of golf; 8 tennis courts (4 lighted). Services: PC, secretarial services; massage. Small pets only, $25 extra charge. Children 17 and under stay free. Senior discount. Reservation deposit required; 3-day refund notice. AE, CB, DI, DS, MC, VI. Dining room, restaurant; 6:30 am-11 pm; $18-$35; cocktails. 24-hour room service.   Ⓓ Ⓢ ⊘

Restaurant

Ranch House Restaurant
Continental $21-$30   ♦♦♦

(805) 646-2360

From jct SR 150 & 33, ¾ mi nw on Maricopa Rd, ⅓ mi w on El Roblar, ½ mi s. Corner of S Lomita Av and Besant Rd (93023). Beef, lamb, chicken & fresh seafood. Homemade breads & desserts. Menu changes weekly. Colorful lush garden foliage, patio dining. Informal atmosphere. Casual attire. No A/C. A la carte. Beer & wine only. Reservations required for dinner. 11:30 am-1:30 pm, seatings for dinner at 6 pm & 8:30 pm; Sun 1-3:30 pm, seatings for dinner at 7:30 pm. Closed Mon, Tue & for lunch 10/2-4/14. AE, DS, MC, VI.   ⊘

SANTA PAULA

Lodging

Santa Paula Travelodge 🅰🅰   Motel   ♦♦
(805) 525-1561; FAX (805) 525-4230   *AAA Special Value Rates*

All year [CP]   1P 46.00   2P/1B 52.00   2P/2B 62.00   XP 5

¼ blk n of SR 126; exit Peck Rd. 350 S Peck Rd (93060). 50 rooms; 2 stories; interior corridors; meeting rooms. 3 efficiencies, no utensils. Cable TV, free movies. Some whirlpools. Fee for refrigerators. Heated pool, whirlpool. Pets, $20 extra charge. Children 17 and under stay free. Weekly rates available. Reservation deposit required. AE, CB, DI, DS, ER, JCB, MC, VI. Restaurant nearby.   Ⓓ Ⓢ ∅

The White Gables Inn   Historic Bed & Breakfast   ♦♦♦
(805) 933-3041   *Rates Subject to Change*

Fri-Sun [BP]   1P ...   2P/1B 85.00 -115.00 2P/2B ...
Mon-Thurs [BP] 1P ...   2P/1B 75.00 -105.00 2P/2B ...

From SR 126 exit 10th St (SR 150), ½ mi n then 4 blks w. 715 E Santa Paula St (93060). 3 rooms; 3 stories; no elevator. 1 room with balcony. Spacious 3rd floor suite with sitting room, bedroom & bath. Historical 1894 Victorian Queen Anne house located in a designated historical district. Shower or combination baths. No A/C; no phones; no TVs. Designated smoking area. No pets. Reservation deposit required. MC, VI.   Ⓓ ∅

Restaurant

Familia Diaz   Mexican   Up to $10   ♦
(805) 525-2813

Adjacent northside of SR 126, exit 10th St (SR 150). 245 S 10th St (93060). Casual atmosphere. Children's menu; carryout; a la carte. Casual attire. Cocktails & lounge. 11 am-2:30 & 4:30-9 pm; Sat & Sun 11 am-9 pm; closed major holidays & 8/2-8/13. DS, MC, VI.

Appendix & Indexes

Chambers of Commerce/ Tourism Offices

The following list of chambers of commerce and tourism offices is provided to help members obtain more information about Santa Barbara and Ventura counties.

Camarillo Chamber of Commerce
632 Los Posas Road
Camarillo 93010
(805) 484-4383

Carpinteria Valley Chamber of Commerce
5036 Carpinteria Avenue
Carpinteria 93014
(805) 684-5479

Conejo Valley Chamber of Commerce
1489 East Thousand Oaks Boulevard
Thousand Oaks 91362
(805) 499-1993

Fillmore Chamber of Commerce
344 Central Avenue
Fillmore 93015
(805) 524-0351

Goleta Valley Chamber of Commerce
5730 Hollister Avenue
Goleta 93117
(805) 967-4618
(See ad below.)

Lompoc Valley Chamber of Commerce
511 North H Street
Lompoc 93436
(805) 7364567

232

Ojai Chamber of Commerce
338 East Ojai Avenue
Ojai 93023-2739
(805) 646-8126

Oxnard Chamber of Commerce
500 East Esplanade Drive
Oxnard 93030
(805) 485-5255

Santa Barbara Chamber of Commerce
504 State Street
Santa Barbara 93102
(805) 965-3023

Santa Barbara Visitor Center
One Santa Barbara Street
Santa Barbara 93101
(805) 965-3021

Santa Maria Valley Chamber of Commerce
614 South Broadway
Santa Maria 93454
(805) 925-2403

Santa Ynez Chamber of Commerce
1095 Meadowvale
P.O. Box 865
Santa Ynez 93460
(805) 688-5318

Santa Paula Chamber of Commerce
Santa Barbara and 10th streets
Santa Paula 93060
(805) 525-5561

Simi Valley Chamber of Commerce
40 West Cochran Street
Suite 100
Simi Valley 93065
(805) 526-3900

Solvang Chamber of Commerce/ Conference & Visitors Bureau
1511-A Mission Drive
Solvang 93464
(805) 688-3317, 688-6144

Ventura Chamber of Commerce
6824 Seaward Avenue
Ventura 93001
(805) 648-2875

Ventura Visitors & Convention Bureau
89-C South California Street
Ventura 93001
(805) 648-2075

Index to Points of Interest

This index contains listings for points of interest and events in Santa Barbara and Ventura counties.

234

Index to Advertisers

For information about placing an advertisement
in Automobile Club of Southern California publications,
please contact

Karen Clyne
Advertising Services H180
Auto Club of Southern California
P.O. Box 2890
Los Angeles, CA 90051
(213) 741-4052